15

Pat Robertson

Also by David Edwin Harrell, Jr.

Oral Roberts: An American Life

All Things Are Possible: The Healing and Charismatic
   Revivals in Modern America

White Sects and Black Men in the Recent South

A Social History of the Disciples of Christ, 2 Vols.

PAT ROBERTSON

A Personal, Religious, and Political Portrait

David Edwin Harrell, Jr.

1817

Harper & Row, Publishers, San Francisco

Cambridge, Hagerstown, New York, Philadelphia, Washington
London, Mexico City, São Paulo, Singapore, Sydney

FIRST EDITION
Designed by M. Haage

Library of Congress Cataloging-in-Publication Data

Harrell. David Edwin.
    Pat Robertson : a personal, religious, and political portrait.

    Includes index.
    1. Robertson, Pat.   2. Christianity and politics—United States—
History—20th Century.   3. Conservatism—Religious aspects—
Christianity.   4. United States—Politics and government—1981—
    .   5. Television in religion—United States.   6. Church and
state—United States—History—20th century.   7. Unites States—
Religion—1965–   .   I. Title.
BX6495.R653H37   1987   973.927'092'4 [B]   87-45176

ISBN 0-06-250380-4

87 88 89 90 91 HC 10 9 8 7 6 5 4 3 2 1

88 - 98

Contents

Preface

Contrary to a July 1987 report in *Newsweek*, I am not a "devout pentecostal." I am not even a fallen pentecostal. I have friends who are pentecostals, and I am reasonably sure they will appreciate my disclaimer. I admire many pentecostals—as I admire some Catholics, Jews, and Marxists. But I do not accept the basic theological precepts of pentecostal or charismatic theology. I sometimes speak tongue in cheek, but I have never spoken in tongues.

I have made such statements in each of my two previous books that studied segments of pentecostal and charismatic history. This personal aside is directed primarily to those inclined to find hidden meanings in all writing about religion. And perhaps everyone needs to know my position before reading this book. To be sure, I have no illusions about writing "scientific history"; I know that my writing is influenced by my own subjective judgments. So, at least I tell you what I am not, though space and time prohibit my telling you what I am.

Since this is also a political book, I suppose I should also affirm that I have no rigid political agenda to promote. Thus far in life I have never voted for any candidate who was not a Democrat or a Socialist. I confess to having developed a certain cynicism about the promises of political liberalism in my time and to a willingness to listen a bit more patiently to other alternatives. But this book is my introduction to New Right conservatism, and I offer it as an exposition of Pat Robertson's views, not a defense of them.

Such statements mark me as an old-fashioned historian with a rigid commitment to an objective study of the past. There are no eternal verities in historical stories, but good historians write as truthfully as possible. A story well told can instruct a wide variety of people. *All Things Are Possible*, a book I wrote over a decade ago, describes the explosive healing revival in post–World War II pentecostalism. To some it is sacred history; to others it is a bizarre tale of ignorance and chicanery. I take some pride in the fact that the book has been used as a text—at Yale University and Oral Roberts University, at the University of North Carolina and at Rhema Bible School.

Telling stories objectively does not imply the absence of interpretation. This book is filled with my interpretations of Pat Robertson's motives, his meanings, and the forces that influenced him and American society. The validity of those interpretations depends on how logically I have used the evidence. What I have not done is offer overt judgments about the morality or the sanity of the story. That, it seems to me, is what a good historian leaves to readers. It is precisely that quality that allows a book to be read by vastly different people, each concluding that here is a true telling of the past.

Not all historians agree with such a definition of historical writing. Much historical writing takes on a tone of polemics, if not propaganda. And, quite properly, most political writing has an instrumental intent. That is all well and good, and I sometimes write polemics myself. But when I am posing as a historian, I try not to plead any case. If I do that job well, the result may be used by a variety of polemicists and moralizers who see the past through different first-principle truths.

While it is particularly precarious to try to write an objective book about a presidential candidate, I believe it is especially worthwhile. American political campaigns beg for nothing more than clear descriptions of the candidates—who they are, what they believe, how they have behaved in the past. No one's life story and belief system cries more for clarification than Pat Robertson's.

This book has three distinct, rather independent parts. The first is a biographical sketch of Pat Robertson and a short history of the growth of the Christian Broadcasting Network (CBN). I was particularly interested in Robertson's pre-Christian life and in his early years as a charismatic. Those periods of his life are less well known and they give important insights into his character and his political philosophy. Part Two of the book explains Robertson's most important religious views and how those views tie him to various religious subgroups—including charismatics, evangelicals, and Southern Baptists. I briefly describe each of these groups and its potential for political organization. Part Three analyzes the evolution of Robertson's political views and outlines the strengths and weaknesses of his candidacy.

A discussion of Pat Robertson's religious and political views raises fundamental philosophical and constitutional questions. For the most part, I have tried to succinctly pose those questions rather than to answer them. What does a charismatic mean when he says "God told me"? What are the foreign policy implications of dispensational premillennialism? What is the proper relationship between religion and politics in America? Has "secular humanism" overthrown the rule of God in America? Can evangelical Christians regain control of American politics? One may or may not agree with Pat Robertson's answers to such questions, but his presidential candidacy will demand that they be honestly confronted.

This is a book about Pat Robertson and his views. It is not a book about his critics and their views. In other words, I have written primarily to make Robertson's views understandable, if not palatable. Whether you like him or not is entirely up to you.

Such a statement imposes clear limitations on what one will find here. Though I interviewed John Buchanan, director of People for the American Way, and other critics of Robertson, my primary intent is to investigate Robertson's beliefs and motives. Consequently, I studied Pat Robertson exhaustively, and I have tried to explain his views thoroughly, letting him answer his critics as effectively as possible. This book does not pretend to exhaust the rebuttals his critics might offer. It is not a book about People for the American Way or the American Civil Liberties Union. It is simply a book about Pat Robertson and his views and it should be judged as nothing more.

Like most historians, I am most comfortable working with the written word, and a large part of this book is based on the publications of the Robertson ministry. I have also let his critics speak largely through published attacks in the press. But I also conducted about forty interviews, including interviews with Pat Robertson, his son Tim, and most of the important officials at CBN. Again, the weight of my research leaned heavily toward Robertson supporters. Partly that is because it is his story; partly it is because those are the sources that tell who he is and what he believes. Most of your enemies know only that you are wrong; they are generally ignorant about how you became misguided.

For a variety of reasons, largely to make the book less formidable for a wider reading audience, the text is not footnoted. When it seemed important, I included information in the text about the location of quotations. I have also written a bibliographical essay telling the most important sources used. I did, in fact, write a footnoted edition of the manuscript for my own use, and, should it be useful for some scholar, I would be happy to share information about the sources.

This book was written under very tight time constraints and I am grateful to the University of Alabama at Birmingham and Harper & Row, San Francisco, for providing financial assistance to undertake the research. Karen Robinson and Karen P. Jermyn at the Holy Spirit Research Center at Oral Roberts University made available to me an extensive file of CBN publications and letters to contributors. My relations with CBN have been formal but cordial. I am particularly indebted to G. Benton Miller, Jr., who coordinated my interviews at CBN. Benton offered more help than was demanded and he became a friend in the process.

PART ONE

A Personal Portrait

1.

Birth

O N MARCH 25, 1930, the "Personals" column of the *Lexington Gazette* included the announcement: "Mr. and Mrs. A. W. Robertson are the proud parents of a son, who arrived Saturday, March 22nd." In spite of the deepening Depression, the other news of the week seemed conventional enough. The weather was unusually warm in late March and Virginia Military Institute had already begun its spring sports activities. An editorial bemoaned the invasion of "chain stores" that imperiled local merchants. As usual, the paper featured a weekly Sunday School lesson. The "Golden Text" for the week was taken from Isaiah 9:6: "For unto us a child is born, unto us a son is given: and the government shall be upon his shoulder. . . ."

2.

Political Birth

SEPTEMBER 15, 1987, was a luminous late summer day in Chesapeake, Virginia. It was the day the Lord had provided for a notable transition in the life of Pat Robertson. Long before the announced ten o'clock press conference, sound trucks and press cars began arriving in the parking lot at 2127 Smith Street, a warehouse where volunteer workers in the Americans for Robertson organization had been coordinating a drive to secure three million signatures supporting Robertson's candidacy for the presidency. On September 17, 1986, Robertson had announced that he would run if three million registered voters signed petitions within the next year saying that they would work, pray, and give to support his race; today he would announce the results.

Robertson appeared in the jammed room precisely on the hour; his brief announcement to the hundred or so reporters and supporters was no surprise. Behind him were piled bundles of petitions that he said contained the signatures of 3.3 million registered voters urging him to run for the presidency. The logistical problems in the petition drive had been formidable, but his organization had done it. He had set a new goal of securing seven million signatures before the beginning of the primaries. But he was now satisfied that the people wanted him to run for the presidency. On October 1 he would formally become a candidate for the Republican party nomination for president of the United States of America.

For about fifteen minutes reporters shouted questions, many of them already familiar. What efforts had been made to validate the three million signatures and how did he know the signers were registered voters? Was he "electable"? What did he regard as the major campaign issues? Would questions about his Marine combat service damage his chances? Would he accept federal campaign funds? Could he escape the image of being a television minister? Had God told him to run for the presidency? Robertson stood smiling and gracious, sometimes nodding understanding as a reporter neared the end of a question. His answers were candid and reasoned—no fanaticism or bombast. He knew the questions, and he knew his answers. This was Pat Robertson at his best, and his best was very good. The challenge before him, he confessed, was to introduce this Pat Robertson to the American electorate.

The press conference was heavy with symbolism. The floor before the candidate was littered with cables and cameras and two score reporters with pads and recorders. It was a profane and unconstrained band who feared neither God nor man. A few minutes before Robertson entered the room, one reporter drolly asked another: "Have you got an accurate count, or do we just agree on the numbers?" They were skeptics by disposition and by training— they were not there to admire but to probe.

But, just before candidate Robertson walked through the curtain, a file of campaign workers filtered into the room and lined the walls surrounding the reporters. They stood quietly, dressed as if for Sunday worship, filled with obvious delight at what they had accomplished. As in all press conferences, Robertson seemed surrounded, a solitary figure before an unruly mob. But, from a more distant vantage, it was the reporters who were surrounded by an ebullient corps that was ready to explode with enthusiasm and hope. At the close of the press conference, Robertson and his supporters disappeared behind the curtains; in a few moments robust cheers echoed from the adjoining room. "They're congratulating one another," said campaign director R. Marc Nuttle.

The ceremonies of September 15 had several levels of meaning. The message to the press and the nation was that Pat Robertson was a candidate—although his formal announcement would not be made until two weeks later. For the volunteer workers in the Americans for Robertson headquarters it was a celebration of one of the most successful organizing campaigns in American political history. For Pat Robertson it was a confirmation that he was walking in the will of God and that he had a chance to win. Robertson was asked whether his success indicated that God wanted him to run. He replied that he had made that decision a year earlier; now he was convinced that the people wanted him to run.

It was entirely appropriate that Robertson's bid for the nomination should start in this warehouse room. It was a loving room where volunteers had counted and recorded the three million names under a banner, "We 'heart' Pat." On one wall hung a quilt bearing the message: "The people of Ohio say yes—Robertson '88." It was also a sanctified room. One wall was lined with signed petitions and letters from supporters—roped off, one campaign worker said, so that unruly reporters could not snatch them from the wall. The letters smacked of the common folk of the nation. Some were on the stationery of village churches. Most began with the words: "Dear Brother Pat."

Clearly, the most pressing task of the Robertson campaign in the months ahead would be to shake the negative connotations that go with the label, "television evangelist." He may never be seen as anything more than a preacher by the news media, or by the American people, and, if he is not, he cannot be elected president. But the next step of his campaign, if there is a next step, must be to show that Pat Robertson is an intelligent and informed man with a remarkably varied background and with a wide-ranging conservative political agenda. The room at 2127 Smith Street in Chesapeake was a startlingly Christian place; it was filled with artifacts of faith. That was fitting. It was Christians who got Pat Robertson to this room on September 15. The question that was now before Robertson and his political advisors was how he would do when he left the room.

3.

Ambience

NESTLED HARD on the banks of the North Fork of the James River, later called the Maury, Lexington lay near the center of the Valley of Virginia. Cut off from the east by the imposing, rugged facade of the Blue Ridge and from the west by the Alleghenies, the village was located on the historic "Great Road" (later the Lee Highway), which led southwest from Winchester to Roanoke and on to the West. The town was founded in 1778; by that date, Rockbridge County had acquired a population of four thousand pioneer settlers without the appearance of a village. The rolling hillsides and meadows of the area were lush and fertile; the vistas surrounding the town site, dominated by nearby House Mountain, were exquisite. Thomas J. "Stonewall" Jackson, a resident of Lexington for ten years, uttered an endorsement later enshrined by the Chamber of Commerce: "Lexington is the most beautiful place I remember of having seen when taken in connection with the surrounding country."

The Valley of Virginia is as celebrated for its history as for its beauty. The names of the nation's founding fathers weave throughout its history. The natural rock bridge a few miles from Lexington, for which the county was named, was a part of a land patent granted to Thomas Jefferson in 1774. As a young man, George Washington visited the bridge, one of the natural wonders of a virgin West, climbing a nearby rocky ledge and carving his name in it to be beheld by later generations. In 1796, Washington made a sizable gift to endow a small college established in Lexington in 1749. The college was subsequently renamed Washington College. In 1839, Washington College was joined in Lexington by Virginia

Military Institute, the oldest state-supported military college in the nation and a veritable Southern West Point.

It was Southern history, however, that was to leave the deepest imprint on Lexington. In 1851, the village became the home of Thomas Jonathan Jackson, professor of natural philosophy at Virginia Military Institute. For a decade Jackson lived quietly in a modest brick home on East Washington Street. A retired army officer, he was one of the Sunday School teachers in the local Presbyterian church. Then, in two violent Civil War years beginning in April 1861, before dying of wounds received in the Battle of Chancellorsville at the age of thirty-nine, Jackson established himself as a genius of military movement—his brightest triumphs coming in his beloved Valley of Virginia. The memory of this most exalted martyred saint of the Confederacy hung like the mountain mists over the valley he loved; his home in Lexington became a shrine, the Stonewall Jackson Memorial Cemetery the resting place of governors and senators.

To the memory of Stonewall Jackson was added the living presence of Robert Edward Lee. In 1865, Lee accepted the presidency of Washington College; he remained in that position until his death in 1870 and was succeeded by his son. Lee was buried in a crypt in Lee Chapel, which had been built under his supervision in 1867; the bones of his beloved horse, Traveler, were interred just outside the general's office. Dignified, respected, indeed revered throughout the vanquished South, Lee cast a spell of gentility and noblesse oblige that seems still to hover over the village. Immediately after his death, the name of the college was changed to Washington and Lee, a title that somehow encapsulated the prestige and self-image of the remote hamlet nestled amidst the beauty of the Appalachians.

The South changed slowly in the years between defeat and humiliation in 1865 and the coming of the Depression and World War II. Nowhere was continuity with the past more apparent than in the Valley—its inhabitants were isolated, nonindustrial, and fiercely proud of their heritage as Virginians and Southerners. In the census of 1930, the population of Lexington was still less than 3,800. Into the 1950s the town remained much as it was in the days of Robert E. Lee. Lining the streets were tidy houses bearing the names of earlier residents—the Glasgow House, the Alexander-Withrow House, the Jackson House. The main street was dominated by churches and small stores, the Stonewall Jackson Restaurant, the State Theater, and other locally owned businesses. Not until 1950 did Lexington get its first traffic light. It was a wholesome, patriotic, godly place to live. Local churches raised a yearly subsidy to assure that the public schools would be supplied with Bible teachers. The *Lexington Gazette* featured liberal doses of Christian teaching, as well as a regular column on "The American Way."

Through the years the village of Lexington continued to be dominated by the campuses of Washington and Lee and Virginia Military Institute, the two schools standing on adjoining property. The buildings of VMI were totally destroyed when Union troops captured Lexington, but Washington College's buildings were spared out of respect for George Washington's gift to the school. Washington and Lee's gracious, neoclassical Front Campus, designated a National Historic Landmark in 1972, resounded from generation to generation with florid and courtly memorials to Lee and Jackson, to the glory of the Lost Cause.

If Lexington bore the marks of its locale and its history, it also had a singular and rich ethnic heritage. Its settlers were the sons and daughters of Ulster; they came in that massive migration from Scotland and Ireland that began at the end of the seventeenth century. These Scotch-Irish immigrants became the quintessential American pioneers, fighting their way down the Valley of Virginia before dispersing westward across the continent. Hardy, venturesome, shrewd, they left behind them a trail of Presbyterian churches, flourishing mercantile ventures and, a love of language, education, theology, and argument. While the Scotch-Irish mingled uneasily with German immigrants in some parts of the valley, Lexington was a virtual Celtic monopoly including the Paxtons, McDowells, McCoys, Kerrs, Glasgows, and Robertsons. It seemed fitting in the early twentieth century that Lexington boasted of being the smallest town in the country with its own golf course.

4.

Forebears

DURING HIS long career in the House of Representatives and Senate of the United States, Pat Robertson's father, Absalom Willis Robertson, was often asked his pedigree by fellow Robertsons throughout America. Although he maintained a membership in the Clan Donnachaidh Society in Edinburgh, Senator Robertson could never trace his Robertson ancestors more than four generations, mostly because his grandfather, Captain Archie Robertson of the Stonewall Brigade, had been killed in the Battle of Cold Harbor. His father, Franklin Pierce Robertson, was only nine years old at the time, and like so many Virginians in the wake of the Civil War he was reared in genteel poverty. Trained in his youth by private tutors, F. P. Robertson was an outstanding student at Richmond University and the Louisville Seminary of the Southern Baptist church. In later years, Senator Robertson recalled that his father was so proficient in Greek, Latin, and Hebrew that he often read the classics in his leisure time. In spite of these attainments, Franklin Pierce Robertson chose to minister to several small rural churches in western Virginia as a home missionary, riding a mule to his appointments and supporting his family of six children on a salary of fifty dollars a month. Reared in this spartan but moral environment, his sons became successful businessmen, bankers, physicians, and politicians.

On his mother's side, Willis Robertson was surer of his lineage. His mother, Josephine Ragland Willis, was a brilliant and cultured woman, educated at Staunton Female Institute and celebrated for her civic and religious work until her death in 1950 at age ninety-two. Her father, Absalom, for whom the senator was named, had been one of ten Willis brothers to serve in the Confederate army. Her mother was a Gordon, descended from James Gordon I of

Sheepbridge, Scotland, whose grandson, James Gordon of Orange, settled in Lancaster County in 1738 and aided James Madison in drafting the Constitution. The Willis and Gordon families claimed kinship to Benjamin Harrison, a signer of the Declaration of Independence, the two presidents Harrison, and the Churchill family; the two names were proudly handed down in later generations of the Robertson family.

The public career of A. Willis Robertson was a nearly unbroken string of successes. A graduate of the first high school in Franklin County (which his mother had been the driving force in founding), at age sixteen he entered Richmond College and in five years received a bachelor's degree and a law degree, at the same time establishing himself as a campus leader and stellar athlete. He was admitted to the bar in 1908 and was elected to the state Senate in 1915. His political career was interrupted by World War I when he volunteered and advanced to the rank of major in the infantry (he was generally called Major Robertson by his Lexington neighbors). After the war, he returned to the Virginia State Senate until 1922. For the next four years Robertson served as Commonwealth Attorney for Rockbridge County and then was appointed chairman of the State Commission of Game and Inland Fisheries by Governor Harry F. Byrd, who had entered the state Senate at the same time as Robertson and had shared a desk with him in the Virginia Senate Chamber. Coincidentally, Robertson and Byrd, the two pillars of Virginia politics for a generation, had been born two weeks apart in Martinsburg, West Virginia, delivered by the same physician, their parents residing on the same street. Elected to the United States House of Representatives in 1932, Robertson supported the early New Deal, though in later years he became the most anti-administration Democrat from the state of Virginia. Robertson was reelected for consecutive terms until 1946 when, upon the death of Senator Carter Glass, he was chosen by the Virginia Democratic Convention to fill Glass's unexpired term in the Senate.

In 1948, Robertson was elected to the first of three terms in the Senate. During their years in the Senate, Robertson and Byrd drifted apart, as Robertson was never fully willing to routinely follow the lead of his senior colleague. The powerful Byrd, according to one reporter, would "brook no divergence" and in 1954 he apparently gave serious thought to trying to purge Robertson. But Robertson remained immensely popular with the Virginia electorate and sustained his career outside the inner councils of the Democratic party, building a remarkable network of personal acquaintances throughout the state. In 1954, one newsman observed that Robertson "hunted and prayed with everyone in the state." In 1960 he won a third term, receiving an unprecedented 81 percent of the vote.

In 1966 at age seventy-nine, A. Willis Robertson suffered his only political defeat. In a bitter battle for the Democratic nomination, the senator was defeated by 611 votes out of over 430,000 ballots cast. Robertson's defeat was a part of a broad shift in Virginia politics. Senator Byrd, who was in failing health, had retired from the Senate the previous year to clear the way for the appointment of his son, Harry Byrd, Jr. The young Byrd, standing for election in his own right in 1966, disassociated himself from the most reactionary stances of his father and Senator Robertson, particularly their die-hard states' rights segregationism. Robertson's opponent, Congressman William Spong, also projected this new image, accusing Senator Robertson, reported the *New York Times*, of opposing "every form of measure designed to cope with the problems that face a modern, urban society like Virginia today." Although Spong was hardly a political liberal, Robertson charged that he had the support of organized labor and tried to link him with Senators Robert and Ted Kennedy. Spong did receive the endorsement of the Virginia Independent Voters League, which, according to the *Times*, had "influence over 235,000 Negro voters." In all, the election was clearly not a personal rejection of Robertson; indeed, the narrowness of his defeat was in many ways a personal tribute to him. The retirement of the elder Byrd, the defeat of Robertson, and the defeat of Representative Howard W. Smith, an eighteen-term member of the House of Representatives and chairman of the House Rules Committee, virtually transformed Virginia politics.

After a lifetime of public service, Robertson was crushed by his defeat. He reestablished his residence in Lexington, although he continued to maintain an office in Washington and to travel as a consultant for the World Bank. Always an impressive physical specimen, in his last years he developed a "heart ailment"; to many of his old friends, the senator's spirit seemed broken. Nonetheless, he continued to hunt and fish with his friends; he and his eldest son, Taddy, killed forty-five quail shortly before his death. He died of a heart attack on November 1, 1971, at age eighty-four. The funeral service at Virginia Military Institute was conducted by Dr. William L. Lumpkin, former minister of the Manly Memorial Baptist Church in Lexington; the honorary pallbearers included his best friend in the Senate, John Stennis of Mississippi, Senators Herman E. Talmadge and Harry F. Byrd, Jr., and his old Lexington friends D. Allen Penick, Matthew W. Paxton, Richard A. Smith, Col. S. M. Heflin, and Dr. O. Hunter McClung. Five other senators and scores of other political figures attended the service before the senator was laid to rest in the Stonewall Jackson Memorial Cemetery.

Throughout his life, Willis Robertson was a pillar of political conservatism. He opposed the repeal of the right-to-work law and proposed antitrust legislation to control labor unions; he opposed the 1954 Supreme Court decision outlawing public school desegregation, signed the 1956 Southern Manifesto (along with over a hundred other Southern congressmen) denouncing the decision as a "clear abuse of judicial power," and continued to oppose civil rights legislation during the Kennedy and Johnson administrations; when the Supreme Court ruled against prayer in public schools in 1962, Robertson introduced a Senate resolution challenging the ruling; he generally opposed the expansion of the federal government and federal spending, although he did consistently support defense spending and federal projects that benefited Virginia.

Robertson viewed his role in the Senate as that of constitutional and financial watchdog. While his racial views were little different from his Southern contemporaries in Washington, Robertson's opposition to the civil rights movement was couched in constitutional terms. "He believes the Constitution says what it means and means what it says," said his friend Herman Talmadge in 1965. His "love of the Constitution," recalled John Stennis, along with his love for Virginia was "the guide of his life as an individual and as a senator."

While Robertson stood shoulder to shoulder with Byrd and other Southern senators in defense of states' rights, his proudest achievements came as "watchdog of the treasury." His expertise in the areas of taxation and banking was unquestioned; in 1958 he became chairman of the powerful Banking and Currency Committee of the Senate. In that role he drafted important legislation and won the admiration and respect of the nation's banking community. But his financial conservatism reached far beyond his committee responsibilities and through the years he claimed credit for striking billions of dollars from the federal budget. Although he initially supported the Marshall Plan after World War II as a necessary humanitarian act to rebuild Europe (a vote that contributed to his rift with Byrd), he later became a persistent critic of foreign aid. The biographical sketches Robertson's office prepared each year for distribution to his constituency unfailingly put a dollar figure on the amount of money the senator had saved American taxpayers.

In many ways, the public career of Willis Robertson justifies the appraisal of historian J. Harvie Wilkinson that he "personified Spartan discipline, pioneer individualism, and Calvinist morality." He brought to Washington the values of Lexington, of his father's rural Baptist churches, of the willful Scotch-Irish pioneers who settled the Valley of Virginia, neither asking nor giving more than what was just and right. In the late 1950s, the senator, along with others among the nation's leaders, was asked a series of personal questions by the publishers of *Who's Who*. His mother and father had most influenced his life, he replied, because they had taught him "high Christian ideals, sound principles" and had given him "firm guidance." His history professor at Richmond College, Dr. S. C. Mitchell, had taught him "love of country," and Woodrow Wilson had left a model of a "scholar in American politics." Asked

to name, in order, "the five greatest living Americans," the senator
offered a list that was a telling personal commentary: "Cordell Hull
(international cooperation), Herbert Hoover (private enterprise),
James B. Conant (science), John D. Rockefeller, Jr. (philanthropy),
George C. Marshall (military leader)."

In spite of the apparent philosophical and political clarity of such
a sketch of Senator A. Willis Robertson, as in most cases Robertson's life was filled with glaring disparities. Over and over again
Robertson behaved unexpectedly. When he backed the Marshall
Plan, he risked Byrd's ire; when he supported Adlai Stevenson for
the presidency in 1952, he seriously alienated his senior colleague.
In 1966 in the election he lost, he made a tentative effort to court
the black vote; had he been younger he might have mellowed as
did his Southern friends in the Senate. In an interview at his World
Bank office in 1968, the former senator expressed doubts about the
Vietnam War, and he questioned his senatorial opposition to foreign aid. "I never fully understood the problem," he told a reporter. "I was busy. . . . Now I see the need." At age eighty, he had
become a bit of a "missionary," he admitted; "I think I'm reverting
to my boyhood training. I was trained to help people."

The senator's personality was a similar mix—a stern, uncompromising facade and a warm, charismatic presence. When he ran for
the Senate for the first time in 1948, at age fifty-one, he was already the "tall, grey-haired incumbent." Physically, he was an extraordinary specimen—tall and muscular, a college athlete, a
lifelong outdoorsman who loved hunting and fishing, a regular
visitor to the Senate gymnasium to the end of his career. He was,
recalled one friend, a "handsome man" with a "commanding presence." The personification of a courtly Southern gentleman, he was
an untiring worker, frequently spending sixteen hours a day in his
Senate office. He cared little for the social merry-go-round in
Washington and made few close friends in the Senate. To many
acquaintances he seemed stern and aloof.

At the same time, it was Robertson's personal charm that explained his political success. He survived for fifty years in Virginia
politics without personal wealth and without the support of the

state's dominant party machinery. His success was built on a network of personal acquaintances made in countless personal appearances at county fairs and small-town civic clubs. An orator of no mean ability who could hold Virginia audiences enthralled with discourses on Stonewall Jackson and Robert E. Lee, he was at his best on a hunting trip, sipping bourbon and spinning yarns. Matt Paxton, Jr., the son of the publisher of the Lexington newspaper and a friend of Pat Robertson, remembered years later not the senator's dignity and reserve, but rather the magical spell cast by his storytelling.

Willis Robertson's private life revealed the same dualities. Parsimonious as the legend of his Scottish ancestors, he was as frugal with his private finances as he was with the taxpayers' money. Throughout much of his Senate career he lived alone in a basement room in a Washington hotel while his wife maintained their residence in Lexington. He kept careful check on the gasoline mileage of his automobile and regularly lectured his family on financial responsibility. His letters to family members were nearly as businesslike as his Senate speeches, full of sensible information, generous in advice, signed "fondly yours." To many observers he appeared austere and cold. He was, agreed his grandson Tim Robertson, a "formal father," and he was a "formal grandfather." He was from the "old school. . . . Women waited on him. The children were there when he wanted to see them." After all, Robertson had not married until age thirty-three; his older son, A. Willis Robertson, Jr. (Taddy), was born when he was thirty-six and his younger, Marion Gordon Robertson (Pat), was born when he was forty-three.

And yet, the Robertson clan was bonded together as fiercely as their wild and lusty Celtic forebears. The senator was constantly solicitous of the needs of his wife and sons; he was proud of their accomplishments, chastened by their failures. If his letters to his sons were filled with admonitions and instructions, he also chatted easily about football and offered light-hearted tips about the available young females in Washington. Formal he was, but there was never any question about his warmth and love. He was there, the bedrock upon which the family was built—silent, unbending, but sure as granite.

In 1920, Willis Robertson married his first cousin, Gladys Churchill Willis, a beautiful and cultured woman ten years his junior. Mrs. Robertson's father had been a trial lawyer until his middle years, when he retired and became a Baptist minister. She was a graduate of Hollins College, a "splendid musician," and, according to the senator, "a great help to me in my political career." In the early years of their marriage, Mrs. Robertson was active in a variety of women's social clubs and she was a "noted hostess"; Pat Robertson recalled that she gave some "very sparkling dinner parties both in Virginia and in Washington." She and the senator traveled in the Orient together in 1935 and their home was filled with lovely furnishings purchased abroad.

The Robertsons' home life changed markedly with the coming of World War II. Up until that time, the family had lived a major portion of each year in residences in Washington, first in Alexandria and later in the northwest section of the city. The outbreak of the war turned the capital city into a bedlam. Mrs. Robertson and their two sons returned to Lexington, never to live in Washington again. Senator Robertson became a solitary figure in Washington; he visited his family on weekends and when Congress was not in session, and they visited occasionally in Washington, but distances developed in family relationships. In a rare public interview late in her life, Mrs. Robertson explained that "she could provide most effective help to her husband here in Lexington where she was close to his constituents and could handle calls and requests and study press reports." While she did remain in close contact with her husband and often read his speeches before they were delivered, her change in residence signaled deeper changes in her own psyche.

"After she found the Lord," recalled her son, Pat, "the lure of glamorous parties and travel and the social scene just didn't terribly appeal to her anymore. She loved her home." In later years Mrs. Robertson declined invitations to the White House and refused to christen the submarine James Madison; more and more she would not accompany the senator on trips, unless he could entice her with the possibility of attending a Billy Graham crusade. Religion came to dominate her mind; she distributed tracts to the students in Lexington's colleges and befriended an array of local ministers. She remained a gracious and attractive woman, deeply concerned about her family. She continued to have many good friends in Lexington and was noted for her marathon telephone conversations, which rarely ended within an hour. But by the time of her death in 1968, she was regarded as something of a religious recluse by her neighbors.

5.

Before Christ

THE TWO ROBERTSON sons, A. Willis, Jr., called Taddy, and Marion Gordon, nicknamed Pat in honor of his father's college roommate, probably thought little of their peculiar family environment while they were growing up. Over six years apart in age, the two sons had considerably different experiences; Taddy was nearly grown before the family moved from Washington and the gulf began to widen between his mother and father. Many friends felt that he remained particularly close to his father and that he displayed some of the reserve and diffidence that marked his father's personality. On the other hand, Lexington was the home of Pat Robertson during his teenage years. He and his mother were often alone. He was the darling of her life; he was spoiled but solicitous, self-indulgent but loving.

One could make too much of the apparent dichotomies that appeared in the Robertson family. The senator attended to his fatherly duties to the best of his ability even though he did not spend a great deal of time in Lexington. Mrs. Robertson was devoted to her husband and her two sons; she prayed for them constantly in her later years. But it seems clear that there was a natural affinity between Taddy and his father; through the years they continued to hunt and drink together. Taddy, like his father, remained a bachelor until late in life, and often the senator invited him to travel with him. On the other hand, Pat became the answer to his mother's prayers as he more and more turned his life toward the spirit.

Pat Robertson grew up in Lexington. As a little boy, recalled his friend Matt Paxton, his mother had dressed him so well and preserved his childhood tresses sufficiently long that he became a "little pugnacious" in self-defense. But he was no sissy. Always big for his age, he played with older boys; he was "popular," "a round-er," "mischievous," a "real social animal." Little boys found plenty to do in Lexington. There were the football games and other athletic events at Washington and Lee and VMI, they could peek in on the dances that brought the big-name bands to town, or they could loaf around in stores like Tolley's Toggery owned by their families' friends and fellow church members. The State Theater offered a standard fare of cowboy movies and musicals, including the films of popular star Ronald Reagan. At home, Pat was surrounded by an atmosphere of Southern culture—pictures of Robert E. Lee and Traveler were scattered throughout the house. His gracious mother, who more and more eschewed social activities, always welcomed his friends and playmates into their home.

Robertson attended school in Washington for several years, but as a young teenager he returned to the public schools in Lexington. The town had an unusually fine system subsidized by the local community. Many of the students were children of the instructors at the local colleges. Pat was an extremely bright student; he skipped the seventh grade and competed well with those older than him. He spent his last two years of high school at the McCallie School in Chattanooga, a fine prep school that educated generations of male heirs of the South's finest families. He proved to be an excellent student, winning the Prix D' Excellence en Francaise Award. The senator tried to provide his sons with a variety of other experiences. One summer he secured jobs for Pat and several of his Lexington friends in the national park system; Pat worked at Yellowstone. At McCallie Pat roomed with his Lexington friend Edwin Gaines, whose father was president of Washington and Lee. It was during his years at McCallie that Robertson decided to box in the Golden Gloves, even though he was only sixteen. Gaines thought he was too pudgy, and Robertson was never the outstanding athlete his father had been, but he persisted with his characteristic tenacity and later recalled that he had won at least one bout.

In 1946 at age sixteen, Pat was back in Lexington, living at home and attending Washington and Lee. A fine academic institution,

Washington and Lee was described in the paper of a neighboring women's school as "a league of fraternities, bounded by classes and surrounded by women's colleges." "Washington and Lee men," continued the article, "are very charming, well-mannered, well-dressed, slightly suave and sophisticated, and, we are told, sometimes *just too* juvenile. . . . They often carry their own cigarettes and always carry a bottle—both are very carefully guarded. They are fun, witty, fairly good dancers, and very confident of their own charm." Every weekend the boys streaked out of Lexington in their cars to visit the neighboring girls' schools—Southern Seminary in Buena Vista, Mary Baldwin in Staunton, Sweet Briar in Amherst, Randolph Macon in Lynchburg, and Hollins College in Hollins. Or the girls were fetched to Lexington to enjoy the "sweet and swingy music" of Tommy Tucker or attend one of the grand balls on campus that brought to Lexington the likes of Tex Beneke, Glen Gray, and Claude Thornhill. They could cap their evening with an "after-dance snack at Lexington's Stork."

Pat Robertson blended into the environment at Washington and Lee as naturally as the graceful buildings on the campus. His local friends joined him there. Matt Paxton and he were SAE fraternity brothers, though he, like most of the local boys, lived at home rather than in the fraternity house. His roommate from McCallie, Edwin Gaines, remained a close friend. Robertson continued to be an excellent student, graduating magna cum laude in 1950 at age twenty and having received a Phi Beta Kappa key the previous year. It all seemed to come easily for him, thought his friends; his academic life never seemed to interfere with an active social calendar.

Ironically, in view of his later life, young Robertson was not a campus political leader at Washington and Lee, although he did, recalled Paxton, "hobnob with the campus leader types." He was not an athlete, though he did wrestle in the intramural competition for his fraternity, and he was virtually invisible in campus publications. His only appearances were in the gossip columns: "Tom Jacob, Pat Robertson, Jim Moore, and Dick Hynson gave the

Sweet Briar girls a thrill, and vice versa over the week-end." He reportedly spread the thrills around widely, never concentrating too much on a steady date.

The fact that Pat was a senator's son could hardly have escaped the notice of his friends and social acquaintances, but such fame was not extraordinary in a place like Washington and Lee. Friends remembered an occasion when Robertson was stopped by a patrolman while he and two friends were on their way to pick up dates. Pat told the officer that he was the son of Senator Robertson; one friend identified himself as Fred Vinson, Jr., son of the Chief Justice of the Supreme Court; the third announced that he was Robert E. Lee the Fourth. "I am George Washington," replied the officer, "and I'm taking you in."

Senator Robertson was extremely proud of the accomplishments of his younger son; years later he would introduce Pat by harking back to the days when his son had graduated magna cum laude from Washington and Lee. The senator promised Pat that he would finance a summer in Europe if he earned a Phi Beta Kappa key, which he did at age nineteen. And so, immediately after his graduation Pat departed for London. He spent the summer as a student of Fine Arts at the University of London, but he also traveled to France and Italy, drinking in culture and good times, a carefree, spirited young man.

Upon his return from Europe in the fall, Robertson and Edwin Gaines reported for active duty in the Marine Corps. The two young men were the first Washington and Lee graduates ever to receive military commissions upon graduation. They had attended platoon leaders class at Quantico Marine Base for two summers prior to graduation and also completed basic training, qualifying them for commissions in the Marine Reserve. The commission had been arranged by Senator Robertson, a staunch believer in the benefits of military experience. Both Gaines and Robertson were scheduled to enter graduate school in the fall of 1950, but the North Korean invasion of South Korea in June resulted in their activation into the Marine Corps. Assigned to the First Marine division in January 1951, Robertson found himself aboard a transport along with about ninety other young officers headed for Japan.

While most of those officers, including Robertson's friend Edwin Gaines, eventually saw combat duty in Korea, Robertson was assigned to a replacement-training command in Japan. He later was sent to Korea as assistant adjutant in division headquarters and finally served in a forward command post near the battle lines. Though he never was engaged in any fighting, he did serve in a combat zone and, on the basis of his record, qualified for a unit citation for combat duty. Although he was never in any danger from combat, the senator was forced to chide him for his lapses in writing his mother, who always presumed him dead when she did not regularly hear from him. His tour completed in 1952, Robertson returned to the United States a First Lieutenant and was discharged, planning to enter Yale University Law School in the fall.

Robertson's career in the Marines was a clear source of pride to him in later years, even after his conversion caused him to blot out much of his frivolous early life. His biographical sketches through the years reported that he had seen "active duty" in Korea and sometimes indicated that he had seen "combat duty." Not given to frequent personal recollections, Robertson, when he did reach into his past to find moral lessons, most often went to his military career. If he spoke at any length on the subject, Robertson usually did make clear the exact nature of his military duties. He told a reporter in 1979: "I fought in Korea. I wasn't with the first main division; I was not out shooting people, but I was in division headquarters."

It was apparently a personal shock to Robertson when he learned in 1986 that some of his young Marine companions had resented him because they believed he had been given privileged treatment. Congressman Andrew Jacobs, Jr., of Indiana made a number of charges against Robertson based on a letter to him from Congressman Paul McCloskey, Jr., of California, which were published widely throughout the country. McCloskey had been a fellow officer with Robertson on board the USS *Breckinridge*, which had transported the ninety young men to Japan. The heart of the charge was based on McCloskey recollection: "My single distinct memory is of Pat, with a big grin on his face, standing on the dock at Kobe, telling us that his father had gotten him out of combat duty. I remember being amazed at the time that a U.S. senator had that kind of power." McCloskey's letter not only challenged Robertson's public statements about his military role but, perhaps more important, raised questions about his intentional avoidance of combat duty and his father's role in exerting pressure to gain favored treatment for him.

Robertson answered the charges by filing a $35-million libel suit against Jacobs and McCloskey for "wanton and reckless statements." Neither side showed any inclination to back down; lawyers began taking depositions immediately. Actually, both sides agreed about much of the testimony. It was clear that Robertson and his young comrades kidded constantly about Pat's preferential status as the son of a senator. What Robertson apparently did not know was that some of them took the exchanges seriously. Once the charges surfaced, even some of Robertson's friends agreed that he probably did receive preferential treatment; no one imagined that his father's position would have escaped the attention of his Marine superiors. At issue, charged Robertson in his suit, were much more basic questions as to whether he was a "coward and sought to use political influence to avoid combat duty" and whether his father put direct pressure on Marine Corps officials. Those issues lay at the heart of the litigation. McCloskey's friends insisted that he was a man of sterling integrity who would not knowingly distort the facts, and Robertson publicly affirmed his confidence in McCloskey's integrity, but not his judgment. On the other hand, Robertson's old friend Edwin Gaines told reporters that he did not believe Robertson would have asked his father for such a favor. And those who knew the senator well, like Lexington's Matt Paxton, agreed: "I really doubt it. Because the senator was a pretty tough old bird. And there was never a whiff of any scandal around the senator. I don't think it would have been in character." In July 1987 a federal judge refused to dismiss the suit against McCloskey, ruling that there was sufficient evidence to justify a trial.

All of that fuss lay far in the future in 1952 when First Lieutenant Robertson returned to civilian life. The senator rewarded his son with another tour of Europe before he entered Yale Law School. A partying gentleman with impeccable credentials (his Marine buddies had labeled him the "division liquor officer"), his preference in Europe ran toward the Riviera. Coincidentally, he met one of his college friends in a Paris bistro. Pat had in tow, his friend remembered, a "roller derby queen from London."

The senator was quite aware of his son's unbridled lust for life as Pat prepared to enter law school in the fall of 1952. He repeatedly urged him to put the fleshpots behind him, be a little less reckless in financial matters, and get on with the more serious business of life. In later years, Robertson could still remember his father's recitations of one of the favorite proverbs of his minister grandfather: "The tendency of everything is to become more so." But it would take more than fatherly lecturing to catch Pat Robertson's attention.

At Yale, for the first time Pat Robertson reached the limits of his ability to wing his way through life on charm and the casual use of his native abilities. This jarring encounter with failed expectations would provide a setting for his first spells of introspection and self-doubt.

Years later Robertson told *Washington Post* editorial writer Michael Barone that he went to Yale looking for a "noble cause," only to be disillusioned by the brilliant "Legal Realists" who dominated the school in the early 1950s. His instructors were "skeptics who believed with Justice Holmes that the law is not a great omnipresence in the sky, but can be explained by politics, economic interests, and 'what the judge had for breakfast.'" While such intellectual misgivings may have surfaced later in his life and may have fed the emptiness that he began to feel then, they were not apparent at the time.

In fact, through most of his three years in law school, life seemed remarkably the same for Robertson—he was glib, charming, and a smashing poker player and casanova. "Whiskey and women," recalled one classmate, "he was out on the point there." His major goal was to make a fortune and to make it quickly. He spent the summer of 1953 working for the Senate Appropriations Committee, for which he received a note of commendation. He wiled away many pleasant hours during the summer chatting in his father's office and came to know the senator better than ever in the past. The next summer he worked in the office of W. R. Grace & Co. in New York, a large conglomerate with worldwide interests in chemical production; he seemed well on the way to a successful business career.

There was, however, a change in the quality of Robertson's academic performance. At Yale he was a mediocre student for the first time in his life; the senator was openly disappointed and Pat was increasingly disillusioned. In retrospect, it is easy to find reasons for his undistinguished showing. For the first time in his academic life, Robertson found himself competing with very bright young people who were better prepared academically than he was. Furthermore, his hedonistic habits, hardly befitting a serious student, apparently grew worse and worse. Shortly after his graduation, in 1955, he failed the New York bar examination, a prospect his father had seen coming for several months. Unaccustomed to failure, he was shaken and the mood was made worse by his understanding of how disappointed his parents must have been.

Another event even more profoundly interrupted Robertson's life in 1954—he married Adelia Elmer, a nursing student at Yale. In November their first child, Timothy, was born. The marriage came only ten weeks before the birth of their child; it was secret, sudden, and no doubt, the result of much soul searching by the young couple. When their parents learned of it, they were shocked and embarrassed. Friends in Lexington did not know of the marriage until months after the fact, and the senator and Mrs. Robertson were deeply distraught that their son had secretly married an unknown woman, presenting them belatedly with a wife and an unexpected grandson. They did not meet Dede until July 1955, when Pat brought her to Washington, but it was months before they would come to know her well enough to have their anxieties somewhat allayed.

The marriage was impulsive and based largely on physical attraction. Dede was working on a master's degree in nursing and encountered Pat when the law students were invited to the nursing dorm one evening for a party. He was charming and adventuresome; she was strikingly beautiful. Some friends thought she bore a marked resemblance to Gladys Robertson. The years would show that she was also strong and independent, stable and sensible. She was from a conservative, middle-class family; her grandfather had served as a state senator in Ohio. A high-spirited girl who had done her own share of partying in Ohio, she matched Pat and they became a pair in a local beer parlor catering to students. The chemistry was right. It was a physical relationship that had to survive some profound strains before ripening into a marriage. "I guess," said Robertson in later years, "it was just the appropriate time." But at the time, it hardly seemed approriate.

In later years Pat Robertson would look back on his marriage to Dede as the best choice he ever made, as would many of his friends. He candidly confessed that "it quieted me down," that marriage was a generic tonic to humble one. Considering his playboy background, this new medicine must have shocked his system. In 1955, he later recollected, he had been "terribly arrogant," cocksure, and self-centered. Then there was Dede and, almost immediately, Timothy. By the end of 1955, Dede discovered that she was carrying a second child. The year 1955 brought to his life not only the first hints of failure, but also the enforced responsibilities of a husband and father. It was enough to turn one introspective.

There was, however, no overt sign of change in Pat Robertson for a year. Momentum seemed to push him on toward his old goals of success and riches; Dede and his growing family may well have been added incentives. He was still ambitious, charming, and driven; Dede was a stylish partner for a young executive.

Immediately after his graduation, Robertson took a job as a management trainee with the W. R. Grace & Co. in New York.

Assigned to the Foreign Service School of the company to study economic conditions in South America, Robertson worked with the leading executives of the company. He found himself in an executive pressure cooker, beginning his fight up the corporate ladder, assured by Peter Grace that he had a bright future with the company. The senator was delighted with his son's new career and urged him to get on with the necessary linguistic training in Spanish and Portuguese.

At the same time, dreams of a quick fortune still danced in Pat Robertson's head; during the months he worked with the Grace company he viewed Latin America as the "land of opportunity" where he would find some way to enrich himself. And he also looked elsewhere. He repeatedly relayed hot stock market tips to the senator, generally receiving in return lectures on frugality and the futility of investing in the market unless one had inside information.

After about nine months with the Grace company, to the consternation of his father Robertson resigned his position and his regular salary. Along with two of his Yale classmates, he founded the Curry Sound Corporation on West 14th Street in New York City. The hopes of the venture rested largely on a technological breakthrough in sound systems that the company hoped to patent. For several months the partners rode a psychological roller coaster as their prospects rose and fell, but the harsh reality was that Robertson fell deeper and deeper into debt and had to depend upon his parents to provide support for his family.

Pat Robertson's life was not working out as expected, and he unquestionably began to feel pressure. Increasingly, his mother was compelled to act as an intermediary between her husband and her son. The senator viewed his son's actions as financially risky at best and irresponsible at worst. When Robertson's get-rich-quick business foundered in the spring, his personal finances were left in disarray. He brooded over his series of failures. At home Dede observed that he was restless, pacing and drinking beer, filled with thinly veiled anxiety.

And yet none of this seemed sufficient at the time to explain the radical changes that were to occur in Robertson's life in the next few months. In late 1955 and early 1956 Pat and Dede seemed to be adjusting to the life of sophisticated New Yorkers, although their strong personalities led to constant bickering. They lived in a modish apartment on Staten Island that featured avant-garde decorations and a huge Modigliani nude in the living room; they patronized the Stork Club and other nightclubs; Pat seemed at home on the fast track. Life was hectic but exhilarating, he later recalled, "trying to make my way and make a lot of money." In March 1956 he was selected as the Adlai Stevenson leader in the Richmond Borough; his father thought it a nice tribute, though he did not believe that Stevenson could win. If all was not well, all was not lost.

Nonetheless, in April 1956 religion surfaced in Pat Robertson's life when he began considering a career in the ministry. The idea first reared its head politely, perceived in the form of the gracious Protestant churches that lay easily amidst the corporate skyscrapers of the city. Here was a Christianity that offered much to young Pat Robertson—culture, dignity, and, perhaps most important, a regular and comfortable salary. In later years Robertson briefly supported his family on a clerical salary while beginning his television empire, but not for long, and not in the style that ran through his mind in 1956. These early religious perceptions were strongly functional, if not totally self-serving. Pat and Dede shopped around for a suitable church, she being a Catholic and he a Baptist. They ended up liking an Evangelical Free church; neither contemplated changing their fashionable life-style.

Robertson's turn to religion was a natural one. His family was littered with Baptist preachers; his father had a healthy respect for organized religion, and his mother had hovered over the young couple, sending tracts and praying constantly for their salvation. Pat had spent his early years as a typical youth in the Manly Memorial Baptist Church in Lexington, attending Sunday School regularly and enjoying the church socials along with the other youngsters. They were "good kids," recalled his friend George Lauderdale, but "none of us were strong Christians—if Christians." His background prepared him to retreat to a cerebral and cultured Christianity that promised relief, but not change, for his unruly life. His decision to enter the ministry, reported to his parents in April, received the wholehearted support of the senator—though he must have felt some disappointment that his son's extraordinary talents and background were not likely to receive the recognition they deserved. Still, the senator idolized his minister father, and he believed that his son could go far in any career he chose. Pat's mother, to her son's surprise, questioned the self-serving motivations that lay behind his decision. Her prayers had not been that her son would become a minister—she wanted him to be a Christian.

Gladys Robertson's gentle probing uncovered a heart that was ready for conversion. If Robertson's decision to enter the ministry had seemed to be nothing more than a pragmatic career change, it was a choice made by a troubled spirit in search of repose. He later recalled: "It was in that period that there was just this incredible emptiness in my heart and I was looking for something better. I tried it all. I had pleasure. I had philosophy. I had made good grades. I had traveled all around the world. It looked like I was going to be able to make a lot of money. And what I wanted was just not in any of those things. And I didn't know what it was." Confused and depressed, he briefly considered suicide. Maybe Christianity was the answer. That thought, however pragmatically formed, was rooted in a contrite and empty heart that was prepared to wring it empty of meaning. Once begun, his journey of faith was destined to be harrowing and exquisitely rewarding.

What he needed, Gladys Robertson told her son, was not Christianity, but Christ. Mrs. Robertson, though still a member of the Southern Baptist church in Lexington, had grown more and more attracted to the fundamentalist Presbyterian churches in Rockbridge County. She was a friend to several of the pastors of the area, including Pat's old classmate George Lauderdale; she talked with them frequently on the telephone, telling them at length of her concern over her son's spiritual welfare, or, as she put it, her "burden for Pat." She gave money to a number of fundamentalist ministers when she could pry funds from the senator, circulating their literature to her family and the Lexington university students. Among those whom she supported was an ex-Marine, itinerant evangelist, Cornelius Vanderbreggen, whose tract ministry was called the Bible Truth Depot. When Pat asked Mrs. Robertson for advice, she put him in touch with Vanderbreggen.

In the summer of 1956, Robertson met Vanderbreggen for dinner in a swanky Philadelphia restaurant. Robertson's future contacts with Vanderbreggen were few, but their dinner meeting triggered Robertson's new-birth experience, that central validating moment in the life of evangelical Christians. It was more Vanderbreggen's demeanor than his message that moved the troubled young Robertson. The evangelist was from a staunch fundamentalist background, a theological posture Robertson explored but never adopted. But Vanderbreggen was a "very fine person," Robertson later recalled, open, honest, and frank. Most of all, he was a classic, unabashed, born-again Christian, opening his Bible in the midst of the elegant restaurant, guilelessly probing those private and innermost feelings that genteel Christians did not discuss with a stranger.

Perhaps the most objective quality of that subjective Christian experience known as the new birth is the personal peace that envelops the born-again Christian, the sense of beatitude, the appearance of a serene confidence in one's relationship with God. Before his meeting with Vanderbreggen, Robertson felt that he had known only a compartmentalized religion, an intellectual belief that was kept in its place and never allowed to surface in ways that might cause embarrassment or ridicule. What he saw in Vanderbreggen was the born-again commitment—a manner that sometimes seems rude and presumptuous to outsiders but is a living testimony of salvation to the believer. The next day, Robertson later wrote, while sitting in his office the meaning of the experience gripped him. He began laughing, rejoicing that he had been saved. When he told Dede about his experience, she thought his story was the height of presumptuousness. But Robertson would never again be ashamed to witness publicly for Jesus Christ.

6.

The Quest for More

BORN-AGAIN CHRISTIANS observed Pat Robertson's good friend Bob Slosser, "don't talk a lot about their private life before Christ." It is not so much a matter of shame or remorse, though both of those feelings may apply; it is more a matter of changed interests and hopes. When an individual has experienced a rebirth, evangelical Christians believe, he or she really becomes a new person. No one who knew him well doubted that Pat Robertson had changed. Gladys Robertson was thrilled; the senator was acquiescent; Dede was befuddled and resentful. When her husband poured a bottle of Ballantine Scotch down the drain, Dede "thought he had really flipped." Pat Robertson and those around him were about to go through four desperately difficult years of building new relationships.

In the summer of 1956 Pat Robertson began to encounter a network of conservative evangelical organizations and personalities that would shape his life. Vanderbreggen recommended that he spend July at Campus in the Woods, a camp sponsored by the Canadian Inter-Varsity Fellowship at Lake of Bays, Canada. The campus was a kind of Christian boot camp, designed to "train college and university students in discipling." Although Inter-Varsity was not strictly associated with that militant conservative wing of evangelicalism known as fundamentalism, it was viewed by many as "egghead fundamentalism." The organization also bore the brand of its Plymouth Brethren founders; during the summer Robertson was introduced for the first time to fervent dispensational premillennialism, the doctrine that the world is at the end of the fifth dispensation, or age, awaiting the sixth and seventh, the biblical millennium and final judgment. More directly, however, he practiced those unashamed and aggressive techniques in evangelizing known as "discipling."

Robertson entered the evangelical network with a voracious appetite to learn. Upon his return from Canada, he spent several months as a volunteer working on *The Evangel* magazine, a publication of the Faith at Work ministry established by a noted evangelical Episcopalian minister, Sam Shoemaker. The next summer he was a volunteer worker in the Billy Graham crusade in New York City and he and Dede attended a summer camp sponsored by the Word of Life Fellowship on Schroon Lake in upper New York State. Headed by Jack Wyrtzen, the camp was another of those evangelical parachurch organizations designed to "win young people to Christ and Christian living." In the year between the summers of 1956 and 1957, Robertson met many of the foremost evangelical leaders in the nation. One such encounter occurred when he attended a Presidential Prayer Breakfast at which his father spoke. While there, he met Robert Walker, editor of one of the most widely circulated evangelical magazines, *Christian Life*; their conversation left the eager Robertson certain that he had only begun exploring the depths of God's will for him. Such ruminations would lead him far beyond the evangelical network he had encountered thus far.

In the midst of all of this activity, Robertson chose and enrolled in a seminary. He first told his father that he was thinking of enrolling at Fuller Theological Seminary in California, and he also considered Gordon Divinity School in Massachusetts. But some of his friends in the Faith at Work ministry told him of a conservative seminary in New York called The Biblical Seminary, and he decided that New York City provided the most challenging environment in which to win souls to Christ during his years as a student. In the fall of 1956 he began working on a Bachelor of Divinity degree at the New York school.

The Biblical Seminary of New York (in 1965 renamed New York Theological Seminary) was one of the rash of evangelical schools founded around the turn of the twentieth century to challenge the older seminaries, which had grown doctrinally liberal. But the school had a distinctive history and theological emphasis that set it apart from some of the more traditional seminaries. Founded by Wilbert Webster White, the school emphasized White's theory "that Scripture should be studied inductively and that it should occupy the central position in a theological curriculum." "Inductive Bible study," or "charting," insisted that all theological truth could be ascertained through a disciplined reading of the Scriptures. Located in a twelve-story building on East 49th Street, the seminary was foundering with low student enrollments and poor support when Robertson entered, but it had lost none of its distinctive theological traits. The president, Robert Trainer, was a stalwart defender of White's inductive method. "I couldn't have found a better place," observed Robertson in later years. "It was exactly what I needed." William A. Weisenbach, vice-president of the seminary in 1987, was convinced that the Bible-centered, nondogmatic methods postulated by White and honed by Trainer had left visible imprints on Robertson's subsequent religious thought.

During his three years at The Biblical Seminary, Robertson embarked on an exhilarating spiritual quest for "more of Christ." He studied the Bible relentlessly, later recalling: "I just wanted more. . . . I just wanted the experiences of the New Testament church. . . . If they had miracles and they had a very close personal walk with Jesus, I wanted it too." He was an exemplary student, as he had been earlier in life. A seminary friend remembered that Robertson "did not put himself forward or draw attention to himself or his gifts, but sought to put the Lord Jesus first." Like all of the students at the seminary, he took a job as an assistant pastor, working during his first year at the Bayside Community Methodist Church. At the same time, the ebullient young Robertson considered the evangelization of the city of New York to be his "ministry"; the result was countless casual, forgotten encounters for Christ.

More and more, however, in his odyssey Robertson traveled in concert with a coterie of zealous and seeking students at the seminary. A spontaneous collection, they began holding frequent meetings for prayer at 6:30 in the mornings in a tower room at the seminary. The group included Dick Simmons, a Presbyterian who had already graduated from a seminary in San Francisco but had come to New York after a disappointing pastorate, his wife, Barbara, Gene Peterson, the president of the student body (who had been reared a pentecostal, but who, by the time he came to the seminary, was Presbyterian), and Dick White, who worked for Inter-Varsity at Columbia University before enrolling at the seminary. A variety of other students attended, some more regularly than others, including Su Nae Chu, the widow of a Presbyterian minister who had been "martyred" during the Korean War. It was she who first introduced the group to praying in tongues. What united the students, recalled Robertson, was an "intense hunger for God." As the months passed, their meetings sometimes stretched into the afternoon, and sometimes into the evenings. It was, Robertson believed, "one of the most intense spiritual quests I have ever seen."

The seminary students were a sincere, reckless, even fanatical cadre in quest of a deeper spirituality. By the summer of 1957, they were in full pursuit of the baptism of the Holy Spirit. Robertson avidly read the spiritual reminiscences of John Wesley and Charles G. Finney, immersing himself in their cravings for more intense religious experiences.

In 1957, for the first time Robertson was introduced to pentecostal worship and the operation of the gifts of the Spirit. Pentecostalism had its beginnings in the hunger of evangelicals like Wesley and Finney for the Holy Spirit. The hallmark of the movement was its identification of the baptism of the Holy Spirit with speaking in tongues (tongues were the initial evidence that one had received the baptism), but pentecostals also received with open arms the other gifts of the Holy Spirit such as prophecy and healing. Pentecostals were convinced that supernatural power was still available to Christians and opened themselves to the free flow of God's miraculous intervention in the world. But this radical theology, as well as the poverty and social isolation of most pentecostals, separated them from other evangelicals throughout most of the twentieth century. In the spring and summer of 1957, Robertson and his student friends scoured New York City visiting the pentecostal outposts and rescue missions scattered about the city in storefronts and dilapidated buildings. He marveled as he witnessed the spiritual ecstasy that enlivened weary audiences late into the city nights. He watched them vanish rejoicing into the subways, having lingered in the embraces of one another after experiencing the embraces of the Holy Spirit. Here was raw, personal, experiential religion. It was tantalizing; Robertson and his friends wanted it.

The energetic and single-minded search Pat Robertson had undertaken inevitably led him into new friendships as well as new experiences; by 1957 the pattern of his future life was falling into place. It was coincidence or, as Christians would believe, providence that determined the specific details of his biographical journey. Robertson's meeting with Robert Walker came at this crucial moment in his life; it was surrounded by encounters with Harald Bredesen, an energetic and quixotic Lutheran clergyman who was to become Robertson's best spiritual friend.

When Robertson met Walker at the Presidential Prayer Breakfast in early 1957, it was one of those quick and passing encounters— broken short by Walker's departure for another appointment—that leave one feeling that the conversation was unfinished. Robertson approached Walker because he knew that the editor had formerly worked for Inter-Varsity, and Robertson was looking into every possibility, trying to find, as Walker recalled, "the will of God for his life." Walker thought that the conversation was unfocused and nebulous, but toward the end they began to talk of the deeper religious experience Walker encouraged evangelicals to seek. A deeper experience was what Robertson was looking for; he sensed that Walker was farther along on that quest than he was.

Indeed, in Robert Walker, Robertson had discovered an evangelical-charismatic pioneer, one who had opened himself to the pentecostal baptism of the Holy Spirit long before the modern charismatic movement began. In the 1950s Walker had been a lonely, if discreetly timid, charismatic voice within evangelicalism. In 1954 he ran a trailblazing article in *Christian Life* entitled "Are We

Missing Something?" The article urged evangelicals to investigate the Holy Spirit, and, although the magazine avoided the use of pentecostal terminology, Walker continued throughout the decade to quietly support the pentecostal experience. Walker and others always felt that he paid a price for such heterodoxy, both economically and in terms of influence.

A few days after his initial conversation with Robertson in Washington, Walker went to New York on business. At about eleven in the evening his telephone at the Park Sheraton Hotel rang. On the other end was Pat Robertson asking if he could arrange an appointment to pursue further the discussion they had begun. Walker asked when could they meet, Robertson replied that he was downstairs at the moment. Walker invited him up and they were soon deep in spiritual conversation. Pat told Walker of an amazing conversation he had just had with a man named Harald Bredesen and then began reciting the "astonishing things" that had been happening in his life. And so, until daybreak they excitedly and reverently discussed the baptism of the Holy Spirit and the other miracles they believed they had witnessed in their lives.

In the long run, it was a chance encounter with Harald Bredesen that had the most far-reaching effect on the life and career of Pat Robertson. The meeting occurred at Christian Soldiers, Inc., a slum mission that had appointed Robertson to its board. At an annual banquet sponsored by the mission, Robertson met Bredesen, who was working as a public relations director for the Gospel Association for the Blind. Bredesen attended the banquet on an impulse, having been a supporter of the mission years earlier. Once there, he was intrigued by the strapping and handsome young Robertson, who was introduced as the son of a U.S. senator. When the speeches were over, he rushed to meet him.

Harald Bredesen's life had been a bewildering collage of presumptuous ambition and humiliating self-abasement. Born into a family of Lutheran ministers, he received a traditional ministerial education and was ordained in the Lutheran church in 1944. Propelled by a personality that confessed to attacks of insecurity and feelings of inferiority as well as visions of fame and celebrity status,

Bredesen never accepted a Lutheran pastorate. Rather, upon graduation, he went to New York City and secured a position as a public relations secretary for the World Council of Christian Education. Bubbling and energetic, fascinated by the wealthy and famous, he was successful but anxious. Bredesen's life from the end of World War II until he met Robertson in 1957, described in his autobiography, *Yes, Lord,* was a bizarre and mostly downward spiral. He set out to make a fortune and failed; he wandered as a religious vagabond in Florida ministering to the Jesus people and flower children; he lived alone in a boarding house in Pine Bluff, Arkansas, where he was threatened by the Ku Klux Klan after being accused of keeping prostitutes; finally he returned to New York acccpting a job in public relations not long before meeting Pat Robertson at the Christian Soldiers mission. Bredesen was bright and literate (Senator Robertson later introduced one of his papers into the *Congressional Record* as "a timely sermon by a brilliant young pastor of Mount Vernon, N.Y."); but there was an engaging, childlike simplicity about his faith. When Pat Robertson met him, Bredesen had endured the gravest poverty and degradation trying to find his way religiously; he was already a veteran of more spiritual battles than most Christians would fight in a lifetime.

Bredesen's spiritual journey had two foci. The first was his experience with the baptism of the Holy Spirit. Bredesen initially encountered pentecostalism while a student assistant pastor in a Lutheran church in North Dakota; at the end of a summer's apprenticeship, he carried away images of a cold and dying denominationalism in the church where he had pastored and a live, experiential religion he had glimpsed in the homes of pentecostal friends. In 1946 he attended a pentecostal camp meeting and shortly thereafter he spoke in tongues, long before the emergence of the modern charismatic movement. In fact, Bredesen later wrote, in 1946 "not one pastor of the historical churches had ever received the baptism with the Holy Spirit . . . and survived in the historic church." Bredesen did not lose his ordination, partly because he had friends in the church's administrative offices and partly because he was not an active pastor. For many years he was a charismatic oddity submerged in a historic church, a prophet before his time. He found fellowship mostly in independent pentecostal circles, but he was constantly looking for adventuresome evangelicals who might be willing to listen to his testimony about the Holy Spirit.

The second focus of Bredesen's life was a search for notoriety. All of his life Bredesen felt drawn to famous people. His conversations and public speeches bristled with references to his encounters with and influence on movie stars and politicians (including Anwar Sadat), the wealthy and the educated. In later years, a remarkable number of the leaders of the Christian Broadcasting Network (CBN) were in some way spiritually indebted to Harald Bredesen. He sought them out; he fastened himself to them; they were his spiritual prey. And so it was that he riveted his attention on young Pat Robertson at the Christian Soldiers mission, quickly working his way through the dispersing crowd to meet him.

Bredesen and Robertson discovered that they were taking the same subway home after the banquet; their conversation turned immediately to the quest for more of Christ. Robertson told Bredesen of his first encounter with Walker. Bredesen and Walker had been friends for many years, having met at a convention of the National Association of Evangelicals and learned that each believed in the baptism with the Holy Spirit. Robertson related how Walker had told him of the ups and downs in his life, which seemed to parallel the course of his own life, and before their conversation had broken off had hinted that the Holy Spirit had helped him. Bredesen took the cue and began telling Robertson about the baptism of the Holy Spirit. The two talked long into the night, but they parted with much left unsaid. The next morning Bredesen appeared unexpectedly at the Robertsons' apartment, having ridden his bicycle across town. He left behind a copy of a book by pentecostal minister J. B. Stiles on the gifts of the Holy Spirit; Robertson invited Bredesen to meet with the student group at the seminary.

All through 1957 the seminary students' quest intensified; Bredesen now supplied know-how and boundless enthusiasm in their

pursuit of the Holy Spirit. Bredesen introduced the group to Paul
Morris, the charismatic minister of the Hillside Avenue Presbyterian Church in Jamaica. They began holding regular meetings at the
Hillside Church and one by one the students spoke in tongues; by
the time Robertson graduated in the spring of 1959 sixteen of the
seminary students received the pentecostal experience. They also
continued to visit the pentecostal churches in the city; years later
Robertson particularly remembered an Assembly of God minister
in Flushing, Pastor Graves, who, he recalled, "was a very godly
man, his face almost shone." Bredesen was ever present, instructing and encouraging; he rebaptized Pat, who had come to doubt
the validity of his boyhood baptism. After the baptism, Bredesen
recalled, "the glory of the Lord came down on me," and he gushed
forth in tongues. Months later, he baptized Dede in "the frigid
waters of Long Island Sound." But, even though he was ever present during these hectic months, Bredesen did not orchestrate the
group's experiences with the Holy Spirit; he was simply a part of
the common "venture into God" that was the preoccupation of
them all.

Dick White was the first of the students to speak in tongues at
Paul Morris's church; Robertson's experience came in a more private way. He returned home from school one day to find his son
Tim sick with a high fever. Unable to contact the doctor, he
prayed. In the midst of the prayer, he suddenly became conscious
that he was "speaking in another language," a language he later
believed to be an "African dialect." This was the experience that
Robertson had been tracking for months before and it was to mark
him for the rest of his life as a charismatic, though no one used
that term at the time, nor was there yet any movement to be a part
of.

In the fall of 1957 Harald Bredesen received an invitation to
become the pastor of the Dutch Reformed Church in Mount Vernon, one of those struggling mainstream churches in a decaying
urban neighborhood. He transferred his ordination to the Reformed church and for the first time in his life accepted the routine
of a regular pastor. He immediately asked Robertson to be his

assistant. Bredesen's church in Westchester County now became the center for the activities of the student enthusiasts. They spent hours together praying and fasting, exploring their new-found gifts of the Spirit. Bredesen said nothing of his charismatic beliefs when he accepted the call to pastor the church; he and his young friends were determined not to alienate those who did not understand their experience. Robertson later believed that these tentative months taught him spiritual restraint; he learned not to push his experience on others who did not want it. For nearly two years the group of young people met clandestinely, behind the massive stone walls and double-locked doors of the Mount Vernon church. Their meetings, joked the young Robertson, were reminiscent of those of "the disciples who locked the doors for fear of the Jews." Not only did they speak in tongues, but they experimented with the whole range of "Spirit-led worship." Quakerlike, they would "wait on God," until someone received an impulse to lead a song, or pray, read a scripture, or prophesy. In these early meetings, Robertson began to develop a penchant for prophecy that was to mark his later career.

As the time drew nearer for graduation and the eventual break-up of their association, the students' seeking seemed to become more frenetic. On March 22, 1959, at a birthday celebration Harald had arranged for Pat, Bredesen began to speak in tongues and then interpreted the message as a divine directive to share their knowledge of the gifts of the Spirit with Mrs. Norman Vincent Peale, the wife of the Dutch Reformed church's most noted minister. It was an extraordinary idea—Bredesen had had no association with the Peales in the past. But he called Mrs. Peale, told her that he needed to discuss some church business with her, and then announced that he wanted to explain to her the baptism of the Holy Spirit. Mrs. Peale replied that she had little time to discuss his business, but that she was interested in hearing what he had to say about speaking in tongues. She would be willing to listen.

After a dinner with Mrs. Peale in her lovely Fifth Avenue apartment, Bredesen, Robertson, and Dick Simmons gave an exhibition of speaking in tongues and told of their personal spiritual experiences, and Pat gave a prophecy. It was a meeting many look back upon as the fountainhead of the modern charismatic movement. Mrs. Peale was impressed, if not entirely convinced, before leaving to attend an editorial meeting of *Guideposts* magazine. At that meeting she urged John Sherrill, senior editor of *Guideposts*, to write a story about tongues speaking. Sherrill contacted Bredesen and, beginning with that association, Sherrill became the pioneer publicist for the emerging charismatic movement. His two books, *They Speak With Other Tongues*, written after his initial encounter with the New York group, and *The Cross and the Switchblade*, written after Bredesen and Simmons introduced him to the slum rescue work of Assembly of God minister David Wilkerson, sold millions of copies and were milestones in the spread of the charismatic movement into the historical Protestant churches and the Roman Catholic church. "We were just students," recalled Robertson years later, "and we wanted God," but they were present at the beginning of a momentous modern religious movement.

On the Sunday that Pat Robertson preached his final sermon as assistant minister at Mount Vernon, Bredesen made public the group's charismatic beliefs. The intensity of their private religious experiences could be bottled up for only so long. In one of their evening meetings, Bredesen began "twirling around like a dervish," shouting that God wanted him to reveal their secret before his congregation on Pentecost Sunday. The students had been waiting for the public explosion; they were excited and "gung-ho," Bredesen later recalled, but he was "scared stiff" that he would be fired on the spot. The promised message came immediately after Robertson finished his lesson. Bredesen rose and began to speak in tongues and to interpret. The congregation was stunned; some were disturbed, most were tolerant, and a few were sympathetic. But the feared public acknowledgment did not end in disaster; in fact, for a number of years the Mount Vernon church was a charismatic showcase. One of Robertson's fellow students recalled singing at the church shortly after it had taken on its charismatic identity. Although she was not charismatic and was taken by surprise by the pentecostal style of the service, replete with tongues speaking, she also was struck by the "intense commitment" she saw in Robertson and the others present.

When Robertson graduated from The Biblical Seminary in May 1959, he entered a harrowing and indecisive summer in which he struggled to find what God wanted him to do. He was offered several pastorates, including one Methodist church in New York City that offered an attractive salary, but he did not "feel led" to accept a job. Among the churches Robertson considered was the Classan Avenue Presbyterian Church in the Bedford Stuyvesant section of New York. He turned down an offer to become pastor of the church, but he recommended his friend Dick Simmons. Simmons accepted and moved his family into the decaying old church manse, which was located next to a bawdy house.

For several weeks Robertson's explorations ended in dead ends. He applied unsuccessfully to the Dutch Reformed church for an appointment as a missionary and visited Norman Grubb, head of Worldwide Evangelization Crusade, hoping to join that ministry. But nothing fell into place. Then while Dede was away visiting her family in Ohio, Pat sold their furniture, gave a portion of the money to his friend Bob Pierce, director of World Vision, and moved in with the Simmons family. After Dede joined him, their entire family, now including three children, lived communally in one room in the Simmons manse, which also housed fellow student Dick White and an odd assortment of down-and-out vagabonds.

It was a difficult summer and fall, made brighter only by the fact that Dede received the baptism of the Holy Spirit while attending a Bible study at Paul Morris's church. For the first time in her life, Dede acquiesced peacefully to her husband's spiritual wanderings, although she despised living communally in the slums. Pat joined Simmons in trying to minister to the poor, racially mixed neighborhood; they were especially eager to draw blacks into the Classan Avenue Church. A friend who visited in the Simmons home that summer later recalled how impressed she had been by the "unity of spirit" that prevailed and by Robertson's willingness to be there: "It was obvious that Pat was a man of refinement, with a gentle, winsome manner, endowed with natural gifts of leadership. I respected him as a man who displayed some of the beauty of Christ. He was determined to know and do God's will while being willing to sacrifice personal comfort and material blessing to reach God's highest."

During that summer Robertson seriously considered remaining to work among the slum dwellers of New York. The neighborhood brothel was for sale, and he thought of buying it and turning it into a mission. But there were enormous pressures on him to get on with a more conventional career. Dede was miserable, even though she was resigned to following her husband's lead. When her outspoken mother visited, however, she was appalled by their living conditions and tried to persuade her daughter and grandchildren to leave with her.

In the midst of all of this, Pat Robertson was going through a deep personal crisis; there were no new careers to choose, no new schools to enter. It was time to face the world. But where? He entered the old Classan Avenue Church and prayed and fasted for seven days. In his autobiography, he writes: "That week, fasting and praying alone in the gloom and murkiness of that old church, I learned as much about the depths of Scripture as I had learned in three years in the seminary." In the midst of his prayers, he later told reporter Kenneth R. Clark, "God led me to a verse in the Bible that said, 'Thou shalt not take a wife or have children in this place.'" That verse, Robertson added, "was one of the most beautiful verses I'd ever seen because it enabled me to leave that part of the world." In a short time, he set out with his family for a new life in Virginia.

During the three-year period from 1956 to 1959, when Pat Robertson attended The Biblical Seminary and migrated from casual Christian, to fervent evangelical, to pioneering charismatic, his fundamental religious personality was formed. Of the friendships made during those years, that with Harald Bredesen would mark both men for the rest of their lives. But what most dramatically changed Robertson's life during these years was his infatuation with Jesus—it was that torrid love affair that placed fearful pressure on his family.

Dede was the most aggrieved party in this triangular love affair. By the summer of 1959, when the worst was over, the couple had weathered some stormy clashes. Generally speaking, Dede followed her husband's religious pilgrimage to the end, but always a couple of years behind and only with an understandable amount of outrage about Pat's spiritual carousing while she stayed home to attend to the growing family. Always ready to speak her mind, she had fought and fumed trying to make sense of her husband's religious extremism, to say nothing of the sometimes outlandish machinations of his friends. The holy quest that ended on Classan Avenue left Dede, no less refined than her husband, brooding about the limits of her commitment to both Pat and his path to self-sacrificial destruction. But, however outrageous it all seemed to others, Dede lived through the journey day by day. She had seen the spiritual transformation of her husband; she never doubted its reality. He was no longer the man she married, and she could have refused to live with a fanatical stranger. But he was as beguiling in his new personality as he had been in his former life; Dede begrudgingly listened, and she followed.

Robertson's relationship with his father was stormier and more hostile. For the senator, the changes in his son became increasingly nightmarish. At first the senator was supportive of Pat's decision to become a minister, writing to influential clerical acquaintances in hopes of furthering his career. And he continued to be the primary source of financial support for the family, regularly sending hundreds of dollars to his son. In 1957 Senator Robertson claimed Pat and Dede as dependents on his tax return, his son having earned less than $3,000 during the year. While the senator's financial assistance usually carried with it fatherly advice, it was generally good natured, except on those occasions when he felt his son was particularly irresponsible. When Pat informed him in 1956 that he was about to buy a house on Staten Island, the senator indignantly forbade such a step, since his son had no income of his own.

In the summer of 1959, when Pat floundered trying to discern what God wanted him to do with his life, the relations between father and son reached a nadir. The senator pressured Pat to accept one of the pastorates that had been offered to him or to become a chaplain in the Marine Corps; if necessary he could go to some small rural church, as his grandfather had, and learn to rear his family frugally but with dignity, as he had been reared. In the heat of the summer at Classan Avenue as Pat considered starting a slum mission, his father called and lectured him on a misguided spiritual idealism that would subject his family to a dangerous and unhealthy life in the slums. When Pat, still undecided about his future, and Dede returned to Lexington in August to visit Mrs. Robertson, the senator coldly suggested that the least they could do was to help with the dishes.

The visit to Lexington was a welcome respite for Pat, Dede, and the children, a few days of sanity before returning to the rigors of Classan Avenue. It was not a triumphant return for the promising youngster who had left Washington and Lee with a Phi Beta Kappa key in 1950. He came home subdued, his future unresolved, and dependent on the charity of a father whose patience had worn thin. To his former friends he seemed "serious and solemn"; he had ample reason to be badly depressed. But, from all appearances, he was not. Internally he was resolute, even though his life was filled with doubt and tension. He was at peace with himself and with God, and he was waiting, as he had learned to do in those meetings with his fellow students. Mrs. Robertson understood. That summer, she told her friends, her son "walked softly before the Lord."

Fittingly, it was Gladys Robertson who provided the key that led her son slowly to the end of his wanderings. Mrs. Robertson's contacts with the conservative Presbyterian churches of Rockbridge County in the 1950s brought her into a renewed acquaintance with George Lauderdale, a former high-school friend of Pat's who was pastoring a rural church near Lexington. Lauderdale became one of the targets of Mrs. Robertson's long telephone calls; he would listen sympathetically as she told in detail of Pat's "zeal for the Lord" as well as her concerns about the spiritual welfare of the senator. Then in 1958, while preaching a series of mission sermons in Portsmouth, Virginia, Lauderdale heard about a local UHF television station that offered free time to preachers. He sought out the rickety station located on Spratley Street in Portsmouth and was offered free time if his program included a gospel music segment. Lauderdale contacted an old college friend, Earl (Jigger) Jackson, who played the guitar and sang; the two moved into the Norfolk Union Mission for the summer, and they launched a television ministry on the little-watched Channel 27. It was an unpromising beginning, but Lauderdale resigned his pastorate and moved his family to Portsmouth. Lauderdale worked to support himself and preached in the evenings, but by the summer of 1959 Jackson had pawned his prized guitar to get enough money to buy a bus ticket home to Greenville, South Carolina.

Then on August 2, 1959, Channel 27 closed down; owner Tim Bright gave no warning. It had been a fly-by-night operation that, Lauderdale thought, Bright used as a tax deduction to balance his profitable automobile business. One evening during the summer Bright asked Lauderdale if he would like to buy the station. The impoverished Lauderdale frankly admitted that he could not entertain such an idea, but he immediately thought of his conversations with Mrs. Robertson and about his old friend Pat. He told Bright that he had a friend who might be interested, assuming that the senator's son would have the necessary financial backing. In a letter to Mrs. Robertson, Lauderdale included a casual but portentous inquiry, remembered later by both parties as a postscript, asking if Pat might be interested in buying a Christian television station that was for sale. Mrs. Robertson informed her son; he seemed disinterested, but the idea lingered on the periphery of his consciousness during the summer of 1959.

During Robertson's visit to Lexington in August 1959 he and George Lauderdale saw one another by chance. Lauderdale had reluctantly driven up from Portsmouth to be executor of the estate of one of his former parishioners. He made the journey partly because of a dream a few days earlier instructing him that his work in the area was not finished. Robertson later labeled his friend's experience a "vision," though Lauderdale continued to insist that "it was just a dream." Whatever the surrounding circumstances, the two met outside the Lexington Post Office and greeted one

another as old friends. Robertson was on his way to the local radio
station, WREL (named for Robert E. Lee), where two of his mother's preacher acquaintances had arranged for him to preach each
day. Lauderdale accompanied him to the station, led a prayer on
the broadcast, and the two old friends talked about the television
station that had just been closed. Lauderdale sensed that Pat was
not very interested; he had no idea that his friend had not the
vaguest possibility of raising the financial backing needed for such
a venture.

After Robertson returned to New York to live with the Simmons
family on Classan Avenue, the television station almost slipped out
of his mind. But slowly, in September and October, as he and
Dede suffered through the depths of his indecision, the idea began
to surface more frequently in their conversations. In early fall,
Robertson made his momentous choice to buy the television station, and he began to rush with his usual abandon toward his new
goals. In November, he and Dede packed the three children into
their car and their few possessions in a U-Haul trailer and headed
for Portsmouth. Although no one could have known at the time,
the Robertson family was about to find a home, and Pat, as he
neared age thirty, was headed toward the power, affluence, and
fame that appeared to be his lost birthright.

7.

Christian Broadcasting Network, 1960–1970

To SOMEONE with less faith and better judgment, the Robertsons' journey from New York to Portsmouth to acquire a television station would have seemed sheer lunacy. They embarked with seventy dollars remaining from the sale of their furniture, headed for a barn, or something, in the Norfolk area. Bright's asking price for the television station was $250,000, though he immediately came down to $75,000 for the property and the equipment when he thought Robertson was a serious buyer. Robertson decided that when he met Bright in Baltimore, he would offer him $37,000. In fact, all of these figures were ephemeral; Robertson had not the slightest prospect of paying anything for the station. Nonetheless, Bright, whom Robertson described as a "middle-aged country boy from the coal-mining section of Virginia," agreed to sell him the station for $37,000 and to give him a six-month option with no cash payment. Actually, Bright owed RCA around $44,000 and he told Robertson that he would have to try to talk RCA into settling for the $37,000 he was willing to pay. In all likelihood the deal was consummated because Bright believed that Senator Robertson's son surely would be able to raise the necessary finances.

The most obvious person with less faith and better judgment in the midst of these hurried weeks was Senator Willis Robertson. When the senator learned, at the end of October, that his son was about to leave for Norfolk to try to buy the television station, he was irate. He told his vagabond son in no uncertain terms that he was not to incur any financial obligations in his latest outrageous scheme, because the debts would almost certainly fall upon him when the venture collapsed. The whole idea was preposterous. Where would he get the $75,000 needed to buy the station? Furthermore, the senator's staff carefully researched the matter and determined that UHF stations were never likely to be of any value. Even if that were not true, a television station could not operate on less than $500,000 a year. Where would he get the money to operate the station? Not only was the venture sheer folly, his son still had no job, had still not been ordained as a minister in any religious denomination, and had shown no inclination to take the responsibility for supporting his family.

Senator Robertson called several of his son's friends to elicit their help. The senator had always liked Harald Bredesen, partly because he was an ordained clergyman in a historic church and partly because he regarded him as "a brilliant young pastor." He asked Bredesen to "try to talk some sense into my boy." If it was good business sense he was after, he would have been better off talking to his son. He telephoned George Lauderdale, cleared his throat and solemnly said: "George, I want to remind you that my son was a Phi Beta Kappa at the age of nineteen. My staff . . . has researched this thing and it will not work." In later years, Pat Robertson concluded that his father was convinced that he was going to embarrass him in his own political backyard.

The elder Robertson and his son were never farther apart than during the first months of the television venture. When the senator asked practical questions, he got spiritual answers. When told by his son that he would carry it off by faith, the senator curtly replied, "Don't tell me you can do this through prayer." When he reluctantly accepted the fact that the business was going to launched, he urged Pat and Lauderdale to try to get the support of the "leading ministers of Norfolk," only to be politely told that they might disagree about the identity of the "leading ministers." The senator was repelled by his son's new charismatic vocabulary and his claims of divine leading. In June 1960 he wrote to famed evangelical preacher Donald Gray Barnhouse requesting a copy of a sermon Barnhouse had preached denouncing modern miracles. Things would get better later, but not before father and son had some barbed exchanges that betrayed the unwavering common sense of the senator and the unquenchable charismatic faith of his son.

It was in this atmosphere of economic gloom, family turmoil, and spiritual adventure that the Christian Broadcasting Network was formally chartered on January 11, 1960. Robertson did most of the legal work himself, making it clear, recalled Lauderdale, that "the Lord Jesus Christ is the head of this thing." Jigger Jackson sent three one-dollar bills to support the enterprise, the first contribution received by the Christian Broadcasting Network, and Robertson opened a bank account with the donation. It was all "absolutely insane talk," recalled Lauderdale later, "unless he was sure enough speaking the word of faith. And he was."

Perhaps the most fortuitous stroke of good fortune during the Robertson family's early months in Norfolk came when Pat got a job and became an ordained minister in the Southern Baptist church. Robertson visited a number of the churches in the area when he arrived and was rebuffed by the more fundamentalist Baptist churches because of his charismatic beliefs. But after visiting the Freemason Baptist Church, a prestigious old congregation in downtown Norfolk, he was hired as the Minister of Education at a salary of $100 a week. The pastor of the church was Dr. William L. Lumpkin, former pastor of the Manly Memorial Church in Lexington, track coach at Lexington High School, and a respected friend of Senator and Mrs. Robertson. A few weeks after he was hired, in a ceremony attended by Senator and Mrs. Robertson and other dignitaries, Pat was ordained by Dr. Lumpkin and two other Baptist ministers. Robertson proved to be popular with the young people of the church; he did his work well Lumpkin recalled in later years, although he was a bit overzealous in urging deeper commitment on the part of the church's members. But the job was far more important to Robertson than to the church. His father was understandably relieved that he had finally been ordained and had agreed to accept steady employment. His parental relations improved steadily from that point on. From Pat Robertson's point of view, the job provided for his family's necessities while he finagled to get his television station on the air.

The early months of CBN were a comedy of errors filled with false starts and breathtaking escapes from disaster. Robertson assembled a five-person board composed of Dede, Bredesen, Lauderdale, Bob Walker, and himself. Bredesen and Lauderdale were obvious choices to join Pat and Dede on the board; when Pat contacted Walker, the aspiring broadcaster confessed that his plans were so grandiose and nebulous that he needed some "way-out guys" to help him. The four men on the board met for the first time during a Full Gospel Business Men's convention in Washington, D.C. Late in the evening, in a hotel room that was being used for storage, the new board approved the constitution and signed the articles of incorporation for the Christian Broadcasting Network. The whole thing must have seemed slightly ridiculous, but they had too much faith to realize it. There was no substance to the plans, only the vision. Demos Shakarian, the founder and president of the Full Gospel Business Men's Fellowship, came by to encourage the group, but when he left there were still no dollars in the coffer.

The Christian Broadcasting Network did not air its first program until August 3, 1961. That broadcast was on radio station WXRI-FM, broadcasting from a small dilapidated facility acquired in a swap for the use of the tower at CBN's nonfunctioning television station. The radio station, whose call letters were the first three letters in the Greek word for Christ, sent out a weak signal received only in the immediate Tidewater area. When Robertson received his permit from the FCC he announced that his television station would use the call letters WTFC (Television For Christ) and that the station would open by December 1960. Both announcements proved to be an embarrassment. The call letters WTFC had already been assigned and the station's opening was far behind schedule. The new call letters, WYAH, were no less symbolic, however, being the first three letters in Yahweh, the Hebrew name for God. Station WYAH-TV aired its first program on October 1, 1961, at 3 p.m.

The opening of the two stations was the culmination of months of labor and negotiations. There were countless last-minute rescues. In February 1960, when it all still seemed a far-fetched dream, Robertson's charismatic friend from New York City, Paul Morris, paid him a visit and brought an $8,000 check for the network as a gift from his working-class church. But there were many low moments. In early 1961, Robertson seriously considered selling the station before it had ever aired a program, but, bolstered by the faith of his board, who rebuked him for being too proud to beg, he printed a headline in the little paper he was publishing, "God's Decision: No Sale!" In the months that followed, other gifts trickled in and Robertson slowly paid off his debt to RCA and patched together the equipment at the abandoned station. When WYAH did finally go on the air, the equipment was antique and temperamental and financial solvency was a day-to-day problem. But the opening of the radio station provided the first crucial link that gave CBN some access to the people of Tidewater area. The opening of the television station put CBN into the homes of a small but loyal band of supporters.

Those small achievements in Robertson's first two years in Portsmouth may well have been more notable than the multimillion-dollar accomplishments of CBN in the 1980s; the weeks were filled with life-or-death decisions. Ben Armstrong, president of the National Religious Broadcasters organization, has repeatedly stated that the founding of this first Christian television station by Robertson was a pioneering milestone, "that serves as a model even today." But the future of CBN was by no means settled once it had been born. The radio station was housed in a makeshift, refurbished garage and furnished with worn-out turntables. Its message was transmitted from an antenna described in the legal documents as "one creosote pole." The television station consisted of one studio on Spratley Street, one camera, and three offices; the equipment was held together by ingenuity and a prayer. Bob Walker was a veteran observer of wild-eyed evangelical schemes, but the first time he visited the facilities at WYAH he privately thought, "I have seen off-the-cuff operations, but this beats them all." When Ben Armstrong visited the facility in 1964, it still looked like "something put together with coat hangers."

For several years, Robertson scrambled frantically to find employees who shared his vision and who had some expertise in the broadcasting business. It was a volatile business environment. CBN was precariously financed, it was staffed by people who were learning as they went, including Pat Robertson, and it was a Christian enterprise, trying to maintain its spiritual objectives in the midst of overwhelming business pressures. There was considerable turnover in the staff and some hard feelings, but, all in all, Robertson was able to assemble a fairly gifted team within the first five years of the network's existence. By 1965, Jay Arlan, who had worked for ABC, had become the network program director, bringing a new professionalism to the stations. The most important other addition to the staff was the arrival of Jim and Tammy Bakker, a young couple who had been successful itinerant evangelists in the Assemblies of God. In September 1965 they began a popular children's program first called "Come on Over" and later named the "Jim and Tammy Show."

In the early years, finding suitable programs was almost as difficult as hiring a competent technical crew. The station aired all of the evangelical and charismatic films that were available, but there were never enough to fill the time. The employees and local volunteers improvised programming ranging from puppet shows to commentaries on Sunday School lessons. Robertson spent considerable time on the air himself, discovering and honing his native skills as a communicator. Bob Walker remembered an occasion during the early 1960s when Robertson interviewed him. He was amazed at Robertson's erudition as he nonchalantly lectured the single camera on a variety of exacting theological subjects. The station also had to run films to fill the time; they frequently were not well screened and early Christian viewers had to tolerate occasional hula dancers and cocktail-drinking heros.

The critical problem in the network's early years was fund-raising. Robertson was determined to operate the station on a noncommercial basis, funding the station with gifts from the viewers. By 1963, however, the budget of the Christian Broadcasting Network had reached $7,000 a month and it desperately needed some regular source of income. Robertson discussed with a local minister friend, Jack White, a scheme to hold a telethon, asking 700 listeners to pledge $10 a month to guarantee the budget. White suggested that

these supporters be called "The 700 Club," a name that long out-
lived its original intent. In 1963 and 1964 telephones were installed
in the studio during the telethons and viewers were asked to call
and make pledges. The telethons fell far short of their goals, although the 350 supporters who joined "The 700 Club" in 1963
provided the first dependable base of financial support in the organization's history. Furthermore, the Christian Broadcasting Network had discovered the fund-raising technique that would provide
the lifeblood for the organization in the future.

It was the 1965 telethon that established CBN on a firm financial
footing for the first time. A combination of factors contributed to
the telethon's success in eliciting pledges far beyond the proposed
yearly budget of $10,000 per month. In 1963, Robertson purchased
a new 50,000-watt transmitter for his FM radio station, vastly ex-
tending its potential audience, and by the fall of 1964 WXRI had
one of the highest listener ratings of any station in the area. The
radio station became a tool to advertise the television station,
broadening its viewing audience by 1965. Also in 1965 for the first
time Robertson featured a celebrity guest, Tony Fontaine, on the
yearly telethon. But the central figure in the financial breakthrough
of CBN was Jim Bakker.

Jim Bakker, as time would prove, was one of the most gifted
fund-raisers in modern religious history. Some of the components
in his formula for financial success—a shameless willingness to
expose his feelings and his financial needs to the public, a childlike
faith in God's personal presence, and an emotional personality that
swung moment by moment from flights of rapture to fits of de-
spair and weeping—appeared for the first time on the 1965 telethon. Late on the final evening of the event, with the telethon still
far short of the goal, Bakker broke down while on camera. Weeping, he told the audience that all was lost because the goal had not
been reached. The spontaneity of the occasion was electric, the
cameras continued to grind long past sign-off time, and the telephone lines were jammed with calls. Unable to call in on the
crowded lines, scores of viewers came to the station, many with
money in their hands. By the time WYAH shut down in the morning hours, enough money had been pledged to pay off all of the

debts of the network and to underwrite the budget for the coming year. For days after the close of the telethon, viewers continued to call in making pledges and, in a new and important development, asking for prayer and guidance and reporting miracles that had taken place during the telethon. For the first time, the human beings on the television screen had made a dynamic connection with the viewers; upon that linkage hung the spiritual and financial future of CBN.

The 1966 telethon was a similar success; viewers flooded the telephones with calls offering financial support, asking for prayer, and reporting miracles. After a request from Jim Bakker and Bill Garthwaite in November 1966, Robertson agreed to begin an evening program that would combine the telethon's viewer call-in system with a talk show format. Bakker had long been intrigued by Johnny Carson's late-night show and the telethon successes convinced him that such a format would allow the Holy Spirit to move on television. Robertson was less sure that the spirituality of the telethons could be captured on a regular basis, but he agreed to the program, and the decision was made to call it "The 700 Club Program." While Bakker hosted the early shows, Robertson insisted the program be a "team effort." In later years, Robertson and Bakker harbored differences of opinion about who contributed most to the creation of the new program. Robertson felt that the first few weeks were modeled much too rigidly on "The Tonight Show"; after a couple of weeks he insisted on a complete revision, including inserting himself as cohost. But everyone soon knew that they had struck upon a successful formula—a program with prayer and ministry and telephone response from the viewers. Beginning at 10:15 each evening, "The 700 Club" usually continued until midnight, but sometimes the hosts would extend the program far into the morning hours if the viewer reaction seemed to demand it. The early programs avoided overt charismatic demonstrations such as speaking in tongues, as did the CBN network in general, but in the late 1960s, in no small part through the influence of Jim Bakker, "The 700 Club" became more and more an open laboratory for Spirit-filled worship and teaching.

A spat between Jim Bakker and the CBN program director nearly lead to Bakker's departure in 1966, but Robertson resolved the tension, and Bakker continued to contribute to the growth of CBN until he decided to leave in 1972. Bakker felt emotionally depleted when he left CBN, but he soon began the creation of his own television empire in Charlotte. Although relations between Robertson and Bakker remained strained for many years, they later greeted one another warmly on a number of public occasions, including an appearance by Bakker at the dedication of CBN's new headquarters in 1979. In the months before the PTL scandal, friends described relations between Robertson and Bakker as "cordial"; "The 700 Club" broadcast a lengthy interview with Jerry Falwell on the occasion of Bakker's resignation as the head of the PTL Network.

The newfound financial stability of CBN ushered in two unbroken decades of expansion. In 1966 Robertson was able to borrow $225,000 to finance the construction of a new building to house the network. Ground was broken on June 5, 1967 (a symbolically important date, Robertson believed, because it was the opening day of the Six-Day War in Israel), and in May 1968 more than 11,000 people attended the dedication of the new facilities. It seemed an incredible achievement in less than a decade. And yet, at a luncheon shortly before the dedication of the new building, Harald Bredesen delivered a startling prophecy: "The days of your beginning seem small in your eyes in light of where I have taken you, but, yea, this day shall seem small in the light of where I am going to take you." Robertson later wrote: "I was dumbfounded. . . . CBN had started from nothing, but by 1968 God's blessings were evident and everything had changed. As we entered this new building, how could it be that something even greater would eclipse this accomplishment." But, in truth, it had all just begun.

8.

Christian Broadcasting Network, 1970–1987

B Y 1970, WHEN Robertson's autobiographical *Shout It from the Housetops* was completed, CBN had acquired ownership of a radio station in Bogota, Columbia (providing a "toehold on the world"), had been given five radio stations in New York state, and had acquired a license to open a UHF television outlet in Atlanta. Robertson estimated that the combined stations of the network were reaching a potential audience of 10 million people. Then, in the next five years, the network expanded at breathtaking speed. A television station in Dallas was added to the stations in Portsmouth and Atlanta. In 1971, advertising executive Stan Ditchfield joined the network and he and Robertson began buying time on commercial television channels for "The 700 Club," adding several cities in 1972 and 1973 and then tripling the number of potential viewers in 1974. Added were affiliates in such major cities as Chicago, Philadelphia, and Washington, D.C. In 1975, the potential audience was doubled again, and for the first time "The 700 Club" was seen in New York City, Los Angeles, and San Francisco. In addition, CBN plunged headlong into the young cable television industry; by 1975 its programs were being shown on 1,200 cable systems. At the end of 1974, the network estimated its "potential viewing audience" at around 65 million viewers. At the end of the next year, that estimate had risen to 110 million viewers. For the first time in 1975, the CBN fund-raising telethon was aired simultaneously in cities all across the nation.

The network had begun to reshape itself in other ways by 1975. "The 700 Club," which has undergone periodic revision in format throughout its life, was noticeably changed in 1974 under the supervision of producer John Gilman. The new program featured not only new sets but also "a greater emphasis on issue-oriented interviews with nationally known guests." In the long run, it was a format ideally designed to take advantage of the expertise of Pat Robertson; early guests included Prime Minister Yitzhak Rabin of Israel. In many of the major cities where "The 700 Club" was broadcast, provision had been made for viewers to call in to a local counseling center during the live broadcast, but in 1974 a twenty-four-hour counseling center was opened in Portsmouth. It received over half a million calls in its first year of operation. The 1974 counseling summary was typical of the statistical scoresheets published periodically by CBN:

Prayer requests	336,498
Salvations	26,827
Baptisms in the Holy Spirit	4,802
Answers to prayer	25,163
Pastoral referrals	12,830
Total	406,120

For the first time, in 1975 "The 700 Club" was broadcast in several foreign countries.

While the objectives of the Christian Broadcasting Network seemed fairly clearly defined in 1975, Robertson was about to announce a startling new set of plans that would revolutionize the shape of the ministry. The topsy-turvy growth of CBN seemed to demand a new headquarters building, and in 1975 Robertson weighed the purchase of five acres as a building site. But in August, during a charismatic conference in California, he heard the "unmistakable" voice of God telling him to purchase a multimillion-dollar 142-acre tract of land in Virginia Beach and "build a headquarters and school for My glory." The purchase was consummated on December 31; in 1976, the national bicentennial year, Robertson announced bold new plans he believed would help to usher in the religious vision of the earliest settlers of Virginia. On

June 5, the anniversary of the 1967 CBN headquarters ground breaking, a ceremony was held at the site of the new headquarters building. Pat Robertson delivered a prophecy:

Yea, my people, saith the Lord, before the foundation of the earth I planned this moment. Was it not my hand that led from England those settlers who came to these shores? Has it not been my ear that heard their prayer, and my heart that remembered? Are you not walking in a fulfillment of the prayer that has been prayed years before you?

Was not this land sanctified and held apart for you? Did you not marvel that there is nothing built here upon this land, this beautiful land? Do you not marvel that someone does not own it, and has kept it from you? . . .

Walk boldly into the future, for I hold the future, and I Am the future. Fear not what will happen, for I will provide, and I will provide beyond your wildest dreams. I have called you into a ministry beyond anything that you can conceive, and even as you begin to conceive, your thoughts cannot comprehend what I have called you to, so do not try to think ahead of me, but only walk with my plans and my purposes, and I will reveal my plans step by step.

You need not be afraid. You can walk confidently, for I the Lord your God have enfolded you with love, and even as you have spoken, I have sent my angels about this place, about this building, which will be called by my name. . . .

The International Headquarters Building was dedicated in an impressive ceremony on October 6, 1979. It was an elegant, Williamsburg-style structure designed by architect Archie Royal Davis, one of the nation's leading authorities on colonial architecture. The James River–type bricks and Indiana limestone on the exterior were complemented by rich and tasteful interior design. The building housed two state-of-the-art television studios and other recording facilities valued at $22 million in addition to administrative offices. The religious dignitaries attending the dedication ceremonies included Bill Bright, Rex Humbard, Jim Bakker, and Demos Shakarian. In a symbolic act extending a degree of evangelical legitimacy to Robertson, Billy Graham delivered the main address.

The completion of the International Headquarters Building was overshadowed by the master plan for a CBN Center that began to unfold in Pat Robertson's mind. At the beginning of 1978, Robertson told his supporters: "I began to write down what God had assigned CBN to do. He had told us to buy land. He had told us to build a university. He had told us to build a center. He had told us to go to many countries with our overseas outreach. He had told us to start a family-oriented alternative network. And there were other things that I had been praying about, too." The diversification and expansion of the Christian Broadcasting Network could be physically measured by the steady appearance of impressive new structures on its Virginia Beach property, expanded by 1982 to over 380 acres. In the fall of 1979 an administration/classroom building was completed for the newly formed CBN University. In 1984, a 152,000-square-foot, $13.2-million library building was added and in 1986 a new classroom building was completed. In 1986, a huge World Outreach Support Center, which housed many of the support operations of the ministry and additional television production facilities, was added to the complex. In 1983, a Chancellor's home was built just a few hundred yards from the International Headquarters Building. In 1987, the scope of the CBN operation, which included over 4,000 employees and a physical complex valued at around $100 million, was a majestic confirmation that no one could have imagined in 1977. And yet in 1987 a sense of mission pervaded the grounds as much as it ever had. No one believed that it was yet time to stop and count what had been accomplished.

The prime achievement of the Christian Broadcasting Network has been its emergence as an important network in the modern American television industry. That accomplishment resulted from a series of bold decisions made by Robertson and from technological developments that opened the industry to latecomers. Perhaps the most far-reaching of those choices lead to the dedication of a CBN satellite earth station in 1977 that allowed the daily transmission of the network's programs to cable outlets across the nation. Although the number of potential cable viewers was still quite small in 1977, CBN quickly became the "largest syndicator of satellite programs in the U.S.," and Robertson declared that the satellite station heralded "a whole new era in gospel broadcasting." In 1976, Robertson attached prophetic meaning to the technological breakthrough: "In Greek, the word 'angel' means 'messenger.' . . . Could it be possible that the Holy Spirit in the book of Revelation was speaking of the wonders of satellites when he mentioned that another angel would fly in the midst of heaven?"

Satellite transmission unlocked a variety of new opportunities for CBN. In April 1977 the annual telethon was broadcast simultaneously in eighteen cities, greatly streamlining the organization's most important fund-raising event. The most exciting potential of satellite transmission, however, was the possibility of creating a "fourth network." After returning from California in 1977 where he had talked with "leaders of the television and motion picture industry," Robertson bubbled with excitement. "When we told them that CBN was launching a fourth television network in America and a film company for wholesome films," he reported to his supporters, "the response was electric." But even with the ability to transmit programming by satellite, the creation of a fourth network with at least fifty affiliate stations seemed a far-fetched dream in 1977.

It was the dramatic expansion of cable television that made CBN a legitimate alternate network. In 1977 Robertson signed a contract to begin delivering twenty-four-hour programming to cable networks over RCA SATCOM II. "We were the first basic cable network ever," said Pat's son and CBN executive Tim Robertson, although HBO and WTBS did begin satellite transmissions before CBN. But cable broadcasting was not to become an important industry until the 1980s. In 1978 CBN programs were shown on cable outlets serving only about 1.5 million homes; by 1980 that figure had risen to about 6 million homes. But in the 1980s the network blossomed. By the end of 1986 the network's programs could be viewed in the homes of around 33 million people, offered on over 6,000 cable systems.

By 1982 the CBN cable network had become a financially self-sufficient wing within the Robertson organization. While the religious image of CBN caused some early difficulties in selling advertising, the network's aim of producing a "high quality mixture of family-oriented entertainment" became increasingly marketable. Furthermore, the CBN cable network made a major change in its revenue situation at the beginning of 1987 when it began charging the cable systems that received the broadcasts. CBN leaders believed that the financial strength of their cable network would, in the future, allow increased production of original programming. By 1987, CBN officials were certain that the "cable network is going to . . . earn a lot of money that can be used in the Lord's work."

Another key to the growth of the CBN cable system was the decision in 1981 to abandon broadcasting only religious programs, or "narrowcasting." Actually, from its beginnings, about half of CBN's programming had been "family style" entertainment, but the clean break in 1981 eliminated weekly religious broadcasts on the network with the exception of "The 700 Club." Beginning in 1981, the network billed itself "The Family Entertainer" and served up large doses of reruns of "Dobie Gillis" and "I Married Joan."

The abandoning of narrowcasting was both a pragmatic and a philosophical decision. First, it had to do with ratings. A series of studies produced in the late 1970s and early 1980s, particularly the book *Prime Time Preachers*, written by Jeffrey K. Hadden and Charles Swann, and an article by sociologist William Martin published in *Atlantic* magazine, attacked the exaggerated audience claims of religious broadcasters. These studies concluded that the electronic preachers were talking mostly to a shrinking body of people who already shared their beliefs. Scores of other studies have been conducted since 1980, varying considerably in their estimates of religious viewing audiences, but perhaps the most important result of the more accurate ratings was the impact that the studies had on CBN. "Like other religious broadcast entities," reported *Christianity Today*, "CBN found itself preaching primarily to the already converted, and drawing just 2 or 3 percent of the total television viewing audience. Michael Litte, executive producer of 'The 700 Club,' said the shift to a secular appeal began when CBN strategists asked themselves, 'What impact are we really making in response to the Great Commission?'" While the rating debate continued in 1987, a sophisticated Nielsen survey commissioned by CBN in 1985 found that "The 700 Club" was viewed by "significantly more households than any other religious broadcast" and that as many as 28.7 million people viewed the program at least once each month. In short, the secularization of the network along with changes in the format of "The 700 Club" seemed to improve Robertson's ability to reach outside television's religious ghetto.

Ratings were the lifeblood of both secular and religious television, but CBNs switch from narrowcasting also reflected a new evangelical interest in the arts. While this new emphasis was not universally accepted by evangelicals, CBN University's School of Communications became a hotbed for innovative ideas. To some evangelicals, the changes in CBN broadcasting seemed a betrayal of the network's Christian mission. "It must be money," judged one critic, "it's just so expensive to be on the air, the broadcasters have to show that stuff." Network executives were chagrined in 1986 when the National Coalition on Television Violence, one of the conservative groups organized to monitor sex and violence on the networks, charged that CBN's cowboy movies and "The Man from UNCLE" were high in violence and had harmful effects on children. CBN spokesman Tim Robertson insisted that such programming could be considered violent only from the most theoretical viewpoint and that all programs aired by CBN were carefully edited to screen out harmful scenes.

The new emphasis on Christian creativity in the arts pervaded CBN University. In 1980 David Clark, the first dean in the School of Communications, offered a frank critique of contemporary religious programming: "With a few notable exceptions, the programming we have produced appeals to the saints but turns off the sinner. We evangelicals have always known and been able to articulate the message of the Gospel in *our own* terms. . . . There needs to be a recognition that many of these forms of worship and the language of evangelical discourse are culture bound and not necessarily inspired." At least, Christian ministries needed to explore new forms for their religious programs, improving on the traditional church service format.

However, the vision of the evangelical communications experts of the 1980s was much broader than simply revising religious programming. They looked back nostalgically to medieval culture, to a time when Christian themes pervaded the arts. What was needed was Christian journalism, Christian painting, and Christian drama. Somehow, in the midst of the secularization of the modern world, Christians had come to view the arts as enemies rather than as allies. Christians must regain the artistic skills needed to reassert themselves, not by preaching or bullying, but by permeating the society with the leaven of good values embodied in good art forms. CBNU was conceived as a training ground for a generation of new artists, and the CBN television network came to understand its Christian mission in artistic terms as well as in evangelistic terms. Ultimately, CBN would be successful only if it could present Christian programming that was artistically as compelling as that offered by secular television.

"The thing that is really driving the business," observed Tim Robertson in 1987, "is programming." In a sense, that had been true from the earliest days when Pat Robertson had scrambled wildly to put something worthwhile in front of the camera. But in the competitive cable environment of the 1980s, the pressure to provide attractive programs was consummately important. In 1978, Robertson announced that within three years CBN would be "producing up to 32 hours a week of 'morally uplifting' TV movies, serial dramas, and variety programs." In the decade that followed, the network tried to develop a slate of marketable original programming, conceived and performed by a new generation of Christian artists. Most of the network's creations were short lived, however; in *Charisma* magazine, Robertson's friend Jamie Buckingham observed that "CBN is a junkyard of programs which have started with great flourish—and just as quickly fallen by the wayside."

When the network abandoned narrowcasting in 1982, it offered a wide range of original programming including "an upbeat, early-morning show" called "USam" and a "positive, godly soap opera" called "Another Life." In the soap, reported the university's magazine, "CBN has shied away from presenting a Sunday school type of message and has tried to present life as it is." "Another Life" was reasonably successful, running 875 shows from June 1, 1981, until October 5, 1984. But original programming was very expensive to produce and these early efforts failed to attract adequate sponsors to justify the production expenses. An attempt to begin a full-scale news broadcast in 1986 lasted for only a few weeks because of an inability to attract commercial sponsors. The network retained news bureaus in Washington, D.C., and the Middle East, however, as well as remote crews capable of worldwide coverage that furnished news briefs and contributed reports to "The 700 Club."

In spite of these false starts, original programming remains one of the major objectives of the CBN network. Tim Robertson, Pat and Dede's eldest son, was a veteran in the television industry when he became president of the network in 1987 at age thirty-two. He was confident that major changes would follow the network's stronger financial position gained from fees paid by cable companies. That money would be plowed back into the production of original programs "based on Judeo-Christian values." In short, the expensive dream of providing a genuine alternate family network has proven elusive, but it is still very much on the agenda.

Throughout all of this transition, the cornerstone of the CBN network and the Robertson ministry remained "The 700 Club." Constantly revised in format over the past two decades, the program varied from an hour to ninety minutes in length but was generally broadcast live in the morning and rerun in the evening over the CBN cable network. In addition, in 1987 "The 700 Club" was aired over about 190 stations in the United States and overseas in time slots purchased by CBN. While ratings remained an extremely controversial subject among experts, it was clear that "The 700 Club," sandwiched into programming that was nonreligious, was reaching beyond the traditional religious audiences by the mid-1980s.

The drift of "The 700 Club" from a totally religious format toward a news, information, and inspirational program was gradual, steady, and almost completely a reflection of the maturation of Pat Robertson. By the end of 1985, the *Saturday Evening Post* called the program a "daily news magazine." No other religious television personality and few religious leaders in the nation could have carried off a program with the breadth of "The 700 Club." Robertson's gifted intellect and broad éducation became the focus of the program, as "The 700 Club" became the showcase for his talents. While Robertson has never tried to hide the religious content of the program, he would have had to seriously compromise his intellect had the program not been broadened in scope.

By the mid-1970s "The 700 Club" included not only news segments and lectures by Robertson on current topics, but also interviews with a list of guests ranging from Israeli Ambassador Abba Eban and Defense Minister Shimon Peres and sports figures Elvin Hayes and Manny Sanguillan to an unending stream of religious personalities, including evangelicals Francis A. Schaffer, Leighton Ford, and Hal Lindsay and charismatics Dennis Bennett, Nicky Cruz, and Jimmy Swaggart. In the 1980s the drift of the program toward news and information exposed viewers (and Pat Robertson) to a staggering parade of guests. Included were familiar figures such as Robert Walker, Harald Bredesen, Oral Roberts, Robert Schuller, and Billy Graham, but also every imaginable religious curiosity and fad. Andy Comiskey related "how God freed him from homosexuality"; Lulu Roman, "comedienne and singer from *Hee Haw,* told about her walk with the Lord and her weight loss"; Monica Lanza told "how God took away her craving for food"; former Cleveland Browns tight end Oscar Roan and his wife, Linda, "discussed incest, its effect on their marriage, and how God healed Linda"; and John Z. DeLorean recounted "the series of events that led to his conversion to Christ." By the mid-1980s Pat Robertson had met and talked with virtually every important evangelical and charismatic leader in the nation and hundreds of minor figures.

Even more stunning was the list of political experts and government leaders who appeared on the program, including Anwar Sadat, Amin Gemayel, Rios Montt and other heads of state, scores of congressmen and senators, and former presidents Jimmy Carter and Gerald Ford. A five-page list of "topics and issues" discussed on the program, assembled by CBN in 1986 included every conceivable topic of political and religious interest. The "national issues" discussed ranged from unemployment and the budget to religious liberty and church-state relations. In "world affairs" the program had invited experts to speak on such diverse topics as international terrorism, world hunger, the famine in Ethiopia, and anti-Semitism. The program also touched on health and medicine, science, the economy, education, diet, the arts, and personal and family living. The diversity of the show caused some problems and demanded an opening disclaimer on the views expressed by non-Christian celebrity guests, but "eating with publicans and sinners," wrote producer Terry Heaton in 1986, was just another part of the CBN strategy to reach out to "the vast majority of human beings for whom the Lord died—but who don't know Jesus."

The changes in "The 700 Club" were reflected as well in the new cohosts who joined Robertson on the program. Ben Kinchlow was hired by CBN in 1974 as director of the counseling center in Dallas; in 1977 he became a regular cohost of "The 700 Club." Kinchlow's autobiography, *Plain Bread*, tells an extraordinary story of the son of a black Methodist minister in Uvalde, Texas, who gravitated through the bitterness of black militancy to a charismatic ministry working in drug rehabilitation. Kinchlow was first invited to appear on "The 700 Club" as a guest; he felt that he and Robertson established an immediate rapport. Invited back a few months later, Kinchlow assumed that he would once again be interviewed by Robertson, but only minutes before the program was to begin he was told that Robertson was out of town and that he was to host the program. Tall, graying, and dignified, Kinchlow was a natural—he radiated a warmth and sincerity that endeared him to the audience. Shortly after his second appearance, he was asked to become Robertson's cohost.

The addition of a black cohost to the program was a touch that had many practical benefits, including reaching out to the growing black evangelical community and cutting short any lingering doubts about Robertson's own commitment to racial equality. Whether or not race was a consideration in the initial decision, the appointment of Ben Kinchlow had an immensely positive effect on CBN in the long range. He distinguished himself both as a television personality and as an administrator. As cohost of "The 700 Club," the affable Kinchlow was an ever-present symbol of the charismatic spirit, even when the program ventured far afield into secular affairs. His sometimes smiling, sometimes grimacing prayers endeared him to charismatic viewers. But, perhaps more important, Kinchlow was the perfect foil for Robertson's forays into every facet of human knowledge. Like most of the television viewers, Kinchlow was neither polished nor learned, but he was a paragon of common sense. Ben became the student; he listened, questioned, and nodded agreement as Robertson swept across the landscape from supply-side economics to nuclear fusion.

In 1983 Robertson and Kinchlow were joined by Danuta Rylko Soderman. An experienced talk show hostess in San Diego, Soderman fell into the spiritual orb of Harald Bredesen and, at Bredesen's suggestion, she contacted CBN. Soderman added a zest and spontaneity that the program had been lacking. Particularly, she questioned and probed Robertson rather than played the acquiescent student role as Ben had done for years.

But it was Pat Robertson who remained the central actor in "The 700 Club"; it was his vehicle of communication. As such, Robertson carefully crafted the program as "advocacy journalism." He wanted "journalism with a different spirit," "news from a Christian perspective." More than any modern religious figure, Robertson was determined to use television as a tool for instruction, not allowing the message to be overshadowed by the medium. He took Ben and his viewers through extensive technical discussions of theory and current events. He conducted countless interviews with experts and gave his commentary. In the course of two decades, Robertson became the instructor of millions of politically unsophisticated Americans who shared his religious commitment. Furthermore, Robertson consciously reached out to younger viewers, reacting to polls that indicated that news programs attracted younger viewers as well as more men than women.

Robertson's presidential bid led to the most far-reaching changes in the history of "The 700 Club." He hosted the show only sporadically in 1987; on August 14 he made his last scheduled live appearance. Even before Robertson's departure, Danuta Soderman had left the program. CBN officials explained that Soderman had been assigned to new duties as a correspondent, but her sudden departure remained something of a mystery. In the summer of 1987 Ben Kinchlow was the only familiar face remaining on "The 700 Club."

On August 31, "The 700 Club" entered a new era, broadcasting from a new modish set with two new anchors. Joining Kinchlow to host the program were Tim Robertson and Susan Howard. Tim had been appearing on the show for several months and had increasingly filled the gap left by his father's absence. Wholesome, bright, and affable, Tim Robertson was a novice, but he was a charismatic young man who would almost surely win his own followers. Susan Howard was a television veteran, having appeared for seven years on "Dallas," but she was a novice in the role of talk show hostess. In addition, the new program included frequent features by news analyst Sam Walker and creative vignettes by Scott Ross. The final half hour of the program, called "Straight Talk," aired panel discussions on a wide variety of issues, some of them a bit controversial for a Christian program.

Partly, the substantial changes in "The 700 Club" were demanded by the departure of Pat Robertson and Danuta Soderman and the emergence of Tim Robertson as the driving force behind CBN. Not so calculated, but nonetheless fortuitous, the new format moved the program further away from traditional Christian programming in the aftermath of the PTL scandal. The new club was also a continued effort to reach a broader and younger audience. It was all an enormous risk, albeit a necessary one, and it would be some time before the ratings would offer any verdict about the success or failure of the experiment.

In addition to "The 700 Club," probably the most successful original programming produced by CBN was a series of specials that have been aired since the mid-1970s. The first of the specials, "It's Time to Pray, America," was shown on 228 television stations; at the time it was "the largest simultaneously released production from a Christian organization." Often combining religious and patriotic themes, the specials frequently scored well in the ratings. The 1984 special "Don't Ask Me, Ask God" was the "most-watched TV religious special" of the year.

From a financial point of view the most important television event at CBN remained the annual telethon. The nature of the telethons evolved along the same lines as "The 700 Club." While the programs continued to feature the thousands of telephone calls from partners, as those making financial pledges were called, asking for prayers, and reporting miracles, the telethons centered around themes such as "Battle for the Family" and "Lives in Crisis" and featured news reports and commentary. The CBN news department provided more and more sophisticated vignettes for the telethons and "The 700 Club" telling stories of people whose lives had been changed by the CBN ministry.

The financial success of the telethons paved the way for the huge growth of CBN in the decade after 1975, and at the same time that growth aided the telethons. Because of the development of the network, the 1978 telethon was four times larger than any previous effort. In a twelve-day telethon the next year, CBN for the first time surpassed $1 million per month in pledges. By 1983, the ministry reported only new pledges; a goal of $12 million in new annual pledges was exceeded by $9 million. In the mid-1980s, CBN's revenue from gifts surpassed $100 million per year, although the ministry did experience some decline in revenue in the wake of Robertson's announced political exploration. The organization was forced to carry out a budget reduction of $24 million in 1986 when a projected increase of 22 percent in contributions fell well short of expectations, but that setback appeared to be only a momentary pause in the upward financial spiral.

While the telethons continue to be the most concentrated fund-raising drive by CBN, by the 1980s the organization had become so diverse and sophisticated that it raised money in a wide variety of ways and expended it for many different purposes beside television production and distribution. By 1987, the yearly budget of CBN was over $200 million, and the portion coming from gifts was mostly from small contributors. Political expert Paul Weyrich was amazed when he learned that the CBN "big donor" list included those who had given as little as $10,000. Although the number of wealthy contributors to CBN increased through the years, Robertson, like other independent religious ministers, became convinced that a broad base of small contributors was the soundest financial strategy. "Like the raindrops," Robertson wrote to his supporters in 1980, "we can join together to form a mighty river . . . to bring living water to those dying of spiritual thirst." Robertson's autobiography, *Shout It from the Housetops*, closed with a bizarre tale of his gullible entrapment in a hoax that promised to net CBN millions of dollars. Shaken badly by the experience, Robertson resolved never to become dependent on the beneficence of large donors. Furthermore, observed CBN board member Tucker Yates, Robertson did not feel comfortable with "fat cats," as did some evangelical ministers; he related much better to the masses.

Robertson bristled when critics challenged the economic ethics of the fund-raising tactics he used to support the huge costs of operating CBN. When *TV Guide* published a critical article in 1975, he sharply replied that it "reflected the mentality of a 22-year-old reporter with no comprehension of economic reality, particularly because he ignored the sale by Walter Annenburg, owner of *TV Guide*, of his own broadcast properties for 110 million dollars more than the magazine article charges was spent on television programs by so-called 'big-time religion' during 1974." But such denials by no means silenced journalistic critics; in 1986 *Time* noted that "even in CBN's flourishing state today, fund-raising is pervasive, as it is on all Gospel TV."

Actually, the fund-raising techniques of CBN were more sophisticated and less offensive than those of most other religious television ministries. While the telethons were primarily devoted to fund-raising, the annual campaigns largely eliminated pitches for money during the regular broadcasts of "The 700 Club," although special appeals were made for specific projects during the year. In September each year, for instance, the program featured a capital fund drive to raise money for the construction of new buildings. Most insiders believed that the ministry's financial policies were models of responsibility. Tucker Yates, who headed the ministry's development area for several years, believed that CBN's restrained tactics contributed much to Robertson's credibility.

At the same time, CBN overlooked none of the tried and tested fund-raising techniques used by other religious organizations—or in fact those used by nonreligious organizations. In the 1970s the ministry developed a sophisticated Development Department that offered "partners" expert advice on estate planning. But the financial backbone of the organization was its mail contacts with partners, both through various CBN publications and through personalized mass mail. The fund-raising potential of mass mail was first exploited by evangelist Oral Roberts in the 1960s; by the 1970s and 1980s the strategy was used not only by religious organizations but by political and social action groups of every sort. CBN sometimes used mass mailings to solicit new members for "The 700 Club," but, by and large, direct mail was used to communicate with the network's supporters about the progress and needs of the ministry. Few organizations had more sophisticated tactics for collecting names and sorting potential contributors. Members of "The 700 Club" and other potential donors were constantly appraised of Robertson's latest "leading"—the challenge to begin a fourth network, the airing of a new special, an opportunity to broadcast in Japan or Brazil, the demands of the Operation Blessing program to relieve the needy, retiring the debt on the CBN Center—and were furnished with cards that could be marked for gifts of $1,000, or $100, or $25.

While the Robertson ministry used all of the most refined fund-raising methods, CBN sometimes resorted to the kinds of gimmickry many ministries used effectively in courting less sophisticated supporters. Donors' names were listed on microfilm and encased in a cross; members of "The 700 Club" received membership cards, bumper stickers, and "gold-tone lapel/collar pins"; other givers received special mailings of cassette tapes and ministry publications; those who gave "Jubilee gifts" of $100 in 1979 received "a personalized certificate and display holder." In perhaps the most curious fund-raising campaign in CBN history, during the construction of the International Headquarters Building supporters began contributing personal property—"gifts of gold, diamonds, silver, crystal, antiques, stocks and bonds, and real estate are being gratefully accepted by CBN." A couple from Cumberland, Maryland, donated a registered Morgan stallion named "Little Rascal." He was rechristened "God's Horse" and put up for sale.

By 1987, bolstered by the growth of partner support, the Christian Broadcasting Network, Inc., not only produced "The 700 Club" and other special programs and controlled the CBN Cable Network, it also operated counseling centers around the world and supported a major charitable program called Operation Blessing. In 1986, CBN attempted to sell its commercially operated television stations, including WYAH, but in the absence of a buyer, it continued to operate them in 1987. In 1978 CBN University was established under the auspices of the CBN board. In addition, in the 1980s several educational and legal organizations were supported by CBN, including the Freedom Council, a nonprofit organization aimed at political education, and the National Legal Foundation, founded to offer legal assistance to Christian causes.

While these varied programs form the CBN nucleus, in the long run the ministry's highly visible domestic activities may be surpassed in importance by its foreign work. Robertson has long seen his ministry as a harbinger of worldwide revival; he wrote to supporters in 1986: "More people will come to the Lord in the next few years than in all history! Not only in the United States and Canada, but in Asia, in Africa, in Latin America, in the Middle East, even behind the Iron Curtain." Furthermore, supporting revival outside the United States has long been one of the most effective means of raising money from Christian donors. Robertson's 1986 letter concluded, "I believe that we stand at the dawn of one of the greatest spiritual advances in the history of the world, please fill out the enclosed card—and send it today with you special gift or pledge."

CBN's presence overseas began with the acquisition of the Bogota radio station in 1968, but the major increase came with the financial growth in the 1970s. First, the network began purchasing time for "The 700 Club" broadcast on radio and television in Latin America and in the Orient; also popular overseas were the Bible cartoons produced by CBN. In the 1980s, the network began dubbing programs in several foreign languages or providing subtitles; in 1983 a surprisingly popular version of "The 700 Club" was produced featuring a Japanese host. In 1986, Robertson proudly announced that a specially edited production of "The 700 Club" had been shown on government-owned television in China. In 1987, CBN television programs were aired in over sixty foreign nations; in most Latin American countries and in several other locations, "700 Club Centers" were supported to provide the same sort of counseling service carried on in the United States. "We're influencing the nations through Christian broadcasting," Robertson wrote in October 1986. Only time will tell how much.

CBN's most ambitious overseas work has been in the Middle East. On April 10, 1982, with the approval of Christian militia leader Major Saad Hadaad, CBN took over a television station in southern Lebanon that had been established by George Otis of High Adventure Ministries. Robertson told supporters that it was "the greatest day in CBN history," bringing together his destiny with that of Israel and the Middle East. Robertson named the station MET (Middle East Television) and managed to keep it on the air despite two bombings in 1983 that caused several hundred thousand dollars in damages. By 1987 CBN operated a counseling center in Cyprus to handle letters from the Middle East and employed several Arabic-speaking translators in Norfolk to prepare programs for MET.

Whatever the long-range import of these worldwide evangelistic efforts, probably the most effective of CBN's domestic support programs has been the counseling centers. The counseling centers grew out of Robertson's desire to establish a real linkage with his television viewers and a desire to react to their needs. Other methods were tried in the 1970s, such as holding local rallies where supporters could meet Robertson or some other ministry representative, but the counseling centers evolved naturally out of the telephone-response system developed on "The 700 Club." By 1979, twenty-one centers were operated on a twenty-four-hour basis with trained employees of CBN in charge of volunteer counselors. At that date the counseling centers had used over 10,000 volunteer workers to staff their telephones.

The number of calls received by the centers exceeded a million in 1978; in 1983 the figure reached three million. At one point in 1985, CBN surpassed American Airlines as the nation's heaviest user of toll-free 800 numbers. Supporters were given scoreboard-like reports on the achievements of the centers. For instance, in the first quarter of 1985 the ministry reported:

Counseling Centers

Total Calls	1,284,333
Salvations	47,467
Answers to Prayer	23,057

In addition, in the first quarter counselors ministered to 167,356 callers about family problems, 46,473 about emotional problems, 12,351 about drugs, 15,523 about alcohol, and 3,477 about suicide.

The calls, no doubt, were an expansive collage of the misery of the underside of American society and other societies. The Japanese center reported an appeal for help from a "famous baseball player" who "called in from a hotel room where he was committing adultery."

The people who took these calls were mostly untrained volunteers from local churches, but they were fortified with a counsel-

or's handbook that represented the accumulated wisdom of years of experience, and trained experts were always available for crisis cases such as potential suicides. Through the years millions of people had at least a casual personal link with CBN through the counseling centers. The following was typical of the letter every caller received from Robertson:

Dear Friend,

Thank you for calling the CBN counseling center. I thank God for using this ministry to help you in your relationship with Him. It is our privilege to help you know Him better, in whatever way He will use us.

I'm sending you some literature which I believe will help you in the areas you expressed. Please pray before you study the material, and ask God to give you understanding. Look up each Scripture reference in your Bible, and He will make it come alive to you.

I can't overemphasize how important it is for you to read your Bible regularly. You'll grow in wisdom, understanding and faith as you read and meditate on the truth of God's word. You can also find good Scripturally-based books written on many subjects that affect your daily life. You can find these in Christian bookstores.

The Lord will reveal Himself to you as long as you continue to seek Him with an open heart. I pray that He will bless you through this literature I'm sending.

And anytime you have questions, anytime you need a partner in prayer, write to me or call the counseling center. We love you!

Your brother in Christ,
Pat Robertson

In 1987 the ministry developed a "call-back system" that allowed a follow-up on some of the calls received by the centers.

The counseling centers also tried to establish ties with local churches. Robertson was always sensitive to criticisms that the electronic church undermined local churches; from the beginning his counseling centers made "referrals to local, Bible-believing churches." Thousands of churches throughout the country cooperated with the centers, most of them charismatic, and many of the pastors praised the referral system as a means of building local churches. "The 700 Club helps us reach a lot of people," wrote black pastor Otis Anderson of Cathedral Baptist Church in Chicago. Based on telephone calls received by the counseling centers, Ben Kinchlow estimated that 600,000 people had been added to local church roles through the efforts of CBN.

Millions more were touched by CBN's benevolent program Operation Blessing. In 1978 while reading Isaiah 58, Robertson felt a strong urge to do something to aid the poor. The program was made possible by the tie that had been established between the counseling centers and local churches, and it did much to strengthen that cooperation. Almost all of the relief work was actually done by local groups; Operation Blessing contributed only a portion of the needed funds. By 1987, the ministry had cooperated with nearly 15,000 local churches and thousands of other relief agencies throughout the country in various projects. The efforts ranged from providing food, clothing, and blankets to victims of natural disasters to providing vegetable seeds for self-help gardens. Operation Blessing also funded famine relief in Ethiopia and Sudan (prompting Vice-President Bush to invite Robertson to accompany him on a trip to Sudan) and provided relief for refugees in Central America. By 1985, CBN estimated that it had contributed to programs helping nearly 9 million people. The total cost of these benevolent schemes was over $50 million, though CBN contributed only a fraction of that amount. In 1985 in cooperation with CBN University Operation Blessing launched Heads Up, a program to combat illiteracy in the inner city. Featuring an innovative system of phonetic reading, Heads Up claimed to have enlisted 25,000 teachers by 1987 and to be reaching 100,000 students in cooperation with local churches.

By far the most ambitious expansion of the CBN ministry was the founding of CBN University in 1978. Robertson first conceived of building a school in 1975 when he acquired the property for the CBN Center. Initially, he announced plans to build a training school for Christians from Third World nations, but by 1977 he had decided to build a graduate university. When the university opened the next year, it had 77 students working in the field of communications; by 1987 the enrollment had risen to over 700 students drawn from a wide variety of undergraduate backgrounds. Full accreditation was granted by the Southern Association of Colleges and Schools in 1984. In the fall of 1986 the university added a School of International Studies and a Law School, aided by Oral Roberts's donation of a law library worth around $10 million. With those additions, CBNU offered graduate work in communications, education, public policy, biblical studies, business administration, journalism, international studies, and law. The first president of the university was Richard F. Gottier, former president of Western New England College, but he was replaced in 1984 by Bob Slosser, a noted author and journalist who was also one of Robertson's best friends.

In hindsight, the founding of the university seemed a natural development for the Robertson ministry. The uniqueness of CBN, in the words of executive Walter Harrelson, was the "intellectual depth behind it." The university immediately became a source for the kinds of artistic expertise the entire CBN operation demanded. But CBNU embraced a concept of Christian vocation that reached beyond the arts. The world needed ministers and missionaries, but just as needed was a commitment to excellence by every Christian in her or his vocation. The school offered an alternative to "secular humanism," allowing students to "integrate Biblical principles into the disciplines they study." CBNU's goal was to permeate society with Christians trained for leadership in the media, education, and politics.

CBN University is "Robertson's school," one journalist wrote recently, and its emphases are reflections of his interests. Robertson's growing concern about politics was shown also by the founding of the Freedom Council in 1981. Funded by CBN, the council was formed to "increase participation by Christians in the political process." Actually, it was only one of a number of political organizations founded and supported by CBN in the 1980s. In 1986, the *New York Times* reported that several of these organizations were being audited by the Internal Revenue Service for abuses of their tax-exempt status and improper reporting of financial transactions. Under particular scrutiny were the activities of the Freedom Council in supporting Robertson's presidential bid. "Mistakes were made, confusion did reign," a former council attorney told the *Times*, but he insisted that "there was no attempt to defraud." Tim Robertson maintained that he welcomed the investigation, confident that CBN was guilty of no wrongdoing. In the meantime, most of the political activities of CBN were curtailed as Robertson's political campaign heated up. The ministry became almost schizophrenic in 1986, determined not to damage its tax-exempt status as a religious organization by supporting Robertson's political adventure. All political projects moved out from under the CBN umbrella in 1986; they were no longer housed at the CBN Center, and they organized their own fund-raising operations.

By the 1980s, CBN had become a huge and complex organization; scores of individuals had come and gone as significant administrators. By and large, outsiders were impressed by the quality of the CBN employees. "For all the vibrant positivity and relentless goodwill, make no mistake," wrote journalist Kenneth R. Clark in 1985, "the 4,000 people who labor in his vineyard are neither blissed-out 'Jesus Freaks' from the 1960s nor Moonies hawking flowers at the airport. Credentials at CBN, professionally and scholastically, are awesome, and business is taken just as seriously as if it were being conducted on Wall Street." At the beginning of 1986, the ministry listed Pat Robertson as president of CBN and chancellor of CBN University. Bob Slosser was president of the university and CBN had three executive vice-presidents. Allen Rundell was in charge of finance and administration and managing the properties, legal staff, and treasury functions. Ben Kinchlow was Vice-President of Ministry and Development, overseeing the counseling centers, Operation Blessing, and all fund-raising. Tim Robertson was in charge of television operations. When Robertson's increased political activities put more and more pressure on his time in 1986, a major reorganization was announced, making Tim Robertson president of CBN, responsible for the day-to-day operations of the ministry beginning January 1, 1987.

Slosser, Kinchlow, and Rundell had years of service behind them and were dedicated to Robertson and his goals. But the emergence of Tim Robertson as a leader gave unexpected stability to the ministry. Vivacious and intelligent, Tim Robertson worked his way up through the CBN television ranks, learning as he went. He was widely respected within the organization; there was no apparent jealousy or recrimination when he was named president.

Within this structure, CBN functioned much like any other large business. The various subdivisions of the ministry competed for the available funding; there was never enough money to go around. In a ministry such as CBN, however, there are some unique administrative problems. One of the weaknesses of a Christian organization, observed Tim Robertson, was that people were not willing to "fight it out." Meekness was a Christian virtue, as was personal kindness, but they were traits that could dampen the needed give-and-take in high-level meetings. Honest confrontation was sometimes sacrificed out of Christian courtesy, usually to the detriment of the ministry.

Compounding this tendency toward corporate conformity was the presence of Pat Robertson. Although one coworker observed in 1977 that Robertson became more humble as the network grew, others viewed the ministry as an autocracy. A certain degree of authoritarianism goes with the territory when a leader gets his directions from God, but debate was also blunted by the sheer force of Robertson's personality. Tim Robertson acknowledged that the biggest problem his father faced was getting good advice. Former black militant Ben Kinchlow confessed that he had long been frightened by Robertson's intimidating intellectual presence. He recalled an evening in a Burbank, California, hotel when he blurted out to his cohost, "Pat, I'm afraid of you." "When you couple the force of his arguments and his undying conviction . . . with the fact that he has been trained in sophistry at Yale Law School," said Tim Robertson, "it is a very devastating array. You better be darn sure that you are absolutely right and that you've got the facts to back [you] when you tangle with him." Through the years not many had been willing to tangle; his son Tim and his wife, Dede, were in the most advantageous positions to do so. Bob Slosser and Tucker Yates, who served both as CBN executives and members of the Board of Directors, could also offer independent judgments.

But not many people felt they could challenge Pat Robertson on his own turf.

In 1987 control of CBN was still vested in a five-person board. Three members remained from the original board, Pat and Dede Robertson and Harald Bredesen. George Lauderdale resigned in the mid-1960s when he became offended by Robertson's willingness to work with nonfundamentalist ministers and churches, though he later came to believe he had been wrong and remained a loyal friend to CBN. Robert Walker left the board in the 1960s because of other commitments. By the mid-1970s, the present board had been formed. One new member was Bob G. Slosser, who became one of Robertson's best friends as well as president of CBNU. The other was S. Tucker Yates, Jr., a member of a wealthy North Carolina merchant family who was appointed to the board in 1972. Both Slosser and Yates became charismatics under the teaching of Harald Bredesen. The spiritual influence of Bredesen on CBN was marked; on the Board of Directors it was complete.

At first glance, Bredesen's impact on CBN appears so pervasive that he looms Rasputin-like behind the spiritual scenes. Though he has never been an employee of CBN, the ministry became the central focus of Bredesen's life. But his influence on Robertson and CBN has been totally benign and spiritual. On practical and financial matters, Robertson regarded his old friend as one of the world's worst guides; if you take him on a trip, Robertson joked, you will probably end up paying the bills. But in spiritual matters, Robertson believed that, more than anyone else he had ever met, Bredesen did "hear from God." "I would say that on spiritual matters," judged Bob Slosser, "Pat pays more attention to Harald than anybody else. Harald doesn't abuse that. But at board meetings or on social occasions, when Harald speaks . . . Pat listens." Though they were "complete opposites," Slosser concluded, "there is a relationship there that is very deep and very profound and rich and good." But whatever Bredesen's influence, it did not extend to the practical day-to-day operation of CBN.

Some people have suggested to Robertson that the size of the board should be increased in view of its power and the dominating influence that he and Dede exercise on a five-person board. At the same time, every board member firmly denied that its sessions were autocratic or even dominated by Robertson. It is an "independent board," insisted Harald Bredesen; "those men are strong men." Robert Walker looked on their gatherings as "spiritual meetings" of "men and women of great faith." Lauderdale recalled that the clear "point of our board meetings" was to "find out what God wants in this situation." Typically, when a question came before the board, Robertson asked the group if anyone had a "leading" about what they should do. Frequently, they would pray individually for guidance, then one by one relate their feelings; sometimes Bredesen or Robertson would speak a "word of knowledge" under the leading of the Holy Spirit. And, while every board member agreed that Robertson was hard to swerve when he had made up his mind, all of them could remember occasions when he was persuaded to change. "I never felt less than a total peer in a board meeting," said Tucker Yates. "That really is to his credit."

Whatever the dynamics of the CBN Board of Directors, no one would deny that the intellect and personality of Pat Robertson was the soul of the ministry. "I always felt," said Robert Walker, "that Pat was better alone than he was with a group of people." Bountifully gifted as a communicator, a television personality, a public speaker, Pat Robertson was most persuasive in a small room, speaking softly and reverently face to face. He also listened, and that added to the power of his personal presence. But in the end he would probably work his will, not by intimidation, but by argument and fervor.

9.

Private Side

A FTER 1960 THE private life of Pat Robertson was virtually subsumed in the larger drama of his multimillion-dollar business empire. In the early years of CBN, he worked a long and exhausting schedule—sometimes twenty hours a day—trying to master every facet of the business. In later years as "The 700 Club" became increasingly important, he adjusted to the confining routine of daily live performances. On the positive side, his television schedule kept him at home. Unlike more conventional evangelists who often roamed the country alone, Robertson and his family lived most of the CBN adventure together.

It was with a very profound sense of togetherness that the family had headed south from New York City to Portsmouth in 1959. Whatever the future held, Dede was relieved to be leaving the slum commune in Bedford Stuyvesant. She had never felt that she shared in her husband's decision to live there; now they had embarked on a new life in which she was a partner. She rode south holding seventeen-month-old Gordon in her lap; Timmy and Elizabeth played in the back seat of their 1953 blue DeSoto, which had been given to them by her parents.

When they arrived, George Lauderdale had arranged for the family of five to share the small home of a friend, Jean Mayo. Within a few days Pat and Dede had managed to rent a small apartment (without a deposit), and they invited the Lauderdales to share Thanksgiving dinner with them. Dede prepared a turkey that had been given to them and the two families gathered for a candlelight dinner, using an old trunk for a table and the stairs for seats.

During their early months in Portsmouth, the Robertson family survived on Pat's irregular preaching appointments at area churches and the benevolence of their parents. To ease their financial distress, Dede took a job nursing at Portsmouth General Hospital. After a few months, when Pat was hired by the Freemason Baptist Church, the family's income was sufficient to allow them to move into a farmhouse on Deep Creek Boulevard, though they continued to thrive on a diet of soybeans that drew frequent protests from the children.

In the summer of 1962, the Robertsons' home life changed once again. As Robertson devoted more and more of his time to getting his television station on the air, it became obvious to everyone that he could no longer do justice to his job at the church. On the other hand, CBN could hardly afford to support him in the early 1960s. At this crucial juncture, a local philanthropist who had long been a friend to Senator Robertson, Fred Beasley, offered to pay Pat $100 a week salary from funds in the Beasley Foundation and also to provide a rent-free home for the family. The regular salary provided by Beasley was the backbone of Robertson's support for a decade; the house was a more mixed blessing. Located on B Street in a rundown section of Portsmouth, the house subjected Dede and the children to two more years of slum living. In 1963 the fourth Robertson child, Anne, was born, and Dede became more and more insistent that the family move to a safer neighborhood.

When Robertson mustered up the nerve to tell his patron that he no longer wanted to live in his free house, Beasley offered the family the use of a lovely country mansion on the campus of Frederick College. It was a gracious and beautiful home, surrounded by woods and marshes. For the next nineteen years it was the Robertson home. The family did not move again until 1983 when they occupied the chancellery on the campus of CBN. That magnificent Williamsburg structure, valued at $385,000 when it was completed, was built half by CBN funds, and half by Robertson's private funds. The home remains the private property of the Robertsons during their lifetime, but at their deaths it becomes the property of CBN.

Once the Robertsons moved into their country home, Dede recalled, they settled into a life-style "similar to that of a super-busy

Pat Robertson as a cadet at the McCallie School, a prep school in Chattanooga, Tennessee.

Marine Lieutenant Pat Robertson. Robertson was in the Marines from 1950 through 1952 and was discharged as a first lieutenant.

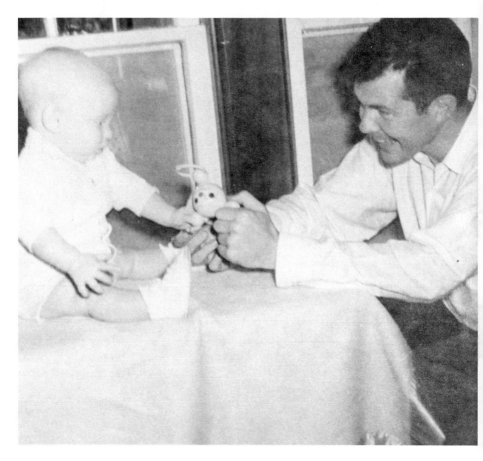

Pat and Dede's first child, Timothy, was born in 1955 while both his parents were still students at Yale.

When Pat and Dede left New York for Virginia in 1959 he had just graduated from seminary. They already had three children—Timothy, Gordon,
and Elizabeth—when Pat headed south without a job.

Robertson graduated from Washington and Lee University in 1950, having earned a Phi Beta Kappa key in 1949 at age 19.

Lt. Robertson reviews his platoon, 1951.

Pat Robertson visiting his father in Washington, D.C. On the extreme right is Robertson's father, Senator A. Willis Robertson. On the extreme left is Senator John Stennis, one of Senator Robertson's best friends.

Pat and Dede, 1982. *Photo by John Loizides.*

corporate executive's family." Pat left home early in the mornings and returned late in the evenings; his family sometimes complained about his absence. But when he was there he played enthusiastically with the children, and they thought he was a "pretty rigid" family disciplinarian. "When he was home we all had a great time playing together as a family," recalled his son Tim; "I never sensed any kind of absence." Not until Tim had left home to attend McCallie and after the television stations in Atlanta and Dallas had been added to the CBN network in the late 1960s, did Robertson's schedule take him away from Virginia Beach for extended periods.

Both Robertson's mother and father lived long enough to see their son's family comfortably settled into the country home and to see CBN firmly established. Gladys Robertson's death in the spring of 1968 came just as CBN was preparing for the dedication of its new building. Her sudden death was a great "emotional shock" to Pat, but she had witnessed the answers to many of her prayers.

Robertson's relations with his father improved in the senator's declining years. In 1964 Senator Robertson went to Europe as an official delegate to a conference of the Interparliamentary Union and he took Pat with him. During the trip, Pat preached in Copenhagen and Stockholm. The senator seemed reconciled to his son's new career. He wrote affirmatively to friends about the television enterprise in later years.

Completely engrossed in his spiritual mission during his father's 1966 campaign defeat, Robertson did nothing to support the senator's bid for reelection. He was stunned and heartbroken by his father's defeat and always felt that he might have been able to reverse the narrow loss had he campaigned in the Portsmouth area. A reporter who was in the senator's office when he took a call from Pat just before delivering his concession speech was impressed by the warmth of the conversation: "He said a few words to cheer Pat up. Then he read his concession statement for the radio in the fine resonant voice. And then he had some advice for Pat who was leaving with his wife and children for a camping trip in Canada; 'Now you try to find a good camping place where you

have electricity and don't have to chop a lot of wood.'" One of
Dede's fondest memories of the 1960s was "a dinner we had in
1966 when we unveiled the plans for the new building, and my
father-in-law came down as guest. The tremendous ovation the
people gave him just thrilled my heart, and it thrilled him, too."
In his last years, the senator vacationed occasionally at the stately
old Chamberlain Hotel at Point Comfort and enjoyed visits with
Pat and Dede and the grandchildren. "I know that my grandfather
ended up having a lot of respect for my dad after he saw what he
had done," observed Tim Robertson. It was surely so. The senator
had always been able to appreciate results. In the end, he must have
seen that his Phi Beta Kappa son might yet realize the fine potential
that had often seemed completely wasted.

The life-style of Pat and Dede Robertson changed in the 1970s
as the demands of CBN became greater and as the children began
to grow up and leave home. In 1970, Dede accepted a job as a
nursing instructor at Tidewater Community College; by that time
Anne was in the second grade. She also became increasingly active
as a speaker at Christian schools and women's groups, particularly
at meetings of the women's charismatic organization Aglow. In
1979 Dede collaborated with author John Sherrill in writing a popular autobiography, *My God Will Supply.* But aside from her family,
Dede devoted most of her attention to CBN.

She was an active member of the Board of Directors. "She has
great instincts," observed Bob Slosser, in the CBN board meetings, "many of the times that Pat has been challenged on something
that he wanted to do, has come out of Dede's mouth." A woman
of impeccable tastes, she personally supervised most of the interior
decoration of the elegant CBN Center. As a tribute to her public
accomplishments, in 1986 she was named Christian Woman of the
Year in a poll of leading evangelicals.

The Robertson children who came of age during these busy
years turned out to be attractive, loyal, and predictably independent
young adults. They had matured in a home where one had to fight
for his or her intellectual life against a father who "would tear us
apart" and a mother who was "tougher than everybody."

"Throughout my whole family experience," recalled Tim Robertson, "ideas were constantly tested and hammered out and argued about and we would yell at each other." With a family full of Type A personalities, they occasionally "blew the roof off the house," but there was never any doubt about the bond of "loyalty and love" that held the family together. Although each of the children experienced an adolescent rebellion, sometimes becoming a potential embarrassment to their father, friends of the Robertson family agreed that the children reflected well on their parents. By 1987, Tim had risen to the head of the CBN ministry and he and his wife had presented his parents with three grandchildren; Elizabeth and her attorney husband lived in Dallas and had one child; Gordon was a handsome young lawyer in Norfolk with all the devastating charms of his father thirty years earlier; and Anne worked for CBN while contemplating the values of a college education.

Outside of CBN and his family, Pat Robertson had little time for other activities. His work frequently came home with him after long hours at the station. Robert Walker remembered spending an evening in the Robertson's country home in the mid-1960s and being told that he would likely be awakened by the telephone during the night. Robertson invited his friend to get on the line if he wished; the calls were being forwarded from the station and he would be praying for those who needed help. In the 1970s, when Robertson began to turn his attention more and more to the complicated political and economic issues of the day, friends watched him day after day leave for home loaded down with an armload of books to pour over late into the night. To a remarkable extent, Pat Robertson's work was his life.

For many years, Robertson's main personal diversion was long walks through the woods and marshes surrounding his country home. He and Dede frequently walked together in the evenings. Walker remembered walking through the countryside for two hours on the evening he visited, talking fervently about Pat's plans for the future of CBN. In later years Robertson took up jogging, and he sometimes played tennis with close friends. But the love of his life in recent years has been a stable of horses housed in stalls behind the chancellery. Otherwise, when he was home he tried to rest, particularly on Sundays.

There has been little room in the lives of Pat and Dede Robertson for "social life." As is the case for many public figures, Robertson's public appearances left him craving privacy. The Slossers were good friends, as were some of the other employees at CBN, but mostly Pat and Dede spent their private time together and with their children. Robertson more and more prized his time with Dede. "He listens to her," observed Bob Slosser. "He probably listens more now than he did back in his young days, because she has proven that she is right." In the lonely, demanding world of celebrity, understanding and friendship are hard to find. In Pat Robertson's world, Dede knows him best and loves him most.

Pat and Dede Robertson have come a long way since the poverty-stricken days in Bedford Stuyvesant, even since the years when Mr. Beasley supplied them with an income of $100 a week. In the 1980s he was paid a salary ranging from $60,000 to 90,000 per year as chief executive officer of CBN and the value of their mansion home in 1987 was estimated at around $750,000. The chancellery was lavishly furnished and was surrounded by gardens and stalls for Robertson's horses. It was also surrounded by a sophisticated security system that assured that intruders could not approach the house.

Robertson long ago ceased to be a direct financial burden to CBN, however, and in recent years he has repeatedly stated that he donated his CBN salary to worthy causes; in 1986 he listed his contributions to CBN at $90,000. He and Dede have accumulated considerable personal wealth, mostly from the best-selling books they have written in the past decade. Like most religious figures, Robertson has been criticized for his luxurious life-style, as CBN has been chastised for its fund-raising techniques. And, like others subjected to such investigations, he has sometimes reacted testily. But in spite of periodic confrontations, more than any other charismatic television personality Robertson has escaped the swirl of controversy that surrounds the financial affairs of the likes of Jim Bakker and Oral Roberts.

In part, Robertson's success has seemed more palatable because he is a less traditional religious figure. He repeatedly stressed as his political ambitions became more open that he considered himself a successful businessman who had created a major television network. As the head of a large corporation, or as a bestselling author, or as a television personality, his life-style seemed unexceptional. Considering his talents and accomplishments, argued his friend Harald Bredesen, he had lived a "very self-sacrificial life."

There is perhaps another reason why Pat Robertson's success seemed unoffensive. He wore it naturally; it seemed to be his birthright. Robertson was reared to gentility and good taste; he has never been overwhelmed by or self-conscious about his life of abundance. When he was selected the most influential charismatic in the world in 1985 by *Charisma* magazine, the editor noted that Robertson had gained the trust of his fellow charismatics because he had "class." Pat and Dede Robertson saw a lot of life on the way to the top; when they arrived there, it seemed to be the place they belonged.

10.

Person

Pat Robertson is charismatic, not just in the theological sense but in the broadest definition of the term. His friends testify endlessly to his personal charm, his persuasiveness, his genuine friendliness. But so do neutral observers. "Don't take Pat Robertson lightly," advised *U.S. News and World Report* in a 1986 article. "Party leaders note that the experienced performer's charm and platform style stole the show from half-dozen veteran political rivals at a party meeting in Nashville." And so do his political adversaries. "I like him personally," John Buchanan, director of the liberal lobbying organization People for the American Way, said incredulously. "I like him. I think he's dangerous. . . . But it is hard for me to personally dislike Pat Robertson." Many observers agree that Robertson is blessed with the same mysterious personal charisma that made Ronald Reagan such a formidable public figure.

The sources of Robertson's charisma are at least partly exposed in the telling of his life story. Through all the meanderings of his life, Pat Robertson always knew who he was—he had a profound sense of place and family. He was a Virginian, a child of Lexington and Washington and Lee, and the son of Senator Robertson. Such roots breed assurance and self-confidence as well as manners. Added to his breeding was the later confidence he gained from his religious experience. According to Harald Bredesen, "Pat is secure in God." Even when Robertson was a young charismatic, remembered Robert Walker, when he joined a group, he would "take authority." Robertson's air has sometimes been seen as condescending and snobbish by those who dislike him; it was an unsettling demeanor in a television preacher. Robertson's friends in the 1960s repeatedly compared him to John F. Kennedy, both in looks and in the calm self-assurance that breeding brings.

Friends and foes agree as well that the key to Robertson's charm is his pleasing and smiling public presence. No matter how straightforward his message, his manner is persuasive and reasonable. Robertson's personal manner, wrote Jim Castelli in an article released by People for the American Way, is "smooth, polished, smiling, reassuring—not threatening." Robertson is a "paragon of diplomacy," observed a Memphis reporter, when compared to Jerry Falwell and other television evangelists who make thundering pronouncements. No doubt, the Robertson of the 1980s was a master of personal television communication skills; he told a Tulsa reporter that he could handle interviews in his sleep.

But the Robertson charisma is not simply a product of glib articulateness or of a pleasing personality and smiling countenance. He is persuasive because he is extremely bright, and he is informed. To state that Pat Robertson is intelligent is superfluous; everyone from Billy Graham to George Will has commended his mind. More impressive is the extent of his learning. According to conservative political analyst Paul Weyrich, "Robertson is perhaps the brightest of all of the potential presidential candidates, in terms of intellect, and in terms of sheer understanding of the national forces. . . . He is not without the ability to speak on virtually every subject. That comes not only from being very bright and very well read but also from the fact that as a television talk show host he has interviewed thousands of people over the years and he has absorbed a good deal of their knowledge. . . . He is one of the few people whom I brief, and I brief a good many, who can repeat back to me virtually everything that I said six months later."

In short, there is an undeniable reasonableness about Robertson's personality and presence. His critics insisted that those qualities showed up when Robertson appeared on "Meet the Press" but disappeared on "The 700 Club." To some observers, a combination of rationality and charismatic religion defied even the mental agility of Pat Robertson. But, in fact, "The 700 Club" was a startling combination of supernaturalism and logic. In a 1980 article in *Har-*

per's magazine, writer Dick Dabney gave his reaction to listening to "The 700 Club": "If it was the old-time religion, Biblical fundamentalism with a stiff jolt of speaking in tongues mixed in, it was presented not in any stupid or even ignorant way but as the centerpiece of a remarkably sophisticated, unified view of modern life."

If self-assurance and intelligence account for Robertson's charm, intensity and drive account for his success. At every point in his life, Robertson has struggled to wring his experiences dry of meaning—from hedonism, to experiential religion, to public service. One can only speculate about the sources of such primal drives. If Robertson's loving mother provided security and assurance, his father constantly held before him lofty goals. Added to that mix was a family environment that gave him exceptional freedom to develop his own individuality. Whatever the sources, Robertson's drive propelled his life. He frequently has been euphoric and thankful about his successes, but never satisfied. The "sense of mission" that Ben Kinchlow felt when he first visited CBN and others found pulsing through the ministry was no more than an extension of Robertson's restless ego, or as he described it, his "divine discontent."

A healthy, hungry ego is Pat Robertson's strongest asset and his most dangerous threat. People who attract millions of followers, who build financial empires, who run for the presidency have large egos. Some of his critics saw his interest in national politics as nothing more than "an enormous gratification to his ego"; many questioned whether he really cared about winning. And some of his best friends quietly and privately prayed that it was God that was speaking to Pat about the presidency and not selfish ambition.

Robertson has tried to force himself, not always successfully, to listen to criticism, to avoid sycophants, to be civil in confrontation. In his autobiography, he candidly discusses repeated internal disputes and controversies in the early years of CBN. There was no denying, confided his friend Tucker Yates, that Robertson was "headstrong" and "difficult to work for," relatively easy to reason with in a private conversation, but difficult and testy in public confrontation. "Sloppiness or slothfulness," agreed Ben Kinchlow, would "send him on a tear." Those who remained loyal to him did so because they knew that he never asked more of others than he gave of himself and because they appreciated his own struggle to keep his ego and aggressive disposition under control.

He has not always kept it under control. Robertson admits that he is sometimes impetuous: "When anybody ad libs a show for . . . twenty years . . . the chances of foot-in-mouth disease are very high." On occasion, he has lashed out in anger in the midst of a program. In 1982 he angrily charged that the behavior of the attorney general of Arkansas in a case testing the state's creation science law had been "crooked." Robertson has been successfully sued and, on the other hand, he has been accused of being thin-skinned and overly sensitive to criticism. He has repeatedly threatened to sue critics. And on occasion he has turned his guns on his fellow believers with such vehemence that his friend Jamie Buckingham admitted that Robertson could be "cutting" and "dogmatic" as well as charming: "He laughs a lot, but when he is crossed he is downright mean." Thinking back on the days when they were pastors together in Mount Vernon, Harald Bredesen remembered that they chastised their listeners so regularly that their wives gave them lectures on charity.

It is, of course, Robertson's forthrightness, his combativeness, and his willingness to fight, that have led him to the forefront of American religious conservatism. The question of whether he is an extremist or a representative of the religious and moral values of a majority of Americans implicates not his personality and character, but his beliefs. Both Robertson and his critics insist that he should be judged by what he has said. But the crystal clarity of those views and their pointed expression are products of his personality.

It is also true, however, that neither Robertson's personality nor his views have been completely rigid or uncompromising. He has, in fact, often described himself as a "pragmatist"; Robert Walker found him to be a "realist." In religious matters, he prided himself on his toleration of views that differed from his, although he refused to compromise his own convictions. On social and political issues, he insisted that he was neither "liberal or conservative," but rather an individual determined to expose every question to the light of common sense, to see what was "smart." In the context of a religious movement that harbors many extremists, most insiders consider Robertson a centrist, one who has almost always shown restraint and balance.

It is balance of a sort that is one of Robertson's most intriguing personality traits. Nothing fascinates casual observers more than his ability to adjust with ease in what seem to be wildly incongruous worlds. "Robertson will switch smoothly from leading a learned discussion of, say, national defense or mythic themes in contemporary American literature, to conducting a fervid pentecostal prayer meeting," wrote journalist Dick Dabney. What is intriguing is his paradoxical mingling of the first families of Virginia with storefront pentecostalism, of Bedford Stuyvesant slums and Williamsburg architecture, of elegant discussion of neo-Keynesianism and an exercising of the gift of the word of knowledge. Other human beings are fascinated by the raw power of personalities in such tension, personalities held together by a will strong enough to unify such diverse intellectual and social universes. And one who has existentially known so much of life has advantages. "It's as easy for Pat to talk to a pauper as it is to a prince," observed Tucker Yates. "I've watched him do both." Robertson's pedigree and intellect attracted many disciples, but when Oral Roberts announced that Robertson was his choice for president, he insisted that he trusted his friend not because he had been rich, but because he had been poor.

Perhaps the most basic and certainly the most persistent question asked of a religious leader is: Is he honest? The public can be as undiscriminating in its judgments of evangelists as of politicians. In the minds of many people, if you have seen one fundamentalist Elmer Gantry, you have seen them all. In fact, Robertson's sincerity and honesty are closest to the surface of all of his traits of character. "The man is honest," said Ben Kinchlow in an article in *People* magazine. "He will stop himself in the middle of a phrase to correct one mistake." More discriminating observers agree. Rice University sociologist William Martin, one of the most perceptive observers of modern American religion, wrote in 1978: "Success and stardom can corrupt the purest of motives and may one day count the Christian Broadcasting Network among their conquests. Still, after ten years of looking rather closely at radio and television ministries, with a good—though not perfect—record of assessing their genuineness, I came away from Virginia Beach convinced that I had been talking to people who believe what they say and practice what they preach."

Honesty and sincerity do not sanctify one's religious and political views, they do not qualify one for public esteem or public office, but they are a starting place. Their absence is a fatal flaw. Pat Robertson's personality has sufficient flaws to make him eminently human, but the absence of a dogged faithfulness to his beliefs is not one of them. Buried deep in his psyche are things most truly believed; he has shared them with his wife through over thirty intimate years; he has taught them to his children. Pat Robertson's problems in the future will almost surely not arise because he believes too casually or compromises too freely, but because his backbone bends too little. But therein also lies his future hope.

PART TWO

A Religious Portrait

11.

Christian

THOSE REVERED and historic Protestant names passed down to the twentieth century—Lutheran, Episcopal, Presbyterian, Methodist, Baptist—have become relics from a distant past; they are now little honored, less understood, and almost beyond definition by most who wear them as a matter of inheritance or convenience. It was not always so. In their time they told much about the people who wore them. They were titles carefully chosen by godly, learned Christians who surrounded them with intricate creeds and catechisms. People taught their children the distinctive truths giving rise to their name, lest they be condemned to hell. One could die because of a name, and many did.

It is true that denominations remain highly visible and economically powerful in twentieth-century America. They command the formal allegiance, sometimes even the doctrinal loyalty, of millions of people. But modern Christians are rarely simply Presbyterians or Baptists, and, save for pockets of sectarianism here and there, few think they must be a part of a particular denomination to gain God's favor.

There are many reasons why religion has so evolved in America. Separation of church and state and the establishment of genuine religious pluralism demanded that competing denominations live together peacefully. As Old World religious battles faded from the nation's collective memory, American Christians came to know one another, often to respect one another, sometimes to marry one another. By the twentieth century most American Protestants (and many Catholics) thought of themselves first as Christians. Asked in 1986 about his "religious commitment" by *Conservative Digest* magazine, Pat Robertson gave a generic answer that seemed typically American: "I am a Christian, and that means my relationship with the Lord Jesus Christ is the most important in my life; that my life belongs to the Lord; and, that my desire is to please Him in all that I do."

This new ecumenical spirit also flourished because of the twentieth-century secularization of the nation that created a pervasive anxiety among Christians. The meticulous and wearisome religious debates of centuries past seemed less and less relevant in a society where the rule of Christ was challenged. Furthermore, mass evangelism, the characteristic American style of religious recruitment, demanded a more vague and less factious message, a pruning of the denominational idiosyncracies that divided.

It may also be, as modern experts in communications argue, that the twentieth century is a more frothy age, conditioned to receive intellectual stimulation only in ninety-second television spots. It is difficult to imagine modern Americans pouring over the ponderous tomes of eighteenth-century theologians or listening intently for hours to learned debaters. If the theological content of popular Christian thought is bounded by television time slots, the historic theological battles of Christendom are not only no longer relevant, they are not possible.

In the twentieth century's looser theological environment, many Americans selected individualized theologies from the smorgasbord of denominationalism. Uninhibited by creeds and dogma, having general religious loyalties that outstripped denominational ties, Americans were the ultimate religious individualists, shopping for and swapping churches, spinning television dials to savor whatever seemed agreeable and right. A majority of modern Christians were willing to accommodate truth from anywhere on the religious landscape; most believed that they would not find all of it at any given spot. "In terms of the succession of the church I'm a Roman Catholic," said Pat Robertson in a 1987 interview. "As far as the majesty of worship, I'm an Episcopalian; as far as the belief in the sovereignty of God, I'm Presbyterian; in terms of holiness, I'm a Methodist; in terms of church government, I'm a Presbyterian also; in terms of the priesthood of believers and baptism, I'm a Baptist;

in terms of the baptism of the Holy Spirit, I'm a Pentecostal. So I'm a little bit of all of them."

Pat Robertson was consciously committed to the ideal of being an interdenominational Christian. All television ministers overlook minor doctrinal issues (and sometimes major ones) in order to embrace all who share with them the fundamental tenets of Christianity. But Robertson's ecumenism predated his successes on television. He has commended Protestants ranging from fundamentalist Jerry Falwell to liberal Albert Schweitzer. He has consistently spoken well of Roman Catholics and has been shocked and chagrined on occasions when he has been criticized by Catholic leaders. After a skirmish in 1987, he said defensively: "I've attempted all during my twenty-five years to build bridges with traditional bodies, be they Catholic or Protestant."

Robertson's vision of a united Christian community surmounting historic and contemporary denominational schisms was highlighted at the ceremony dedicating the CBN International Headquarters Building in 1979. Billy Graham, the unrivaled chieftain of evangelical Protestantism, gave his blessing to CBN and to Robertson by delivering the opening address. Every charismatic knew that the occasion was laden with symbolic significance as the leader of American evangelicalism praised Robertson's ministry. Bob Slosser summarized the ecumenical overtones of the occasion. First, he wrote, Graham spoke warmly of the pope. Then he turned and "verbally embraced one of the world's most prominent evangelical, Spirit-filled leaders, Pat Robertson." "Thus, on October 6, 1979," Slosser believed, "thousands watching in person and millions watching by television underwent a touch—perhaps the merest of glimpses, but still a glimpse—of the spiritual unity that Jesus had asked His Father to send upon His Church."

Of course, real Christian unity remained only a vision in the twentieth century, despite the collapse of the formidable theological barriers inherited from the Reformation. As denominational names waned in significance, new religious categories came to speak of new divisions. Less well defined than old denominational barriers, the new labels—liberal, evangelical, fundamentalist, charismatic—cut horizontally across Protestantism, often slicing denominations into homogeneous theological and cultural subgroups. These words increasingly came to describe distinctive interdenominational communities speaking unique religious languages and supporting separate collections of educational institutions, periodicals, and parachurch organizations. Outsiders frequently were bewildered by the untidiness of these new religious categories, but insiders understood them well; they knew where they fit, they knew the rules for entry and exit, and they knew the distinctive beliefs that made them a part of the group. Only in recent years could one comfortably fit into more than one of these communities, and even now some of the barriers are impassable. But, like millions of other Christians, Pat Robertson has long insisted that he rightfully wore several religious names. While others in those communities have not always welcomed him into their company, his life and his theology gave him a legitimate claim to at least three—charismatic, evangelical, and Southern Baptist, in that order of importance.

Each of those religious communities provides a potential political base for Pat Robertson. Of course, religion is only one factor influencing voting patterns. "Where people live, what they do for a living, and how much education they have attained are significant factors in the way they vote," reminded political analyst Albert J. Menendez. But religion has played a controversial and influential role in some twentieth-century elections, beginning with the 1928 and 1960 campaigns in which the Catholic faith of Al Smith and John F. Kennedy was an issue. But it was Jimmy Carter's 1976 campaign that most clearly roused the political consciousness of a generation of evangelicals. While it remains extremely difficult to quantify the relationship between religion and voting patterns, most political analysts agree that in recent years such categories as "the self-reported importance of religion," being "born-again," belief in a "literal interpretation of the Bible," and even denominational affiliation can be linked in quite specific ways to voting preferences. In the years after the election of 1976, evangelical voting has been tied to a conservative social agenda; that is, it has become more issues oriented and also has been better coordinated than ever before in the twentieth century.

Pat Robertson's political views alone make him an attractive candidate to evangelical conservatives, but those views do not greatly distinguish him from other conservative Republican aspirants. Robertson's candidacy clearly involves who he is religiously, as well as what he believes politically. "Members of groups which have been long excluded from political participation will tend to vote for 'their own,'" observed analyst Albert J. Menendez. If that observation is valid, Robertson's triple religious identification is laden with meaning.

To some degree, charismatics, evangelicals, and Southern Baptists all fit the Menendez description of groups entering the political mainstream. Each of the groups has felt some alienation from the American political process, and each has combined an intense religious pride with its awakened political conscience. To a large degree, evangelical support for Jimmy Carter in 1976 was a matter of pride; evangelicals voted for Carter not because they agreed with him, but because he was one of them. Evangelical support for Ronald Reagan, on the other hand, rested not on a religious identification with him, because Reagan has never understood the nuances of evangelical culture, but on Reagan's support for the conservative social agenda. Evangelicals voted for Jimmy Carter because of who he was; they voted for Ronald Reagan because of what he said. Pat Robertson comes to the campaign of 1988 as a charismatic-evangelical-Southern Baptist with conservative political views. He both acts and talks like an evangelical. Asked by a reporter in 1986 what "Christian groups" might support his candidacy, Robertson speculated: "The ones who are supportive, at the present time, have been most of the leaders of the major independent ministries, plus a number of heads of denominations affiliated with the National Association of Evangelicals, as well as my own denomination, which is Southern Baptist. Both the independent Baptists and especially the charismatic churches are showing a great deal of interest. The full gospel and Pentecostal churches and the Assemblies of God have been extremely supportive." It was a sweeping and impressive listing.

12.

Charismatic

IN AUGUST 1985 *Charisma* magazine, the most widely circulated journal in the charismatic movement, asked its readers to name the "persons I consider the most influential in the Charismatic movement." Pat Robertson led the balloting, finishing ahead of such older leaders as Oral Roberts and Kenneth Hagin. But *Charisma* insisted that the vote was not a surprise; Robertson was no "flash-in-the-pan." "He's been around for a long time and has proved himself to be reputable, credible, and often right." In all, Pat Robertson had earned the right to be declared leader of the movement.

By the mid-1980s the charismatic movement had become so diverse that it virtually defied description. Defined broadly, the word described a religious family that included all Christians who believed in the presence of the "gifts of the Holy Spirit" (the charismata) in the contemporary church. While speaking in tongues (glossalia) and divine healing were the most emphasized gifts, charismatics believed in a pervasive miraculous presence in the natural world. In fact, a *Christianity Today*–Gallup poll survey in 1980 revealed that only about one-sixth of those who claimed to be charismatics had actually spoken in tongues, but all believed in the broader operation of the gifts of the Holy Spirit.

In the 1980s the charismatic movement spawned huge independent megachurches across the United States; a survey in 1985 estimated that there were about 8,000 churches in the nation with over 1,000 members. While the first megachurches were mostly Baptist, by the 1980s the Assemblies of God and other pentecostal denominations and independent charismatic groups had become leaders of the megachurch revolution. Several independent churches, including the Word of Faith Church in Dallas, The Church of the Way in Van Nuys, California, and the Crenshaw Christian Center in Los Angeles, claimed over 5,000 members. But the charismatic movement also reached into virtually every American denomination and included millions of Roman Catholic supporters in a Catholic Renewal movement that received the blessings of the pope.

The size of this huge and amorphous religious movement, united only by the personalities of highly visible leaders and influential parachurch organizations, is very difficult to estimate. The Gallup poll conducted for *Christianity Today* in 1980 estimated that 29 million adult Americans considered themselves charismatics. Of that number about 10 million were members of traditional pentecostal denominations; the remainder were identified with the Catholic Renewal or were charismatics within mainstream Protestant churches. But the charismatic movement has grown at an astonishing rate in the 1980s. By 1985 some religious demographers believed that charismatics were the largest Protestant family in the world, estimating that there were 50 million charismatics around the world. Others placed the number much higher. At the 1985 international conference of pentecostal denominations, leaders claimed nearly 60 million members in their churches. In addition, according to one speaker, there were 38 million "non-affiliated indigenous Pentecostals," around 16 million Protestant Charismatics and between 30 and 50 million Catholic Charismatics. Particularly in Third World nations, where the charismatic belief in miracles merged easily with prevailing supernatural worldviews, the charismatic message was spectacularly successful. In recent years, this expansion was also encouraged by the active mission programs of American pentecostal churches and the worldwide media blitzes sponsored by charismatic leaders including Pat Robertson.

Historically, the charismatic movement was the product of American pentecostalism. The pentecostal movement began around the turn of the twentieth century, born of cravings within American evangelicalism for the baptism of the Holy Spirit. In the first decade of the century, the basic tenets of pentecostal theology became clear. Pentecostals believed that the baptism of the Holy Spirit was followed by speaking in tongues (tongues speaking was the "initial evidence" of the baptism), basing that belief on the Pentecost Day experience described in Acts 2. Dubbed "pentecostals" because of their emphasis on the Pentecost experience, the early leaders of the movement also emphasized the imminent second return of Christ and a general belief in miracles, or, as they put it, a restoration of the "full gospel," or the "apostolic faith."

During the first half of the twentieth century, the pentecostal movement grew rapidly among the poorer classes in America, but it also was vexed by repeated divisions into small squabbling sects. By World War II, however, the Assemblies of God, headquartered in Springfield, Missouri, had emerged as the largest of a group of stable pentecostal denominations. Furthermore, by 1945 these more stable churches were filled with a new generation of pentecostals, the children and grandchildren of the pioneers of the movement, who were less interested in the trivial debates that had racked the movement for years and who yearned for a demonstration in their time of the same miraculous outpouring of the Holy Spirit that the first generation pentecostals witnessed at the beginning of the century. In addition, the pentecostal churches of the postwar period were filled with a generation of upwardly mobile workers who had escaped the grinding poverty of their parents and who were seeking a place of respect in the broader society.

It was in this setting that a broad panpentecostal revival erupted in 1947 that for a decade stirred ecumenical cooperation in most of the pentecostal denominations. In a highly significant act in 1947 the major pentecostal denominations formed a fellowship where church leaders consulted and formed new friendships. More significant in the origins of the charismatic movement, however, was the explosion of a healing revival in the late 1940s. The revival featured the gifts of a varied assortment of brash and talented pentecostal ministers. They roamed the country preaching in huge tents to audiences of thousands of people, claiming literally millions of miracles as their legacy. These ministers became larger-than-life heroes in the pentecostal community and they drew millions of dollars of support from the people who attended their meetings. The ablest of the evangelists, led by Oral Roberts, expanded the healing revival dramatically, taking it on television and building sophisticated organizations capable of communicating with millions of people.

For several years after the eruption of the massive healing revival, the pentecostal denominations supported the gifted ministers who had triggered it. But church leaders soon began to withdraw their approval. By the early 1950s scores of ministers had established independent ministerial associations that were beyond the supervision and control of the leaders of the pentecostal churches; some of those organizations had become more powerful than the small denominations that had ordained their founders. Partly, denominational leaders became jealous of the success of the revivalists, but they also became concerned about the clear financial irresponsibility of some of the ministers, their exaggerated miracle claims, and the unregulated theological environment that the evangelists had created. By the mid-1950s the pentecostal churches had withdrawn their support from most of the ministers, though many pentecostals continued to subsidize them.

The strongest of the independent ministries survived and continued to preach the pentecostal message in tents and on television. In addition, a number of important parachurch organizations grew out of the healing revival, the most important being the Full Gospel Business Men's Fellowship International. The FGBMFI was formed by Los Angeles dairyman Demos Shakarian in 1954 with the encouragement and support of Oral Roberts. The fellowship became a pentecostal Rotary Club; pentecostal car dealers and small-town merchants suddenly had a venue for sharing their experiences in settings more appropriate to their newly won economic and social status.

It was these flourishing independent organizations, along with countless local pentecostal pastors, that first piqued the curiosity of growing numbers of other religious Americans in the baptism of the Holy Spirit. Oral Roberts noted in the 1950s that thousands of people from mainstream churches were attending his tent meetings and standing in his prayer line. The first public recognition of the spread of pentecostal theology into mainstream Protestantism, however, came in 1960 with the public announcement by Episcopalian priest Dennis Bennett that he had spoken in tongues. Bennett's confession attracted the attention of the national media. A second milestone came in 1966 when students at Notre Dame University introduced tongues speaking into the Catholic church. In the 1960s thousands of Christians in the traditional churches began to claim the experience; they were first called "neopentecostals," but subsequently the name "charismatic" became the most widely used title for all of those, Protestant and Catholic, who shared the pentecostal experience but who did not become members of pentecostal denominations.

From its beginnings, the intensity of the charismatic movement was captured in thousands of joyous worship services where Christians from diverse backgrounds shared the exhilaration of private spiritual ecstasy. United by this "hallelujah factor," charismatics easily shared worship. But beneath their joyous unity lay immense practical and theological problems. By the 1980s, it was obvious to leaders of the charismatic movement that "preserving unity will not be as easy today as it seemed in the first flush of Charismatic enthusiasm." The new charismatics combined their new spiritual experience with a respect for historic theology and liturgy; they frequently were shocked by the looseness of pentecostal thought. Pentecostals, on the other hand, clung to their old sectarian theology of the baptism of the Holy Spirit, which in its severest forms insisted that only those who had spoken in tongues had received the promised Holy Spirit. Increasingly, pentecostals viewed charismatics as spiritual novices preoccupied with a subjective experience they did not understand. Within these basic theological conflicts were embedded scores of smaller sources of friction.

Finally, the spread of the Holy Spirit into the traditional churches complicated existing institutional tensions. The pentecostal churches had long resented the powerful independent ministries that had emerged in the 1950s; they were slow to see the opportunities afforded to them by the outbreak of tongues speaking in the traditional churches. The older pentecostal churches, or "classical pentecostals," related very stiffly with charismatic Christians who remained in the mainline churches. Many pentecostals retained a sectarian disdain for nonpentecostal churches. Jimmy Swaggart, an Assembly of God minister, spoke a widely held pentecostal belief when he allegedly asserted that "Catholicism is not Christian." Roman Catholics, particularly, complained of the "wall between these 'classical Pentecostals' and other Spirit-filled believers." On the other hand, non-Catholic charismatics frequently protested that the Catholic Renewal was closing itself to communication with outsiders, emphasizing such objectionable practices as "praying to Mary." In the 1960s most of the mainstream Protestant churches denounced charismatics, sometimes driving them from their churches. But in the 1970s as denomination after denomination came to tolerate the movement, charismatics were urged to remain loyal to their church and were warned against the theological and cultural excesses of pentecostalism.

By the end of the 1970s the charismatic movement had reached a series of accommodations. Increasingly, charismatics in mainstream Protestant denominations and in the Catholic church felt welcome in their churches; they existed in cells that were often viewed as revitalization movements within moribund churches. While such charismatics generally associated loosely with Spirit-filled believers outside their denominations and often supported independent ministries, they defined themselves primarily in denominational terms. Many openly opposed the simplistic theology of traditional pentecostalism, its covert anti-intellectualism, and the "pentecostal pride" that insisted that the "a second baptism was and is normative for all Christians at all times." The Catholic Charismatic Renewal was particularly successful in placing the gifts of the Holy Spirit within a historical theological and ecclesiastical context. The Catholic movement was sanctioned by the pope and institutionalized in an International Catholic Charismatic Renewal Office in Belgium. More and more Catholic Charismatic leaders emphasized loyalty to the church.

Some of the old pentecostal denominations, particularly the Assemblies of God, abandoned their fiercest hostilities toward the Protestant and Catholic charismatics in the 1980s and began to woo those who were dissatisfied with their old denominations. As a result, the Assemblies of God grew rapidly in the 1980s, drawing people whose charismatic experience was more important to them than their denominational affiliation. In 1986 the church passed 2 million in membership and was the fastest growing American denomination.

In short, in the 1980s the term "charismatic" described a theologically loose and institutionally diverse movement that cut across the American religious landscape from the Roman Catholic church to a nondescript assortment of independent pentecostal and charismatic churches. In 1985 charismatic spokesman David du Plessis judged that "the charismatic movement has become the most unifying force in Christianity." There were some notable efforts to give practical expression to the symbolic unity of the movement. In 1977 a Charismatic Conference drew thousands to Arrowhead Stadium in Kansas City. One evening the same stage was shared by a Roman Catholic cardinal, an Anglican bishop, the general superintendent of the Assemblies of God, and the leader of the largest black pentecostal denomination, the Church of God in Christ. A similar conference was held in the New Orleans Superdome in 1985. In addition, some of the older charismatic parachurch organizations, such as the Full Gospel Business Men's Fellowship International, and some publications, such as *Charisma* magazine, gave coherence to the movement. By the 1980s, however, the most important foci for the movement were the charismatic television ministries; the most important of those was Pat Robertson's "The 700 Club."

Pat Robertson's emergence as the most visible leader of this amorphous movement was a tribute to his success. Robertson, his student friends in New York City, and Harald Bredesen were pioneers of the charismatic movement in the traditional churches, their quest for the Holy Spirit predating the publicity surrounding the charismatic experience of Dennis Bennett. As the movement began to assume an identity of its own in the 1960s, Robertson became an instant celebrity because of his father's political position. He was befriended in the 1960s by the pacesetters of the revival—men like Oral Roberts and Demos Shakarian. In 1969 he became a member of a junior advisory board at Oral Roberts University and he spoke at some of the regional conventions of the FGBMFI during his first decade at CBN. But in the end only the talented survived in the freewheeling environment where the gifts of the Holy Spirit were the badge of authenticity. It was the success of CBN that brought Robertson to the fore of the movement.

In the 1970s Robertson slowly became more and more visible. In 1973 he was a featured speaker at the first World Conference on the Holy Spirit, held in Jerusalem, joining Kathryn Kuhlman, David du Plessis, and Corrie ten Boom on the program. In 1977 for the first time he gave a major address at the national convention of the FGBMFI. The next year, at the twenty-fifth anniversary meeting of the fellowship, Robertson was headlined along with Oral Roberts, the spiritual mentor of the organization, and other rising charismatic stars such as Jim Bakker and Father John Bertolucci. By the mid-1980s, Robertson's accomplishments and talents clearly justified the charismatic vote that he had become "our 'most respected' Christian leader in America."

More than most pentecostals and charismatics, Robertson was tied to a body of evangelical thought that historically preceded charismatic theology. Like some other charismatics, he was well aware of the writings of Norman Vincent Peale. It was a short step from Peale's positive thinking to the charismatic trust in miraculous faith. After reading Peale, one charismatic editor wrote: "I have made up my mind to think positively, based on who I am and what I have in Christ." Robertson was also familiar with the teaching of evangelical Norman Grubb, whose emphasis on "speaking the word of faith" could easily be translated into charismatic language. Charismatics simply added an overtly miraculous dimension to the body of positive thinking and success theology already present in American evangelicalism. In his 1982 book *The Secret*

Kingdom, Robertson acknowledged that "positive thinking will more often than not lead to successful action," but he believed that charismatic faith was needed to unlock all of the secrets of success.

In *The Secret Kingdom* Robertson explored the "secrets" of success available to those who were a part of the Kingdom of God. The Kingdom, an invisible realm of existence, was ignored by most people, but it was the dwelling place of Christians. To claim the power of the Kingdom one needed only to *"have faith in God."* In a series of tapes distributed to his supporters Robertson offered insights into a series of biblical secrets—the "Secret of Wealth," the "Secret of Success," the "Secret of Greatness," and the "Secret of Miracles." "Are you tired of money worries?" asked an advertisement. "Begin to apply the dynamic principles outlined. And you'll see your personal finances revolutionized! You'll experience material wealth and prosperity you never thought possible. These methods are Scriptural. They are tested and proven." On success: "This is the formula for success you've been looking for—God's unbeatable formula!" Robertson's discoveries would also "set your feet on the road to greatness." Finally, those who listened to the tapes were told "how your words can bring about miracles."

In his book, Robertson's findings were summarized in eight Kingdom laws. The "law of reciprocity" was a restatement of Jesus' declaration "Give, and it will be given to you." The "law of use" demanded a conscientious use of one's talents. The "law of perseverance" meant that one's triumphs often came only after struggle and apparent defeat. The "law of responsibility" meant that one had to take advantage of "opportunity" and "favor." The "law of greatness" called for each Christian to be a servant, ready to learn and help others. The "law of unity" called for Christians to be single-minded in their spiritual and worldly objectives and for the church to be united in its mission. The "law of miracles" depended on the application of the other rules. It was possible for God to disrupt the natural order and perform miracles, and he would do so if petitioners would have faith, envision the miracles, refuse to doubt, and speak as if their requests had already taken place. Finally, the "law of dominion" asserted that God had given his people dominion over the earth, a promise that offered freedom from bondage to sin and distress, including hunger. All of these laws were based on scriptural principles, Robertson believed, and their faithful application would restore Kingdom power.

Robertson insisted that he not only believed these principles, he also lived by them. "I put them to work in my life," he wrote. "I wasn't interested in abstraction. I wanted to determine if they worked." His books were cluttered with episodes from his personal life and his experiences in building CBN that illustrated that the Kingdom laws worked. And most of Robertson's friends agreed that his life had been marked by personal generosity and unwavering faith in the principles he preached.

Robertson's teachings about the Kingdom came perilously close to allying him with the most extreme theological party within the modern charismatic movement—a group known as the "faith teachers." In *The Secret Kingdom* he seemed to endorse the basic teaching of that group: "We have a title deed to what God has promised. Our role is to believe in our hearts that it has been accomplished, according to what God has given us the deed to, and then to speak it." Sometimes called the "name it and claim it" theology, the faith teaching caused a serious rift in the charismatic movement in the 1980s; particularly under attack were Kenneth Hagin of Tulsa and widely known television minister Kenneth Copeland.

The faith movement was rejected by other charismatics for two reasons. First, some faith ministers placed great emphasis on claiming material wealth. Second, the teaching seemed to allow no room for failures. Several charismatic theologians labeled the doctrine "gnosticism" and "Christian humanism" and warned that it could lead to feelings of guilt when it failed to heal and enrich and that it sometimes led to tragedy. "Never box God in with your own ideas about how prayers should be answered," warned a Catholic charismatic leader. By the mid-1980s the theological battle had cooled, partly because the leading faith teachers had moderated their presentations and also because the two sides had little real contact with one another.

Robertson never became directly involved in the controversy. While he talked of the power of faith in the strongest terms, he remained an intensely practical man and never eliminated the inscrutable from his theology. He wrote in *The Secret Kingdom*: "At the same time, the Lord has called for us to be honest and truthful in the innermost being, so we are not to delude ourselves and to say something is true when it is not. We are not to engage in superstition or silliness. We merely are to have confidence that with Him all things are possible." And Robertson never argued that God intended for all people to have great "material wealth." Nonetheless, he remained "convinced that if a person is *continuously* in sickness, poverty, or other physical and mental straits, then he is missing the truths of the Kingdom." Pat Robertson lived in the real world, but he firmly believed that a "hidden world" existed and that Christians could and should gain dominion over all evil by establishing contact with that world.

Charismatic belief in the power of positive faith was often difficult to distinguish from the positive thinking emphasis found in evangelical circles. It was their belief in miracles and the gifts of the Holy Spirit that most clearly separated pentecostals and charismatics from other evangelical Christians. While most Christians have remote notions that there is spiritual world surrounding them, charismatics viewed that spiritual domain as luxuriously present, peopled with angels and demons in active combat. When Robertson moved to the Virginia Tidewater in 1959, he believed that the whole area was in "the grip of demon power"; the evil influence had been attracted there by the presence of the Edgar Cayce Association for Research and Enlightenment. Demons were "fallen angels," Robertson theorized, and they were "interested in tormenting people, possessing them, and leading them away from God and His truth."

Robertson maintained that all natural events took place within a universe that included not only the visible but also the invisible. Angels and demons roamed the spiritual layers of existence, but they could be controlled by the Christian through access to the power of God. When Robertson attacked witchcraft on his television programs in the 1970s, he maintained that his adversaries were "laying witchcraft curses on us and on my children." He wrote: "I got so mad that the devil would *dare* to come against the servant of God that I commanded the spirit of witchcraft to *leave my household*; to go right back where it came from; and to give them trouble when it got there!"

Charismatic belief in a real spiritual world provided a foundation for the understanding of the miraculous. "A miracle," wrote Robertson, "might be defined as a concrete breakthrough from the invisible, supernatural world into our own visible, natural world." Such divine interventions were more than God answering prayer in natural ways; they were extraordinary happenings that produced "wonder in those who observe them." Robertson conceded that his own belief in miracles grew gradually; only after hearing thousands of testimonies was he convinced. But ultimately he believed because "more and more I've seen God doing remarkable miracles through me."

While Robertson's listing of miracle testimonies sounded little different from the thousands of stories recited by pentecostals and other charismatics, he developed a far broader intellectual underpinning for his beliefs than most charismatics. In his book *Beyond Reason*, he blamed modern science for creating a "closed system of reality" that excluded the existence of the spirit world. Early modern scientists such as Isaac Newton were Christians, but in the nineteenth century a secular-minded science put "human reason on a pedestal that left little room at the top for an infinite, unsearchable, dynamic Deity." However, Robertson argued, modern science has become less and less confident that all experience can be understood empirically. Humankind had entered a post-Enlightenment era, and it seemed both honest and reasonable to explore supernatural perceptions. The existence of truth beyond reason explained miracles, and miracles, in turn, bore witness to the reality of that truth.

Robertson superimposed this relatively highbrow understanding of the spirit world over a popular belief system that demanded no such explanations. Miracles of healing were the lifeblood of CBN;

hundreds of thousands of testimonies of miraculous healings have poured into the ministry through the years. The list stretched on endlessly—teeth miraculously filled, operations performed by God in the midst of prayers, cancers vanishing without explanation. In recent years, CBN television crews have been dispatched around the world to document miracles—"taking their stories, interviewing their friends," providing, whenever possible, "medical verification." While CBN pursued verification more seriously than most charismatic ministries, its efforts depended mainly on the testimony of the believers. CBN discovered, as others had before, that the scientific documentation of miracles was a tricky business at best. When Anne Kiedeman testified that God had straightened her "tipped uterus" after Robertson had a word of knowledge that Jesus was performing an operation on someone in the audience, she offered as evidence her recollection of a statement by her personal physician, "I understand that no way could this just happen by itself."

Robertson's emphasis on miracles placed him squarely in the center of the charismatic movement—his claims on "The 700 Club" were no less sensational than those of other pentecostal or charismatic ministers. Furthermore, he repeatedly cited his own experiences with divine healing. When his youngest son, Gordon, became ill with a staph infection in a New York City hospital, he recalled: "I turned to that seemingly empty room and I said in a tone of command, 'Virus, in the name of Jesus Christ of Nazareth, I take authority over you. Get out of here.'" But in spite of such statements of faith, Robertson conceded that perhaps 80 percent of all illness was psychosomatic and that much of the healing that was viewed as divine was the result of the "power of suggestion." And he, like most moderate charismatics, insisted that medical care as well as prayer was a divinely ordained means of healing.

Important as divine healing was in the building of CBN, Robertson was most fascinated by the broader intervention of God in the natural world—by the sweeping powers implied in human dominion over nature. In his book *Beyond Reason*, Robertson acknowledged that "many people are reluctant to consider" the ability of

Christians to influence the "forces of nature." Even many of the faithful drew back from efforts to influence natural law, Robertson wrote, believing that such claims "crossed the line that separates the extraordinary from the absurd." In 1986 Garry Trudeau and other cartoonists found the idea that one could alter the working of nature not only absurd but also humorous.

While Robertson did not believe that human beings had the power to "control the elements," he insisted that Christians had far more authority than they realized. It was in this context that, on several occasions, Robertson prayed that CBN would not be destroyed by hurricanes. He was certain that supernatural power spared Norfolk from disaster on those occasions: "Skeptics may offer other explanations for these events. But I know it was God's power that spared this region and also our CBN tower. As a matter of fact, we haven't had a major hurricane hit Tidewater since then, and that was about twenty years ago. The hurricane activity in our area has apparently been stopped, at least for the present. It's as if God Himself from that time forward has set a kind of shield around us."

In a more specific vein, Robertson believed in the operation of the nine gifts of the Holy Spirit listed in 1 Corinthians 12, or the charismata—receiving a word of wisdom, receiving a word of knowledge, discerning spirits, performing miracles, healing, having faith by the Spirit, speaking in tongues, interpreting tongues speaking, and prophesying. It was these gifts that he and his student friends in New York City had sought so zealously. The gift that operated most conspicuously in Robertson's life was the "word of knowledge," which allowed the "discerning of something that is not available to the senses," but he believed that all of the gifts were available to those who had been baptized in the Holy Spirit.

Robertson's view of the baptism in the Holy Spirit was linked to his early entry into the charismatic movement and to his early associations with pentecostals. Robertson, like most nonpentecostals who spoke in tongues before 1960, accepted pentecostal theology with little modification; for instance, he laboriously argued that early evangelical seekers of Holy Spirit baptism, such as

Charles G. Finney, spoke in tongues. Robertson believed that all who were born again received the "indwelling Spirit," but they did not receive the supernatural gifts. The baptism in the Holy Spirit was a subsequent experience designed to "empower for service," and that experience, Robertson believed, was always signaled by speaking in tongues. Robertson, Harald Bredesen, and their early charismatic comrades also accepted the pentecostal assumption that, at least some of the time, spiritual tongues were a foreign language. Robertson thought that his initial tongues speaking experience sounded like an African dialect; Harald Bredesen believed that he had first spoken in Polish and in his autobiography he included sworn testimonials that "an Egyptian heiress" had heard him speaking "archaic Arabic." On the other hand, in practice, Robertson and CBN never emphasized speaking in tongues.

The most characteristic Robertson spiritual gift was the "word of knowledge." Nearly every program of "The 700 Club" featured prayer sessions in which Robertson, Ben Kinchlow, and other guests spoke of healings they sensed were then occurring in the television audience. In 1986, Robertson explained to *Time* magazine: "This is a very quiet word, brought forth in the spirit of a human being dealing with a problem that somebody has that God cares about and wants to help. The first time that it happened to me, I thought it was something I don't really want to do. But I worked up my courage and mentioned what I felt was being spoken, and somebody called in and said that at that moment they had been gloriously healed." Robertson knew that many people would consider him a "psychic screwball" when he began using the word of knowledge on television; he acquiesced because he was willing to be a "fool for Christ." Robertson and other charismatics understood that many Christians, to say nothing of non-Christians, would never be persuaded that the gifts of the Holy Spirit were real. But he was convinced that he had seen many miracles that were fulfillments of words of knowledge spoken on "The 700 Club."

In explaining the word of knowledge, Robertson probed the central issue of charismatic theology and the question that most concerned those outside the movement—the belief in the supernatural leading of God. The word of knowledge was sometimes sparked in him by a physical sensation, such as a pain, Robertson wrote, but usually "it's a very still, small voice in your inner man. It's God's voice as he speaks to you—through your spirit, through your inner man—to those who are sensitive and listening." Charismatics, like Methodists of the nineteenth century and Quakers of the eighteenth century, rejected the modern triumph of reason over emotion, of the objective mind over the subjective spirit. Like nineteenth-century transcendentalists and Romantics, they were intent on listening with both soul and mind. In every age such seekers have run the risk of being stigmatized as "screwballs" by those who are less comfortable with subjective leadings.

In short, charismatics were modern advocates of the very old notion that God communicates through people's feelings as well as through their minds. In an influential book, *The Emerging Order: God in the Age of Scarcity*, Jeremy Rifkin and Ted Howard describe charismatic theology as an "unconscious challenge to the modern worldview." They view the challenge to reason as a healthy one, suggesting that it might "provide the kind of liberating force that could topple the prevailing ethos and provide a bridge to the next age of history." Subjective insight could be an alternate method of "securing answers to some of the problems of life." For Robertson and other educated and thoughtful charismatics appealing to subjective leadings was not sheer obscurantism, it was a conscious effort to see past the limits of reason. Divine guidance was one's subjective leadings placed in a framework of unwavering faith.

The word of knowledge, then, was but one example of God's subjective communication with human beings. If, in the minds of many Americans, Pat Robertson's use of the word of knowledge placed him on the lunatic fringe, his broader claims to divine guidance, conventional enough in charismatic circles, seemed particularly disconcerting when spoken by a presidential candidate. Many Americans were not as receptive to the idea of a postrational society as were Rifkin and Howard. In one of the most penetrating critiques of Robertson as a political candidate, evangelical historian

George Marsden focused on Robertson's claim to "extrabiblical revelations." "Once in office," he wrote, "someone who thinks he has such powers would certainly want to draw on these powers in times of crisis. The results could be disastrous." The "great danger" in mixing religion and politics, Marsden believed, "comes when claims to divine power and guidance are combined with real political power. The combination could be lethal and will soon lead to injustices done in God's name." Sociologist Jeffrey Hadden focused on the same issue in *People* magazine: "Deep in your heart you wonder where would Pat Robertson go if he felt that God were leading him in directions that were in radical contradiction to the principles of American democracy." On few other issues did Robertson's religious rhetoric demand closer examination.

Most broadly stated, charismatics believe in the direct and personal guidance of God in their lives. "As you go to each decision that comes before you on any given day," wrote Robertson in 1982, "you'll know immediately whether the things you do and the things you say are of God. And He will lead you in dealing with matters that will come about in the future. All you have to do is to follow the leading of God in your heart for today." The language of a faithful charismatic bristles with confident assertions about the leadings of the Lord, often announced in a triumphant sentence beginning "God told me . . ." Although most charismatics, including Robertson, believe that God's guidance sometimes comes in dramatic "supernatural visitations" and in audible voices as in the case of Balaam's ass, almost always their language is simply a confident announcement about their subjective peace with God. The "peace of God," Robertson affirmed, is the key to understanding God's directions. "As long as the peace is there, you can go forth, confidently assured that your heart is fixed on the course that God has set for you. When the peace lifts, it is the Holy Spirit telling you that you are going in the wrong direction."

In spite of such confident rhetoric, however, the charismatic belief in God's leading is not a pure subjectivism. First, charismatics accept the Bible as the ultimate authority in all matters religious as do all evangelicals. When confronted with conflicting revelations, like other Christians charismatics appeal to the authority of the Scriptures. Robertson expressed a common view: "I frankly believe that about 98 percent of all the guidance that you and I need is contained in the Bible." Any charismatic leader who ventures too far from conventional Protestant theology will ultimately be called to account.

Perhaps the most important limitation that charismatics place on God's leading is their practical use of trial and error. Robertson readily confessed that Christians are not always "sensitive enough to God's voice to know when He is saying yes and when He is saying no." In such cases, one could only live by trial and error, understanding that God might "close doors" to guide in other directions. This pragmatic understanding of guidance flows into a general belief in beneficent providence; when one is uncertain about the future the best course is to "wait on God" and take advantage of whatever opportunities life provides.

Furthermore, every charismatic knows that even when one is certain about the leading of God, he or she might be wrong. After a mistake in judgment in the early years of CBN, Robertson confessed: "It looked bad, because once you admit a mistake in the area of guidance, it indicates you are prone to make others. I had already made several." Only the wildest extremists would imagine that their leadings might not be misguided. The key to success is a deeper spirituality: "As we know Him, we will also know what He wants for us. We will know how to make decisions today which will put us in a correct position for tomorrow." But no one is a perfect listener.

On the question of God's guidance, for better or for worse, it is rhetoric that separates charismatics from other Christians, not practice. When faced with the imponderable, with decisions that transcend rational investigation, most Christians pray and consult the Scriptures and then try to make a spiritual choice. Even non-Christians in similar circumstances make subjective decisions, passing the possible alternatives through a network of accepted beliefs. In effect, charismatics do the same. They perhaps have more confidence in their feelings, or at least they say they do, but their actions are studied guesses. Every charismatic knows that he or she may be wrong—that the voice of God may have spoken indistinctly. "When a person declares, 'The Lord told me . . .' what is he really saying?" asked Don Matzat in *Charisma* magazine in 1985. He answered: "He is really saying that he has a thought, an impression, an idea or an insight regarding a specific area of decision or direction, which he believes is prompted by the Holy Spirit who dwells within. . . . Therefore all statements relating to the will of God or the leading of the spirit are faith statements." In the final analysis, a charismatic is saying, "I *believe* this is what the Lord is saying to me through His Holy Spirit."

Pat Robertson's conduct conforms precisely to such a definition of God's leading. Robertson has always had a profound confidence in the prophetic gift of Harald Bredesen, noted Tucker Yates, but "he doesn't buy everything Harald says. He knows that prophetic words come through human lips. . . . The Bible tells us to try them." Very early in his own charismatic life, Bredesen concluded that supernatural insight was never "directional": "I came to see that prophecy can never be by itself directive. It may be preparational or confirmational, but it never by itself is directional." Thoughtful charismatics proceed with caution, ever testing, believing and hoping that they are acting within the will of God.

The pragmatic limitations of charismatic rhetoric are nowhere more obvious than in the actions of the successful charismatic television ministers. While all of the notable evangelists claim uncommon abilities in discerning the will of God, few deny that they sometimes fail. Their massive ministries were not built without mishaps and reconsideration. Robertson veered back and forth making "spiritual course corrections" on the way to his present eminence, ever following the leading of the Lord, but never presuming that his hearing was perfect. In the end, successful charismatic leaders believed simply that they had good batting averages; their success rate was God's pragmatic confirmation that they were good listeners.

For over a decade Pat Robertson has refrained from identifying himself publicly as a charismatic, although both historically and theologically he stands near the center of that amorphous movement. Robertson's reticence is a reaction against the theological excesses that flourished in the subjective environment of the charismatic movement. A theology founded on the rapturous leadings of the Lord opens itself to an endless parade of self-proclaimed prophets and exotic revelations. It was precisely that lack of intellectual order that had splintered American pentecostalism in the first half of the twentieth century. Most evangelicals and Catholics who received the baptism in the Holy Spirit in the 1960s and 1970s were both attracted and repelled by the freedom to follow the Spirit's leading. But by the mid-1970s the charismatic revival was in the throes of its first major dispute in trying to establish the doctrinal limits of prophetic authority.

Pat Robertson was a principal actor in what came to be called the "discipleship controversy." The debate erupted in 1975; in question were the teachings of a group of pioneer charismatic leaders, including Derek Prince and Bob Mumford, who had formed the Christian Growth Ministries in Fort Lauderdale, Florida. In some ways their teaching appeared to be an effort to bring a measure of order to the chaotic charismatic movement. They encouraged all believers to form "covenant discipleship" relationships with "shepherds," more mature Christians who could give them guidance. But the movement was soon awash with "horror stories" about alleged abuses that gave to the shepherds dictatorial control of the lives of those who "submitted" to them. Robertson was enraged when two young men who had worked at CBN reported to him some of the problems they had experienced as a part of a "submitted assembly."

Robertson lashed out at the discipleship leaders, labeling the teaching the "cult of submission." He wrote Mumford "a scathing eight-page letter attacking the discipleship teaching point by point." Robertson attacked the teaching on the "The 700 Club," naming the leaders; he warned that the "cult" demanded "slavish submission to other human beings." In a memo to two CBN executives that was subsequently widely circulated in the charismatic movement, Robertson banned the five leaders of the discipleship movement from his radio and television stations and ordered his employees to erase any tapes in their possession featuring the teaching. Robertson allied himself in the controversy with Demos Shakarian, the powerful president of the Full Gospel Business Men's Fellowship International, and with Kathryn Kuhlman to try to quarantine the Fort Lauderdale ministers. Shakarian barred them from appearing as speakers before the FGBMFI and, reportedly, Kuhlman refused to speak at an International World Congress on the Holy Spirit until Bob Mumford was removed from the program.

The charismatic movement had been an unbroken success story in the 1970s, and the discipleship controversy stunned its leaders. While a majority of charismatics probably questioned the teachings of the Christian Growth ministers, many were stunned by the ferocity of Robertson's attack. "Not only the teaching coming from CGM bothers us," wrote charismatic author Jamie Buckingham, "but also those who have reacted radically and are racing through the Kingdom waving red flags." A summit conference was convened in Minneapolis in the fall of 1975 to try to quell the debate. "The discussion was heated with charges and countercharges passing back and forth," reported *Logos Journal*, and the meeting concluded with "the major problems still unsettled." Many felt that the discipleship teachers had offered adequate assurances against future excesses, but Robertson, who left the meeting early after delivering his own speech, was far from satisfied. He told reporters: "My concern is for the grave doctrinal error and resulting practice which has been and is harming the body of Christ nationwide, and yet has been and is being covered up by a cloak of deception of which we saw only a part in Minneapolis." The altercation abated in the late 1970s; some reconciliation took place in later years, although tensions still exist. In the end, the dispute probably had a dampening effect on the ministries of the discipleship teachers; nonetheless, by the mid-1980s some of the leaders of the Christian Growth movement had become supporters of Pat Robertson's political aspirations.

The discipleship debate identified Pat Robertson as a figure with immense power within the charismatic movement. But perhaps the most important legacy of the controversy was the theological reassessment it triggered in Robertson's mind. From his earliest days as a charismatic he had been wary of the divisiveness of the charismatic experience and rhetoric. In recent years, he has become increasingly wary of charismatic extremists.

It was not, Bob Slosser believed, that Robertson was "backing away" from charismatics; rather he was "embracing" evangelicals. But, in fact, the discipleship controversy caused Robertson to seriously rethink his identification with the loose and undisciplined charismatic movement. "I was really angry," he later recalled, and "I blasted them and . . . it stopped that thing right in its tracks." But he continued to be upset that "the independent charismatic group per se never took official action to condemn this. And they never have." For the first time, Robertson realized the dangers of being a part of a religious movement were "everything goes," where every prophet had equal access to divine leading. He was much too rational a man to tolerate such chaos, and he was much too traditional in theology to leave unchallenged what he regarded as heresy. "From the moment of that controversy," he later recalled, "I felt more comfortable identifying myself as an evangelical."

Politically, Robertson's charismatic beliefs are appealing to the millions of Americans who have the same subjective confidence in the leading of the Lord. And while his political opponents find charismatic rhetoric outrageous, even dangerous, they are keenly aware that no candidate dare criticize the religious beliefs of an opponent. Not only would one run the risk of alienating the millions who share Robertson's beliefs, but also many Americans would consider such criticism the height of religious bigotry. Who would be willing to suggest that all charismatics should be disfranchised as dangerous religious fanatics? Or who would suggest that any candidate for the presidency should be barred because of his or her religious beliefs? In short, those opponents who are honestly shocked by Robertson's charismatic rhetoric are trapped in a political dilemma. "If I were running against Pat Robertson, I would be very reluctant to talk about the hurricane or the faith healing or anything like that," said John Buchanan, director of People for the

American Way, "because that could be interpreted as attacking his religious belief and the belief of *x* million other Americans. . . . But I would want somehow for those facts to be known."

Robertson admitted that he was "an easier target to ridicule" because of his long years as host of an extemporaneous television program. But Robertson knew as well that his opponents were treading in dangerous territory when they attacked his religious views. He told a reporter in 1986: "I believe the American people are very fair, and I believe they dislike intolerance and bigotry. If any opponent or if the press itself begins to ridicule the deeply held convictions of a religious person, it will boomerang on them. The people want strong convictions and they're willing to tolerate strong convictions. As a matter of fact, I think what seems at this point a potential negative is going to wind up becoming a positive, because the people would much rather have a president who has strong Christian convictions than they would a president who has no beliefs at all." When Democratic National Committee Chairman Paul Kirk circulated a letter sharply critical of Robertson in early 1986, Robertson retorted: "Does this mean that the Democratic Party is declaring war on Southern Baptists or does your opposition include all 60 million evangelical Christians, of which I also am one?"

In his defense, Robertson could point to a long tradition of subjective religion in American history; many former American political leaders have held religious views similar to those of Robertson. The nineteenth century was the great Methodist century in American religious history, and Methodist rhetoric, while slightly less enthusiastic than modern charismatic language, bristled with allusions to the leadings of God. Large numbers of Roman Catholics and Eastern Christians in the United States believe in miracles as strongly as charismatics. Some Robertson supporters contended that his major rhetorical challenge was communicating his beliefs about the supernatural to those who shared his convictions but spoke different religious dialects.

Stung by attacks on Robertson's charismatic beliefs and particularly by the satire surrounding the Hurricane Gloria incident, in

1986 CBN commissioned a Gallup survey of the religious beliefs of the American people. The poll showed that 74 percent of "all adult Americans believe God has a plan for their lives"and that 69 percent "believe that at some time in their lives God has led or guided them in making a decision." More than one-third of those surveyed believed that "God speaks to them directly" and nearly half felt that "God speaks through an internal feeling or impression." When asked the possible political significance of the poll, George Gallup told the Associated Press: "The public is perhaps more open to a person saying he is receiving guidance from God than the press has indicated, and not just in terms of Pat's statements about hurricanes . . . but also in a broad sense." In short, Robertson and other charismatics claim to be a part of a mainstream American religious tradition that has furnished the nation throughout its history with God-fearing political leaders.

On the other hand, as a political candidate, Pat Robertson will be called on repeatedly to explain his charismatic rhetoric to Christians from other traditions and, even more, to an increasingly secular nation. Many Americans were shocked by Jimmy Carter's candid allusions to his born–again experience; some found it difficult to judge him solely on the basis of his political philosophy. But Carter's moderate evangelicalism was sheer rationalism compared to the subjective experiences of charismatics. In the judgment of John Buchanan, Robertson's theology must eventually eliminate him as a contender for the presidency: "It is too extreme, even for people of faith."

The central political question raised by Pat Robertson's charismatic theology was whether or not he could be trusted to behave rationally as president of the United States. To those unfamiliar with charismatic theology, the combination of rationality and supernatural leadings from God seemed inconceivable. In 1986 a Central American pentecostal politician explained his rhetorical dilemma: "If I talk to the general public with the language I use with Christians, they might stone me, . . . but if I use political language with the brethren, they question my Christianity." As a political candidate Pat Robertson will be held to strict account for his charismatic rhetoric. Bob Slosser believed that Robertson would be able to bridge the rhetorical gap: "He can make his point without lapsing into Christianese as well as anyone I have ever known." But Robertson's best hope with non-Christians was to direct attention from his religious language to his practical conduct.

If Pat Robertson's charismatic religion placed him in some political jeopardy, it also was his chief political asset. The emergence of pentecostals and charismatics as a political coalition constitutes a third political wave of evangelicalism since World War II. Beginning in the 1950s with Billy Graham and the more virulent anticommunism of Carl McIntire and Billy James Hargis, evangelicals began to influence conservative politics. A second major group became politicized in the fundamentalist-led Moral Majority movement of the 1970s. While pentecostals and charismatics are far less organized and united than the predominantly Independent Baptist fundamentalist movement, they dwarf Jerry Falwell's clientele in size and represent a sociological and theological diversity that offers extraordinary political promise.

More than any other group of white Protestants in America, pentecostals lived the first half of the twentieth century in insulated spiritual enclaves. Spurned even by working-class fundamentalists as the lunatic fringe, pentecostalism spread like wildfire among the urban and rural dispossessed. Pentecostal hope nurtured those with broken lives, teaching them to view the world as a hostile but temporary abode; it glorifyied anti-intellectualism, poverty, and deprivation, both soothing and feeding inferiority complexes. Pentecostal theology was largely escapist; it emphasized an individual's direct link with God and the bypassing of clerical elites through the gifts of the Holy Spirit. Divine healing eliminated the need for medical elites. Pentecostals waged a relentless war against the "world" and all its pleasures and lived with an expectation of the imminent second coming of Christ. Such fanaticism, wrote a Church of God minister in 1986, reenforced pentecostals' "outsider status" and "vindicated their experience and their theology."

Such thinking did not mix well with social and political activism and, with rare exceptions, into the decade of the 1970s pentecostals were remarkably apolitical. In 1976 Pat Robertson reported that he asked a "great man of God" who had "stirred miracle faith in millions of people" to join him in a campaign to "pray for America." He was stunned when he received a predictable pentecostal answer, a declination: "It was as if I were talking to existentialist philosopher Jean-Paul Sartre. . . . Was this great man of God correct? Should we give up on prayer for national revival and concentrate solely on ministering to individuals while we await the ultimate degeneration of our country and the world?" The political system rarely recruited candidates or asked advice from pentecostals' social class; on the other hand, political reform in America, except perhaps for the rural socialism of the 1920s and 1930s, seemed to have little relevance to their desperate needs.

By the 1980s the pentecostal denominations had changed dramatically. Many churches were filled with a joyful, upwardly mobile middle-class, and their theology, while still emphasizing the miraculous, was far from escapist. The gifts of the Spirit had become a source of personal enrichment and divine healing offered supplementary health care. Contemporary pentecostals embraced a culture-affirming theology that sanctified success and wealth. By 1986 some older pentecostals complained that they were "faced with a continual battle" to preserve the movement's original values. That battle was the price of pentecostal success—economically, socially, and religiously. By the 1980s pentecostals were self-consciously aware that they were considered "evangelicals," that they had joined the "mainstream" of American religion.

The upward mobility of pentecostals brought changes in their social and political perspective. In many ways pentecostals had never been so isolated from society as they imagined, and they adapted quickly to success. Church of God minister John A. Sims wrote in 1986: "Rhetorically denying that it wanted, in any way, to be part of this world, the church showed an amazing ability to adapt to prevailing currents. For a group that was supposed to be 'outsiders' in the culture, there was an astounding adaptation to 'insider' fashions, music, promotional techniques, and institutional/ bureaucratic structures as the movement experienced social and economic mobility." In short, it was the lack of opportunity, rather than insurmountable theological barriers, that separated pentecostals from American society. As pentecostals in the 1970s and 1980s perceived that they were becoming insiders in American culture, they began to explore the classical Christian "social concerns." By 1980 pentecostals were poised for entry into the American political process.

Charismatics were a more diverse group socially and theologically than pentecostals. Most had been members of mainstream churches before receiving the baptism of the Holy Spirit and had never felt so alienated from society as pentecostals. Many charismatics simply imposed a new spiritual perspective on traditional evangelical social and political concerns. Charismatic Catholics formed a naturally conservative theological and political vanguard of the church, winning the blessings and praise of the church's conservative leaders. On the other hand, not all charismatics felt at ease as political activists. Many charismatics had roots in conservative evangelical circles that shared with pentecostals a sense of social alienation. Other evangelicals and mainstream Protestants entered the charismatic movement because of its emphasis on personal religious experience; often they had been repelled by the social and political preoccupation of more liberal churches.

By the 1980s, however, there was a clear political awakening under way among charismatics and pentecostals. "For too long we Christians have neglected our responsibilities toward our government," wrote Harold Hostetler in *Logos Journal* in 1980. "Because of our past neglect (sometimes because we've considered politics an 'unclean' profession) we have had forced upon us laws that favor abortion, pornography, and the elimination of almost all mention of God from our public schools." "The thing we are beginning to understand—and I didn't understand this myself for years," said Reagan's charismatic director of public liaison, Carolyn Sundseth, "is that if Jesus Christ is going to be your Lord in every area of your life, He has to be the Lord of your politics, too." By 1987 the charismatic movement rippled with perceptions of potential political power. In 1986 after George Bush held a "dialogue" with several charismatic leaders in Florida, Phil Derstine wrote: "As the church grows, so does its influence. . . . Never before in history has the evangelical church been so strongly positioned to influence the entire WORLD through television and satellite communications."

To some extent charismatics had been a part of the evangelical political awakening led by Jerry Falwell in the late 1970s. One of the charismatic "decatrends" noted by *Charisma* magazine in 1985 was: "During the past decade we Christians have discovered that not only can we voice our opinions, but by actually getting involved in the political process we can have great significance." By the mid-1980s charismatic publications teemed with calls to political action. "It is God's will that we have good government," wrote Michael Coleman in *New Wine*; "if God wants us to pray for it to come about, then He also wants us to take action so that it will come about." *The Forerunner*, the publication of Maranatha Churches, Inc., a flourishing charismatic campus ministry, was filled with articles urging young Christians to "invade the political arena." Charismatic magazines also introduced their readers to New Right political strategists like Paul Weyrich and to the assortment of Christian conservative organizations that had been born in the decade of the 1970s.

Of course, pentecostals and charismatics were not a uniform political community. Some charismatics identified with the more liberal political agenda of evangelical Jimmy Carter. In the midst of the 1980 presidential campaign, Jamie Buckingham, writing in *Charisma*, delivered a broadside toward the Moral Majority: "It is imperative that Christians be involved in politics. But God forbid that we join our corporate voice with the chorus of legalistic pharisees who seem determined to inflict on this nation a government run by religious zealots." The magazine's evangelical columnist, Richard O. Lovelace, was a persistent voice for political moderation; in 1982 *Charisma* even ventured the publication of a Mark Hatfield condemnation of the "simplistic notion of certain New Right religionists."

On the whole, however, the newly aroused pentecostal and charismatic alliance was almost solidly conservative. Jerry Falwell was often commended by charismatic leaders, and in some cases charismatics and fundamentalists cooperated in political action groups. But theological and cultural dissimilarities made that cooperation tentative and difficult to sustain. James Wright, charismatic director of the highly successful Family Protection Lobby in Maryland in the early 1980s, despaired of coordinating his work with the Moral Majority and settled on a strategy of activating charismatics in his state. Fundamentalist-charismatic tensions surfaced in a variety of ways before the 1980 election. Pat Robertson never gave formal support to the fundamentalist-led political movement; before the election Jim Bakker had withdrawn his support. "Like the 99 men in the boarding house bed," wrote Jamie Buckingham, "one wonders if they will all continue to roll over when Jerry Falwell says, 'Roll over.'"

In short, the charismatic political awakening was akin to the religious Right movement that emerged under the direction of Falwell; it was in many ways sparked by the success of the Moral Majority, but it was never a fully committed part of that movement. By the mid-1980s a charismatic/pentecostal political revival was under way, and at the center of it was Pat Robertson. In the mid-1970s Robertson began to politically educate "Spirit-filled" Christians. First he urged them to "pray for America," but soon Robertson was lecturing on "The 700 Club" and at Freedom Council rallies on every conceivable political topic. And combined with the education was an exhortation for Christians to become politically involved at the local level. "We must get ready for this staggering task by training leaders," Robertson wrote in 1985, "not just leaders in the Church but leaders for positions in state, local, and national government—people who know how to direct foreign policy, how to oversee social welfare operations, how to operate major educational programs." "The results of this massive education effort," believes Tim LaHaye, "will show themselves in '88 and on into the 21st century."

Increasingly, charismatics felt that they were surging to the lead in the nation's moral and political reform. Charismatic reports of conservative political successes frequently noted not only the election of Christians, but of "Spirit-filled Christians." There was a growing sense of awe that God and Pat Robertson had led them to center stage. And there was an unquestionable pride that one of their own could be a presidential candidate. "Next year," wrote Phil Derstine on a triumphant note, "we approach a Presidential election with a viable born-again, Spirit-filled Christian candidate on the ballot." Others observed that the White House would provide Robertson with a "bully pulpit" and that his religious beliefs made him more attractive than other political conservatives: "With a firm political viewpoint and a strong grasp of biblical truth, Robertson can drive home a message that other candidates might accept but would not articulate."

Pentecostals and charismatics form an imposing political group as the election of 1988 approaches. Pat Robertson's strongest religious identification is with the charismatic movement; and it is that community that most lately has perceived that this is its moment in the American political sun. Millions of charismatics and pentecostals quietly resent the religious ridicule heaped on Pat Robertson, and they will likely stand up for him in the voting booth. Jamie Buckingham, influential charismatic minister and writer, was among the charismatic ministers who received a private audience with George Bush in 1986. Buckingham liked Bush, and he had never been a supporter of radical Right ideology; but as he weighed Bush and Robertson in the balances, he raised the same hurricane question that Robertson's detractors had been guffawing about: "The question is a good question: Do you want a man to whom God has given command over hurricanes to command our nation? Or do you want another politician?" If that is *the* question in the minds of the millions of charismatics in the United States, Pat Robertson's religious-political base could be far larger than that of any presidential candidate in American history.

The economic and racial diversity of the charismatic movement has made the movement's political potential even more intriguing.

American fundamentalism and evangelicalism are almost entirely white and middle-class movements. The charismatic movement, on the other hand, has spread rapidly among Hispanics and blacks; the independent charismatic megachurches generally include notable minority memberships. Among Pat Robertson's supporters when he appealed for three million supporters in September 1986 were Bishop J. O. Patterson, president of the Church of God in Christ, the second largest black denomination in the country, and Rosie Grier, a leading black charismatic personality. Whether the appeal of a "Spirit-filled" presidential candidate could attract minority votes to the Republican party was a political question never before raised.

Because of its cell organization, the charismatic movement appeared to be a religious movement peculiarly adaptable to political organization. While the 1980s were marked by the rise of huge charismatic churches and by the remarkable growth of the old-line pentecostal denominations, the movement survived for decades as cells within mainline Protestant churches and in Roman Catholic parishes. Well organized at the local level, loosely connected to other cells and to the movement's independent leaders, highly motivated and intent on spreading their message, charismatics were masters of grass-roots organization. No group in American history has been better situated to permeate the nation's political system than charismatics.

In his 1986 book, *America's Dates with Destiny*, Pat Robertson reminded his "evangelical Christian friends" of his personal efforts to rouse their political consciences. It was a reminder that particularly rang true to charismatics: "During the last two years, I have visited your homes and churches in every state across the nation. I have talked and listened to your clergy and your laity. I have addressed your conventions, your rallies, and your citywide meetings. I am excited about your new commitment to the nation's spiritual and political renewal." Pat Robertson was casting about for new supporters in 1988, but he was intimately acquainted with his home base.

13.

Evangelical

THEOLOGIAN KENNETH S. Kantzer has suggested two "funda-mental principles" undergirding evangelicalism from the days of Martin Luther to the present: "The first sees justification occur-ring at the beginning of one's Christian life rather than the end. God's loving favor is entered into through faith in Jesus Christ; it is not a reward for moral earnestness or ecclesiastical obedience. The second principle asserts that Scripture, as illumined by the Holy Spirit, is the only trustworthy guide in moral and spiritual matters." These principles provide a general umbrella covering most conservative Protestants; since the beginning of the twentieth century, the term "evangelical" has been applied more particularly to the conservative wing of Protestantism that, to some degree, rejected the liberal Protestant accommodation to modern thought. These conservatives, often called "fundamentalists" in the early twentieth century, seemed to be routed in the 1920s; they lost con-trol of the most powerful northern Protestant denominations and faced public ridicule after the Dayton, Tennessee, Scopes trial in 1925. Their defeat was always more apparent than real, however, and evangelicals began rebuilding amidst the defeats of the 1920s.

But exact definitions of evangelicalism remain elusive. "The evangelical movement is precisely that—a movement," wrote the editor of the *Evangelical Newsletter* in 1985; "you can define its di-rections, but it's hard to rope it in." In a 1977 cover story on the resurgence of evangelicalism, *Time* magazine probed for a defini-tion. First, the word described those who believed in "bringing the word of God to their fellow man." Beyond that, continued the article, "most Evangelicals are basically conventional Protestants who hold staunchly to the authority of the Bible in all matters and adhere to orthodox Christian doctrine. They believe in making a conscious personal commitment to Christ, a spiritual encounter, gradual or instantaneous, known as the born-again experience." Using these parameters, *Time* guessed that there were 45 million evangelicals in the country in 1977, around 12 million in the "mainline churches" and another 33 million in "orthodox Protestant groups" unaffiliated with the National Council of Churches of Christ.

By the 1980s evangelicals boasted that they had become the mainstream of American Protestantism. Post–World War II evangelicals, led by Billy Graham, made impressive gains. In 1986 one evangelical leader listed some of his generation's achievements: "We inherited a religious scene dominated by liberals; we bequeath liberalism in shambles. We inherited 11,000 overseas missionaries; we bequeathed 40,000. We inherited a reputation for anti–intellectualism; we bequeathed a generation of scholars and scholarly work." In the 1980s evangelicals guessed their numbers to be as high as 70 million; they dominated the huge religious television industry and listed over a hundred book publishers and thousands of bookstores throughout the nation. *Newsweek* magazine declared 1976 "the year of the evangelical"; in 1977 *New York* magazine reported "a 500 to 600 percent increase in the number of born-again executives here"; in December 1986 *The Washingtonian* announced in a feature article on evangelicals that "God Is Back."

While it is proper to use the word "evangelical" to describe the collage of Protestants who subscribe generally to Kenneth Kantzer's two Reformation principles, the millions of believers included in that definition are divided into several discrete subgroups. Pentecostals and charismatics were the most numerous subgroup of evangelicals. Long shunned by orthodox fundamentalists, pentecostals delighted in their recent acceptance as evangelicals. But most "Spirit-filled" Christians still lived in segregated communities served by charismatic institutions. Many other conservative Protestants belonged to separatist denominations that have little association with the broader evangelical community. The most notable such group was the Southern Baptist church. While many

Southern Baptists mingled freely with other evangelicals, the church itself remained aloof from formal associations with other churches. Even more secluded was the Churches of Christ, a largely Southern group with several million members. Staunchly conservative, the Churches of Christ maintained a sectarian disdain for all other churches.

The core of American evangelicalism was formed by those Protestants who led the fight against liberalism in the twentieth century. By the middle of the 1950s they had divided into two factions—fundamentalists and neo-evangelicals (or evangelicals). Fundamentalists became concerned about growing signs of liberalism among those who had set out to oppose modernism; they displayed a militant and uncompromising spirit of separatism that demanded constant guerilla warfare against liberal Christianity. Since the 1950s fundamentalists and neo-evangelicals developed distinctive communities, each with its own institutions and leaders, although in recent years the dividing line has become more blurred.

In a tighter sense, then, the word "evangelical" has been used to describe that group of Protestants who in the post–World War II period followed a spiritual migration identified in the popular mind with Billy Graham. In schools like Wheaton College and Fuller Theological Seminary and in publications such as *Christianity Today* and *Eternity* these neo-evangelicals embraced a conservative Protestantism that was more cerebral, less confrontational, and more socially aware than that of the fundamentalists. By birthright and by training they were the leaders of conservative Protestantism in America. Evangelical leaders, particularly Billy Graham, were honored by most of the other subgroups within the larger evangelical community, even though fundamentalists and sectarian evangelicals sometimes viewed them as dangerously moderate.

Fundamentalists, particularly, have been heated critics of the evangelical elite. The rift between fundamentalists and evangelicals opened in 1956 when Billy Graham accepted the sponsorship of several mainstream churches during a crusade in New York City, a crusade in which Pat Robertson and his fellow students were volunteer workers. Fundamentalist leaders like Bob Jones, Sr., and

John R. Rice, long suspicious that liberal ideas were growing in the evangelical community, publicly attacked Graham and an open schism followed. Since that time, fundamentalists have waged war on evangelical liberalism—their chief grievance being the unwillingness of evangelical leaders to break all ties with liberal Christians. In a 1985 poll of evangelical leaders, Martin Marty observed that the differences between the groups were "less cognitive or doctrinal than . . . tonal, personal, and behavioral." At the same time, others suggested that fundamentalists were stricter in their view of Biblical inerrancy, more conservative in "lifestyle," more given to anti-intellectualism, and more confrontational in temperament, particularly on social issues.

By the 1980s the evangelical-fundamentalist rift appeared more as a continuum. The differences between Jerry Falwell, whom *Time* magazine labeled a neofundamentalist, and conservative evangelicals like Harold Lindsell were slight. On the right and left extremes were such separatist enclaves as Bob Jones University and the socially active evangelical magazine *Sojourners*. While the middle of the evangelical community was theologically fuzzy, fundamentalists and evangelicals still tended to support different institutions and leaders.

The fact that evangelicals were increasingly willing to embrace pentecostals and charismatics was to fundamentalists another sign of growing doctrinal decadence. In his book on fundamentalism, Jerry Falwell acknowledged that "most Fundamentalists would not accept the Charismatic Movement as a legitimate representation of Fundamentalism," although Falwell was willing to concede that pentecostalism was "based upon evangelical doctrinal foundation." More orthodox fundamentalists would not concede so much.

On the other hand, according to *Charisma* magazine, one of the major trends of the 1980s was the "acceptance of charismatics" by evangelicals. After years of "rejection and distrust," wrote charismatic evangelical Richard Lovelace, "evangelical churchmen and Spirit-baptized preachers have been brought together." Billy Graham opened the way for a rapprochement between evangelicals and pentecostals and charismatics by symbolically embracing Oral

Roberts in the late 1960s, first inviting him to participate in an international conference in Berlin and later speaking at the dedication of Oral Roberts University. Even more symbolic of the growing acceptance of charismatics was a 1983 announcement by conservative evangelical Bill Bright, leader of Campus Crusade for Christ, that he did "not condemn or condone Charismatic gifts."

In short, the broader evangelical community was composed of several major subgroups—some of them viewing one another as heretical. But in the center was a group of respected leaders who regarded all of the diverse elements as evangelical. It still remained somewhat difficult to be a hyphenated evangelical. In 1984, Larry Hart, the Southern Baptist chaplain at Oral Roberts University, asked a "personal and painful question that still plagues me": "Just where does a believer who is an 'evangelical in theology' and a 'charismatic in experience' fit in the body of Christ?"

No twentieth-century Christian leader confronted this dilemma of identification more publicly than Pat Robertson. Robertson's early connections were with such neo-evangelical institutions as Inter-Varsity, Campus in the Woods, The Biblical Seminary, and the Billy Graham organization. He has been a member of the Board of Directors of the National Religious Broadcasters, a branch of the National Association of Evangelicals. Like other charismatic leaders, Robertson cherished his relationship with Graham. Though Robertson and Graham have never been close friends, Graham appeared as a guest on "The 700 Club," he spoke at the dedication of the CBN Center, and Robertson was one of the featured speakers at Graham's International Conference of Itinerant Evangelists in Amsterdam in July 1983.

More significant has been the growing friendship between Robertson and Bill Bright. Bright's Campus Crusade for Christ was one of the most powerful conservative evangelical parachurch organizations of the postwar years. For many years Bright firmly opposed the charismatic movement, but by the 1980s Robertson viewed him as a close personal friend. Robertson participated in Jesus '76, a youth gathering that also received the support of Bright. When Robertson and Bright became cosponsors of the

Washington for Jesus rally in 1979, it marked an unprecedented cooperation between charismatic and evangelical leaders. They both appeared at Billy Graham's conference in Amsterdam in 1983 and soon afterward Bright announced that Campus Crusade would no longer ban participation by charismatics. In all likelihood, Robertson's relationship with Bright was built on style and upbringing, but it was facilitated by the genuine evangelical underpinnings of Robertson's thought—an intellectual base totally lacking in many pentecostal and charismatic leaders.

If Pat Robertson has always maintained some affinity for evangelicals, he has been less comfortable with fundamentalists. When he first moved to Norfolk, he was rebuffed by the fundamentalist churches because of his charismatic experience. He was received by the Freemason Street Church, a bastion of the more moderate evangelical stance within the Southern Baptist church. That experience was repeated over and over through the years. Robertson was more at home with the theology of Billy Graham and Bill Bright than with that of Jerry Falwell and Bob Jones. Bill Bright was resilient enough to pray with Robertson, Falwell's fundamentalist theology made such spiritual exercises precarious, and ranker fundamentalists considered all charismatics heretics.

In his 1984 book *Answers to 200 of Life's Most Probing Questions*, Pat Robertson betrayed an orthodox evangelical theological base. He argued for the literal truth of the Scriptures, including the Genesis creation story, rejected the scientific theory of evolution, and defended the virgin birth of Jesus. Like most evangelicals, he accepted a modified Calvinism that defended original sin and predestination, salvation by grace through faith, and the "eternal security" of the believer. In short, taking away the sections of his book that outlined his charismatic beliefs, Robertson appeared to be a conservative evangelical.

In view of his political aspirations, Robertson's most controversial evangelical belief is his acceptance of the dispensational premillennial view of prophecy. Conservative American Protestantism in the late nineteenth century became closely identified with the dispensational interpretation of the biblical millennium that emerged first among the Plymouth Brethren and was widely disseminated by the Scofield Bible translation. Generally speaking, dispensationalism argues that there are seven stages in world history leading from the Garden of Eden to heaven. At present, the world is near the end of the fifth dispensation, the church age. That age will be followed by the idyllic scriptural millennium, and that period will be ended by the Battle of Armageddon and the final judgment. While dispensationalists differed about the exact sequence of the end-time scenario, the doctrine is widely accepted among American evangelicals of all varieties and is considered by most to be one of the fundamentals of the faith. While pentecostals generally accepted dispensational views, it was the evangelicals who nurtured and promoted the theory into a major theological system. Two of Jerry Falwell's assistants at Liberty Baptist University recently estimated that dispensational eschatology was accepted by around 50 million Americans, including such ministers as Jerry Falwell, Pat Robertson, Jimmy Swaggart, Jim Bakker, and Jack Van Impe.

Dispensational premillennialism was the most sweeping theory to derive from the general evangelical interest in the literal interpretation of biblical prophecy. Particularly in the late 1970s and early 1980s when he edited his geopolitical newsletter *Pat Robertson's Perspective,* Robertson was intrigued by the interpretation of prophecy. Convinced that he had predicted the Iranian hostage crisis two years before the event, Robertson believed the Scriptures predicted "exact outcomes." "I don't want to appear like a mystical doomsday fortune-teller," he wrote; "I'm not. But look at the facts. Bible prophecies are no longer mere predictions, as is apparent to anyone who has the eyes to see." In 1982 the theme of the annual CBN telethon was Robertson's reading of the "signs of the times," an attempt to take "an in-depth look at what may very well lie ahead in the summer of '82." Robertson always hedged his predictions. In 1980 when he circulated a special issue of *Perspective* on "Prophetic Insights," he included an opening disclaimer: "I underscore emphatically that some of the tentative hypotheses are intended to provoke thought. They are put forth for reflection, prayer, and study—not as something set in stone brought down from the mountain. In certain instances we can speak with great certainty, but in other instances we must speak as those who 'see through a glass darkly.'"

Generally speaking, Robertson's prophetic musings were set in a dispensational premillennial context. In the late 1970s and early 1980s Robertson repeatedly explored the twentieth-century significance of the prophecies of Ezekiel, Joel, Zechariah, Isaiah, and other prophets in the Old and New Testaments. Among other things, he concluded that he would be "alive when Jesus Christ comes back to earth," that the prophetic Antichrist was "a man alive today, approximately 27 years old, who is now being groomed to be the Satanic messiah," and that Christians were entering a period of trouble and turmoil that could be identified as the Great Tribulation that was to precede the ushering in of the millennium.

Like other dispensationalists, Robertson saw a combination of developments in the modern world that seemed to be fulfillments of biblical prophecy. Most important were the international developments surrounding the establishment of the state of Israel in 1948 and the Jewish annexation of Jerusalem in 1967. The return of the Jews to the Middle East seemed to be a dramatic confirmation of the dispensational theory, "the most significant fulfillment of Biblical prophecy in our day." Robertson believed that the establishment of Israel had set off God's clock to usher in the millennium and the creation of a physical kingdom to be ruled over by the returned Christ. The founding of Israel signaled the "ending of the 'times of the gentiles.'" Further evidence of the predicted decline of the West could be seen in the "humiliating U.S. loss in Vietnam," the Watergate scandal, political crises in Portugal and France, the Middle Eastern oil crisis, and the decay of moral and spiritual values in the United States.

By the 1980s most dispensationalists believed that Israel's prophetic preparation was nearly completed. Many "students of the Bible," wrote Robertson, thought that the Jews would soon rebuild a temple in Jerusalem to become the "international religious center for God's chosen people." Then God, "by persecution and otherwise," would "cause a deepening of the Messianic expectation of Israel" and lead the Jews to accept Christ upon his return. Like most dispensationalists, Robertson revered Israel, but at the same time he believed that it was the destiny of the Jews to become Christians. While Robertson believed that the conversion of the Jews would take place on God's timetable and could not be forced, one of the major missions of CBN has been to encourage them to become "completed Jews" who had accepted Christ.

"CBN is vitally interested in prophetical events in Israel, and Dr. Robertson has made three visits there this year," announced a ministry publication in 1975. The fact that the Six-Day War in 1967 erupted on the day that ground was broken for CBN's new Portsmouth television facility was to Robertson "a direct sign from God. Without question. Our destiny was linked with Israel." Through the years "The 700 Club" featured Middle Eastern news and Robertson frequently interviewed Israeli political leaders. CBN attempted to secure permission to build a television station in Bethlehem in the 1970s but failed. Once a station was acquired in southern Lebanon, it became one of the ministry's highest priorities and was viewed as prophetically significant.

On numerous occasions Robertson ticked off the international sequence of events that would lead to the return of Christ—a sequence similar to that popularized by Hal Lindsay in his best-selling book *The Late Great Planet Earth*. In 1979 Robertson wrote: "We read in Ezekiel of a military confederacy composed of Russia, Iran, Ethiopia, and Somaliland and others moving against Israel. This is what God told the prophet about those times. The military confederacy would move on (1) a regathered Israel (2) living in peace with immediate neighbors (3) in the latter days (4) defended in part by the United States ('young lions of Tarshish') (5) in what looks like a nuclear war (6) from which Russia will be destroyed as a major power and (7) God, though Israel, will be exalted." In an extensive examination of the prophecies of Ezekiel in 1980 Robertson concluded: "The coming Middle East war is an absolute certainty, as is the destruction of the Soviet Union. *All available economic and military intelligence pinpoints 1982 as the optimum time for such a Soviet strike.*"

While Robertson's international interpretations of prophecy were most striking, he also wrote about domestic omens of the last days. Generally speaking, Robertson believed that the immediate future of Western society threatened economic and moral disaster. He predicted that the world economy was on the verge of collapse. In 1979 he wrote: "It is my firm conviction that in the '80s most of us are going to live through a major worldwide depression, a major war, and the restructuring of the world as we know it." Over and over, Robertson warned of an economic collapse in the 1980s and gave detailed economic advice to his partners. In 1980 he sent the readers of *Perspective* six suggestions on how to prepare for the impending world economic collapse: (1) Be sure "that your life is founded on God and His Word." (2) "To the best of your ability, . . . get free from the world system which is failing. . . . Achieve as much sufficiency as possible in energy, water sources, food supplies and basic life-support systems, and at the same time get out of debt." (3) "Develop multiple personal skills." (4) "Develop cooperative buying arrangements." (5) "If you own property in one of the older core cities, you should try, if possible, to shift your investment to a smaller community." (6) "Where possible in your personal and business life, try to use less energy."

In spite of these dire predictions, Robertson believed that the world would survive and, indeed, that the millennium would be preceded by "the greatest worldwide spiritual revival ever seen in history." That revival was about to begin—or perhaps had begun, spearheaded by the religious programming of CBN and other ministers. It would result in the conversion of millions: "We are not going to see a million or five million or ten million—we're going to see hundreds of millions of people come to Jesus. If God just takes a tithe out of the world, over 400 million people will be saved!" "For the next several years," Robertson wrote in 1979, Christians would be blessed with "vast sums of money . . . to accomplish God's purposes." During this "brief period of grace" world conditions would remain "at an absolutely optimum point for world evangelism. This can be our finest hour!" While Robertson sometimes seemed to say that the period of revival would precede the world economic collapse and biblical tribulation, at other times the two periods seemed to overlap. In 1983 he wrote: "What's going to happen in the near future? The World is going to see heartache, but God's people are going to see tremendous blessing, tremendous anointing, tremendous outpouring of the Spirit, and tremendous evangelism."

Robertson's prophetic pronouncements often seemed as precise and certain as those of Hal Lindsay and other leading dispensationalists. He undertook his prophetic studies in the 1970s with the same earnestness that characterized all of his study. Those who knew him best, including Bob Slosser, believed that by the 1980s he regretted tarrying so long in Ezekiel. In 1987 Robertson himself acknowledged that some of his prophetic readings were a bit far-fetched—though he also believed that many of his predictions were remarkably accurate.

In the end, the prophetic beliefs that Robertson shares with millions of other evangelical and fundamentalist Christians may require even more political explanation than his charismatic subjectivism. Political observers were shocked when Ronald Reagan made a casual allusion to Armageddon, but Robertson's immersion in biblical prophecy raises to new heights the issue of "Armageddon theology." "Armageddon theology clearly has political implications," warned People for the American Way; "the greatest danger it presents is a disdain for peace, particularly in the Middle East." Critics were particularly mindful of Robertson's comments about the inevitability of nuclear war. Would, indeed, a dispensational premillennialist be more apt to instigate a nuclear war?

Robertson's prophetic scenario seemed to have several safeguards. In the first place, he was a somewhat unorthodox dispensationalist. Robertson never accepted the premillennial concept of the "rapture," a relatively eccentric biblical interpretation that argues that the faithful would be "caught away" before the tribulation began and would escape the trials preceding the millennium.

As a "post-trib" dispensationalist, he stood outside the mainstream of the prophetic movement; in general his view of the whole end-time scenario was less supernatural. In the minds of more orthodox dispensationalists, Robertson's view meant that he "no longer believes in the imminent Coming of our Lord Jesus Christ."

In addition, Robertson was always tentative and guarded in his prophetic interpretations, in spite of the rashness of some of his statements. He hedged his predictions with warnings of uncertainty. His projections were filled with "ifs": "If we are reading the Book of Revelation correctly"; "if any of these projections are at all correct"; "if the approximate dating of events is even close." Even at the height of his prophetic interest, he acknowledged that "dating events in the future is dangerous." Furthermore, Robertson openly admitted to changing his mind. In October 1985 he told *The Wall Street Journal* that he no longer anticipated a nuclear war or the end of the age in the 1980s. In short, Robertson's dispensationalism was never so dogmatic and swaggering as that of most fundamentalists.

Robertson also rejected any sort of rigid determinism. He was convinced, he wrote in 1981, that "not everything in the future is fixed. The Bible assures us that God answers prayers." In the 1980s Robertson still discussed dispensational prophecy, but his speculations sometimes sounded more like the optimistic assertions of nineteenth-century postmillennialism, and he urged tolerance toward "Bible-believers who take differing views of this particular aspect of Scripture." While he still believed in the millennium, he also was convinced that Christians could change the world: "I also believe that the principles of the Kingdom of God can change the world. These principles are so revolutionary that they can change government, education, and social life." In short, Robertson's pragmatism and innate optimism in the 1980s increasingly blunted the dispensational pessimism that marked his writings in the 1970s.

Nonetheless, Robertson's earlier prophetic statements were destined to become a part of the presidential campaign debate. Despite his assurances that he would act rationally as the leader of the nation, his critics highlighted "Armageddon theology." Robertson has, therefore, repeatedly and directly denied that his beliefs implied an end-time death wish: "There's no way I feel I'm going to help the Lord bring the world to an end. God doesn't want to incinerate the world." Only the most biased critics continued to believe that Robertson's prophetic beliefs consciously committed him to destroying the world.

More pertinent were charges that Robertson's convictions bound him to an inflexible foreign policy, particularly in the Middle East. In 1982 he reported to his partners that nearly a decade earlier he "swore a vow to the Lord that despite the opposition to Israel on many sides, we would stand with Israel, come what may." Many political conservatives who agreed with Robertson's Middle Eastern perspective felt uneasy with the prophetic, rather than pragmatic, basis of his judgments. Robertson's nondispensational supporters, however, were convinced that "belief in a prophecy . . . does not commit the Christian believer to making the prophecy come true."

Political conservatives have been aware that the "Armageddon theology" issue might be the most damaging plank in the platform of the religious Right. In 1986 Ed Dobson and Ed Hindson, two of Jerry Falwell's lieutenants, published an analysis of dispensational premillennialism in *Policy Review*, a serious New Right opinion journal. It was a fascinating piece, designed to guide secular conservatives through the prophetic jungles of Gog and Magog. The writers observed that all save "extreme fundamentalists" refused to make end-time timetables, and that dispensationalists encouraged good citizenship while awaiting the Second Coming. Most important, the authors attacked the idea that those who believed in the second coming of Christ would "try to hasten the event." Such thinking, they argued, was based on "a profound misunderstanding of the Bible and what evangelicals actually believe." In an ingenious twist, they insisted that it was postmillennialists and humanists who were potentially dangerous, because they saw themselves as divine instruments who could improve the world. Premillennialists, on the other hand, believed that the future was entirely in the hands of God and that it could not be manipulated by human actions: "A lot of talk about speeding up the apocalypse would be stopped if more people understood that prophecy cannot be altered. There are some conditional prophecies. . . . But prophecies about the end times are unconditional. . . . It is arrogant and sinful to think that we can change them. Pat Robertson has said that Armageddon is 'an act of God Almighty that has nothing to do with human abilities whatsoever. I have no intention of helping God along in this respect.'"

In the end, Pat Robertson's strategy must be to convince the American public that everyone has a view of the future and that his view, while not predetermined, is based on prophetic beliefs he shares with millions of other evangelicals. But he also must assure a majority of his fellow Americans that his views do not limit his foreign policy options and, above all, that they are not dangerous. It was clear that Pat Robertson, the political candidate, was prepared to speak on those points, but he carried into the campaign hundreds of pages of prophetic interpretations that were more extreme than any presidential candidate would feel comfortable defending.

Evangelicals are a much more diverse political group than charismatics, as they are a more diverse theological assortment. To some extent, evangelicals have felt the same social alienation as pentecostals, though never to the same degree. Nonetheless, the evangelical hegemony that shaped nineteenth-century America retired in the 1920s into sequestered bands, in the words of one modern evangelical historian, a "shrinking and defensive minority." It was in this defeatist soil that dispensational premillennialism buried its roots. In the midst of their pessimism, many evangelicals retreated from politics, content to save their souls in an increasingly pluralistic and secular society.

In the 1960s and 1970s, for a variety of reasons, evangelicals began to reassert themselves politically. Partly, they were stunned by the secularization of American society, by the radicalism of the 1960s, and finally by what they considered direct government assaults on them. But the political reawakening also had an intellectual basis. A new generation of evangelicals set out to reclaim their heritage, spurred by the notion that the United States once had been an evangelical nation, that their ancestors had "run the show." Perhaps the first to discover this heritage were a group of young, politically liberal evangelicals who acclaimed the evangelical crusades against slavery and other social injustice in the nineteenth century. But it was the conservative wing of evangelicalism that embraced the vision and set out to seize political power in the 1970s. In the case of both liberals and conservatives, wrote historian Douglas W. Frank, it was power that intrigued twentieth-century evangelicals about their historical legacy; in both cases, he believed, their message was often "shrill and self-righteous."

For well over a decade, evangelicals have been urging the establishment of the Kingdom of God in America. It was this mission, they announced, that had brought the original settlers to America, and modern evangelicals must fulfill the vision. Evangelical journalist Richard Lovelace wrote in 1986: "There is also a new determination among fundamentalists and Charismatics to make Christian values prevail in our society. Among evangelicals, recent theology is full of vigorous statements about the kingdom of Christ, calling us to promote the rule of Jesus through righteous acts and prophetic words." The theological implications of the new Kingdom theology were far reaching; some evangelicals believed it undermined the Calvinistic base of evangelical theology and dispensational premillennialism, both of which seemed better suited to more pessimistic and troubled times. The Kingdom of God theology was a conservative social gospel, urging Christians to battle "the world, the flesh, and the devil, right up to the end of history."

While Pat Robertson was not a theologian and wrote sparingly about the return of the evangelical Kingdom of Christ, he was obsessed by the lost American heritage. He, like many other evangelicals, believed that "the Decade of Destiny will bring a change. . . . They expect to see Christians move more and more into full life under biblical principles of the kingdom of God, taking up major responsibilities in American society in such a harmonious way as to be unmistakable." Even Billy Graham, somewhat subdued from past political liaisons, endorsed the rallying of the evangelical Kingdom. In a 1985 interview with Robert-son, Graham announced: "I think [Christians] ought to be involved. I'm for evangelicals running for public office—and winning if possible—and getting control of the bureaucracy, getting control of the executive branch of government. . . . I would like to see every true believer involved in politics in some way, shape, or form."

The quest for a Christian America was the theme of Pat Robert-son's 1986 interpretation of American history, *America's Dates with Destiny*. The book is divided into three sections: the first chronicles the "exciting days . . . when our forefathers clearly demonstrated the early spiritual directions of this nation"; the second targets "nine tragic dates" that were landmarks in the demise of the evangelical vision; the third suggests steps for recovering the nation's "spiritual heritage." Robertson was convinced that a "moral and spiritual renewal of historical proportions is under way" in the country. Led by evangelical Christians, the nation was returning to the Christian values that had protected it until the late nineteenth century. Robertson believed that he personally was playing a role in the fulfillment of the prayers of his distant ancestors who had settled in Virginia to establish a Christian haven.

The new evangelical perception of political power was partly the result of the growing unity among old-line evangelicals, fundamentalists, and charismatics. In his book, Robertson acknowledged that evangelicals were as "wonderfully diverse from each other as they are from their unbelieving neighbors." But that diversity also made it much more difficult to estimate the political impact of evangelicalism.

In their book *Religion on Capitol Hill*, published in 1982, Peter L. Benson and Dorothy L. Williams estimated that "about 40 percent of evangelicals tilt to the liberal side, 60 percent are more at home on the conservative side, while very few evangelicals take a moderate political position." Robertson was not perfectly comfortable with either evangelical extreme. Liberal evangelicals denounced an "evangelical Christianity . . . enslaved by the political far Right." In 1986 a liberal evangelical dubbed Robertson the "fundamentalist jester for the nation." On the other hand, many fundamentalists rejected the new "political ecumenism" that demanded "yoking together with unbelievers in the Lord's work." It was almost as unpalatable for a fundamentalist to endorse Pat Robertson as it was for *Sojourners* magazine. Many insiders believed that Jerry Falwell's endorsement of George Bush in 1986 had as much to do with "underlying theological tension" as with Falwell's newly won insider status within the Republican party. In short, to fundamentalists Pat Robertson's charismatic beliefs were heresy and to liberal evangelicals they were an embarrassment. In August 1986 Robert Grant, head of Christian Voice, told *Time* magazine: "We've got a badly fragmented Christian community that cannot be lumped together."

Reflecting this fragmentation, several polls of evangelical leaders showed that Robertson had surprisingly little support. A 1986 Gallup poll showed that Robertson was the presidential choice of only 20 percent of those who were "born again," compared to 43 percent who selected Bush. On the other hand, Robertson does have support in the evangelical community. A poll of "100 leaders of evangelical Christian activist organizations" conducted by a conservative news organization in 1986 found that Robertson had the support of 43 percent of those leaders. "Attacks from outside the evangelical community," reported *Time* magazine at the end of 1986, had encouraged "Robertson's rivals within the family," including Jimmy Swaggart, to rally to his support.

Most crucial were the reactions of the hundreds of thousands of evangelical pastors scattered throughout the country. There was no way to measure their cumulative response to the presidential aspirations of Pat Robertson. But Robertson clearly has the support of many for a variety of reasons. "His grasp of prophecy means he would stay true to Israel," a Nashville Baptist minister told a reporter. A Rhode Island United Methodist minister believed that Robertson would raise "the conscience of the nation in godly matters"; Pastor Art McPhee of the Good Shepherd Christian Fellowship of Needham, Massachusetts, observed: "If God called him to politics, I'll support him." The election of 1988 will test the evangelical political conscience more directly than any previous presidential campaign, even Jimmy Carter's race in 1976.

Finally, Robertson's political potential depends upon his ability to attract those who share the evangelical value system. Robertson has repeatedly appealed to those who "support similar spiritual and political ideals even though they are members of other religious traditions or are uncertain of their personal faith." To an extraordinary degree, Orthodox Jews and Catholics backed the Moral Majority movement of the 1970s. Along with Baptists, those two religious groups shifted toward Ronald Reagan in 1980 in percentages well above the national average. Catholics and Jews will probably have no more difficulty in consorting with a charismatic evangelical than with fundamentalists. Mormons became a part of the conservative coalition of the late 1970s and delivered Reagan an 80-percent vote in 1980. The sectarian Churches of Christ has almost uniformly supported conservative candidates, even though the group still shuns formal alliances with evangelicals. Churches of Christ periodicals frequently attack charismatic and evangelical theology, but they rambunctiously support conservative social values. Pat Robertson's summons to return to the nation's evangelical roots, to traditional moral values, will, no doubt, stir the consciences of many conservative Christians and Jews who would not consider themselves evangelicals.

14.

Southern Baptist

The Southern Baptist church is a giant within American evangelicalism. With a membership of over 14.5 million, it is the largest Protestant church in the nation. Now a genuinely national church, in many Southern states Southern Baptists still constitute well over half of the religious population. Although Southern Baptist growth has slowed in the last decade, it remains a dynamic and expansive church, still enlarging at a faster rate than the population. In 1986 one of every four seminary students in America was enrolled in the six seminaries supported by the Southern Baptist Convention. The denomination boasts some of the largest churches in the country, including First Baptist Church in Dallas, pastored by W. A. Criswell, which claims over 20,000 members.

Like the South that nurtured it, the Southern Baptist church has become increasingly diverse in the years since World War II. And yet the church still smacks of the rural and small-town South. In the nineteenth-century South, the Baptists shied away from cities, turning them over to the Presbyterians and Methodists, but they conquered the Southern back country. "Cities frighten Southern Baptists," said Larry Rose, director of the Center for Urban Church Studies in 1981, "because they are big, unmanageable, and can't be controlled." According to Rose, the Southern Baptist church "is still 95 percent middle and upper class, and white," and that description does not fit any American city, even those in the South.

In short, Southern Baptist leaders often preached in huge First Baptist churches in the gleaming cities of the New South, but the denomination became progressively stronger as one headed into the suburbs and the countryside. Of the 36,000 Southern Baptist ministers in the 1980s, probably half do not have college degrees, many are "second-career adults," and thousands are "bi-vocational" ministers who support themselves working in the factories and on the farms of the South. The denomination remains the embodiment of the religious and social beliefs of the Southern yeomen, the folk church of the South.

In the 1980s the struggle within the Southern Baptist church between moderates (or liberals) and conservatives (or fundamentalists) became one of the most important religious stories of the decade. In fact, the battle within the church had been going on for over half a century; several million archconservative Baptists had already left the convention to form independent churches and associations that made up the core of modern fundamentalism. In the early 1980s conservative Southern Baptist Paige Patterson estimated that the convention was still losing as many as fifty churches a year. But most conservative Baptists remained in the convention and in the 1970s they became increasingly vocal about the growing liberalism of the church's agencies, particularly the six seminaries.

In some ways the struggle for control of the Southern Baptist Convention was reminiscent of the modernist-fundamentalist conflict that racked the Northern Presbyterian and Baptist churches in the 1920s. Once again, the central theological issue in the debate was the "inerrancy of the Scriptures." But there were also decided differences. The Southern Baptist Convention harbored few genuine "liberals"; the modernism of the 1920s had few outspoken advocates anywhere by the 1980s. The Southern Baptist confrontation was a clash between moderate evangelicals who felt at home with the likes of Billy Graham and his Northern allies, and fundamentalist conservatives. While the Southern Baptist "holy war" is still far from over, the conservatives appear to have far more enduring power than their Northern counterparts a generation earlier.

The battleground within the Southern Baptist church has been the elected president of the convention, a position long considered honorary and given to a prominent minister. In 1979 the conservatives elected Adrian Rogers, minister of the huge Bellevue Baptist

Church in Memphis. Since that election, a series of conservatives, including Bailey Smith of Del City, Oklahoma, Charles Stanley of Atlanta, and Jimmy Draper of Euless, Texas, have been presidents of the convention. By gaining control of the church's committee structure and the appointive power to various institutional and educational boards, the conservative presidents have pushed the denomination to the right.

The confrontation has pitted against one another the leaders of the church's agencies, the leaders of the seminaries and the editors of most Baptist papers, against the powerful pastors who controlled the presidency. Conservatives believed that it was a battle between the bureaucracy and the people, arguing that 90 percent of the church's membership supported their conservative theology, though they recognized that many of the people did not have the stomach for a fight. It became clear in the 1980s that a majority of the voting delegates at the Southern Baptist conventions did, indeed, support a fundamentalist theology and trusted the leadership of the conservative presidents. A "Peace Committee" was formed in 1984 to try to reduce tensions, but a poll of evangelical leaders in the same year indicated that well over half believed that the denomination would split before the end of the century.

The innate conservatism of the Southern Baptist church made it more resistant to the charismatic movement than any other Protestant denomination. Like fundamentalists, conservative Southern Baptists had "definite doctrinal scruples" against charismatic theology. As late as 1975, debate over the charismatic movement was considered the most controversial issue in the church. Many Southern Baptist churches refused to tolerate charismatic members in the 1970s and as late as 1985 a charismatic church was expelled by a Louisiana Baptist association.

Nonetheless, in the 1980s charismatics made some headway within the Southern Baptist church. In 1983 conservative Harold Lindsell appealed for a renewed emphasis on the Holy Spirit: "I am concerned that Southern Baptists, who represent the largest Protestant group in America, be involved. All too many of them seem to be afraid of the word 'charismatic.'" By 1977 there were enough Spirit-filled Southern Baptists to support the publication of a journal, *Fullness*; by 1985 the magazine's circulation had reached 20,000. In the 1980s charismatic leaders claimed that thousands of Southern Baptist ministers had become supporters of the movement. By and large, charismatic Southern Baptists remained aloof from the conservative–moderate rift in the church. Even James Robison, militant conservative before becoming charismatic in the early 1980s, urged conservatives to refrain from making "blanket accusations" that "would be damaging to the cause of Christ."

Pat Robertson was a Southern Baptist by birth, by heritage, by ordination, and to a very large degree by belief. Particularly with the growth of a substantial charismatic community within the church and the open acceptance of charismatics even by conservative Southern Baptists in the 1980s, Robertson was perfectly at home in the denomination. Only by association were his ties to the Southern Baptist church notably weak.

In 1987 Robertson remained a member of the Freemason Street Baptist Church in Norfolk, though he rarely attended services because of his demanding schedule and his celebrity stature. His daughter Elizabeth was married at the stately old building, however, and Robertson remembered kindly Dr. William L. Lumpkin, the old family friend and retired pastor of the congregation, although Lumpkin expressed reservations about Robertson's conservative political turn. Dede switched her membership to the First Baptist Church of Norfolk, where she was for many years an active member. In his early years, Robertson served as pastor or youth minister of four different Southern Baptist churches.

Robertson's doctrinal beliefs reflect his Baptist heritage. He endorses adult believers' baptism and as a result was rebaptized when he "accepted Jesus Christ as my Savior." On the mode of baptism, he is decidedly Baptist: "In the New Testament the Greek word, *baptizo*, means to dip or immerse. I believe that immersion is the New Testament fashion, although some people believe that pouring or sprinkling are perfectly adequate." In addition to these distinctively Baptist beliefs, Robertson agrees with conservative Southern Baptists on virtually every important question of biblical interpretation, including dispensational premillennialism.

This doctrinal affinity as well as his political conservatism drew Robertson toward the conservative Southern Baptist leaders in the 1980s. Robertson's early associations with his denomination had been with the more moderate Freemason Street Church, forced largely by the anticharismatic prejudices of conservative Baptists in the 1960s and 1970s. But once those prejudices began to abate, it became clear that Robertson's natural affinity was with theological conservatives. By 1987, Robertson counted among his best friends such Southern Baptist Convention presidents as Charles Stanley, Jimmy Draper, and Adrian Rogers. He acknowledged that he had had few "close ties" with his church through the years, and on occasion moderate denominational leaders expressed resentment about his recent public identification with the Southern Baptists. But for a variety of reasons Robertson has drawn steadily closer to the church of his youth and to the denomination's new conservative leaders.

Many believed that it was politics, not theology, that had encouraged the alliance of Robertson and the conservative leadership of the Southern Baptist church. The emergence of the electronic church and the religious Right created a "conservative ecumenism," argued Baptist scholar Walter Shurden, that made possible such unlikely alliances. This ecumenism led Southern Baptists into far more interdenominational cooperation than moderate church leaders would have dared to suggest. In the case of Robertson, however, both his moderate charismatic image and his Baptist heritage made the rapprochement seem natural.

Robertson's identification with the Southern Baptist church may be his greatest hidden political asset. "The Southern Baptist Convention, the church of Pat Robertson and Jimmy Carter," noted *The Washingtonian* in September 1986, "includes among its members nearly one in every twenty Americans. . . . There's a political story in that, obviously. Voting as a bloc, or anything approaching a bloc, the Southern Baptist Convention can shift the ideological center of political parties, if not yet elect a President." Several modern political analysts have suggested that the white Southern Baptist vote "is currently having the most explosive political impact in the country." While it is clear that the Southern Baptist Convention is not monolithic, it seems equally clear that its members overwhelmingly support the social and political agenda of modern conservatives.

There is evidence to support the possibility of a Southern Baptist bloc vote. Southern Baptists supported their fellow churchman Jimmy Carter in large numbers in 1976. Perhaps more significant, according to political analysts, Southern Baptists, disappointed by Carter's policies, switched to Reagan: "In every deep South state, the white Baptist swing to Reagan was the highest for any voting group." Albert J. Menendez argued that Southern Baptists were "solidly conservative," with a long history of political activism when they believed their interests were at stake. Other surveys supported that view. Writing in the conservative journal *Election Politics* in 1985, James L. Guth presented poll data indicating massive switches among Southern Baptist clergy from the Democratic party to the Republican party. Furthermore, observed Guth, these ministers "share common perspectives . . . with their people and often perceive strong congregational backing for activism. . . . Perhaps it is not too much to imagine Southern Baptist ministers providing a part of the informal local organization of the GOP, just as their Northern evangelical brethren did for a much younger Republican party."

The question, then, is whether Robertson can capitalize on his Baptist heritage and yet overcome the Baptist distrust of charismatics. His political views clearly concur with those of a majority of Southern Baptists. If he can convince Southern Baptists that he is one of them, as he has convinced many of the church's most powerful leaders, the Baptist's proclivity to vote their religious convictions could have a stunning impact on the Southern primaries in the spring of 1988.

15.

The Electronic Church

PERHAPS THE most common religious title given to Pat Robertson in recent years has been "televangelist." In many ways, it is the least apt. "The job of evangelist is a very noble calling," Robertson told reporters in 1986, "but I really am not one. I'm a professional broadcaster. I am a religious broadcaster." CBN's communications experts have labored to leave behind "wall-to-wall preaching" formats, the "personal kingdom syndrome," and the other negative connotations of the electronic church and have blazed new trails in audience research and the development of creative programming. Robertson has long tried to appear as something more than another television evangelist.

At the same time Robertson could not separate himself from the modern electronic religion phenomenon, nor would he desire to do so. He was, in fact, at the very heart of it; he appeared on the cover of *Time* in February 1986 as the nation's leading "televangelist." The "quiet explosion in religious television," wrote Ben Armstrong, head of the National Religious Broadcasters and author of *The Electric Church,* began in 1961 with the opening of station WYAH-TV in Portsmouth. Robertson readily confessed that many of the other television evangelists were his "close friends." Among his earliest and most important supporters for his presidential candidacy were Oral Roberts and Jimmy Swaggart. Speaking at the opening of Robert Tilton's satellite network in 1985, Robertson joined with Robert Schuller, Rex Humbard, and Richard Roberts in urging that "petty differences must be put aside to allow the Christian community to band together." He did not like all of his fellow evangelists, but he was forced to tolerate them: "We're all trying to do the same thing in different ways using different styles."

The facts concerning the emergence of the electronic church have been pretty thoroughly explored in the past decade. Since the broadcast of an Episcopalian service on Pittsburgh radio station KDKA in 1921, enterprising religious leaders have used radio and television as a means of broadening their own influence and, presumably, the influence of Christianity. From the beginning, evangelicals and pentecostals used these new mediums most effectively; in 1944 they formed the National Religious Broadcasters organization to protect their common interest. In 1952 Rex Humbard began broadcasting his church services on an Akron television station, and two years later, in an even more portentous development, he urged Oral Roberts to film his tent healing crusades and broadcast them on television. Roberts's programs were an enormous success in widening his influence, but they also raised a cry of indignation from mainstream religious leaders. In the 1950s a battle raged between the National Council of Churches, which urged that the networks give free time for religious programming selected by responsible Catholic and Protestant agencies, and Roberts and the National Religious Broadcasters, who successfully defended the right to purchase time for religious broadcasting.

Having secured the right to use television, evangelical religious leaders spent three decades trying to learn how best to do it. Again, Oral Roberts pioneered the path to the future when in 1968 he abandoned his old television format and the following year returned in prime-time specials produced in Hollywood by Dick Ross. Roberts's new programs featured popular stars in an entertainment format. The Roberts specials attracted new audiences that had never before watched religious television. In the 1970s and 1980s scores of emulators offered variations of the Roberts programs. Religious programming became increasingly well produced, laced with large doses of musical entertainment, and frequently featuring conversational interludes with religious and entertainment stars. "The 700 Club" introduced the talk show format that became the model for scores of other programs in the 1970s.

As religious television matured in the 1980s, predictably the pentecostals and charismatics dominated the medium. While Robert Schuller and Jerry Falwell built major television ministries retaining the older church service format, almost all of the larger ministries were pentecostal and charismatic, and almost all featured the nonpreaching techniques pioneered by Roberts and Robertson. The exuberant pentecostal approach to worship had always encouraged musical talent. The pentecostal environment that produced Jimmy Swaggart, Jerry Lee Lewis, and Mickey Gilley was filled with rambunctious guitar picking and singing that ultimately led all three of them to television. In short, pentecostal music, personal testifying, and camp-meeting preaching were ideally adapted to television. While critics of the electronic church chastised television ministers for "using the latest techniques of Hollywood to convey its message," pentecostals and charismatics did so with a clear conscience, and their tactics were little different from those used under the steamy tents and in the brush arbors a generation earlier.

There can be no doubt about the success of the electronic church; by 1987 television ministries received well over half a billion dollars a year in revenues, the number of ministers trying to support regional and national ministries was approaching 100, and the National Religious Broadcasters in 1985 listed 1,050 "organizational members." On the other hand, much debate surrounded the question of just how successful the television evangelists have been. Many television ministers habitually overestimated the sizes of their audiences, and a furious debate ensued when Ben Armstrong in his 1979 book *The Electric Church* reported that religious television had an estimated weekly audience of 130 million viewers. Although Armstrong also noted that the "unduplicated" average weekly television audience was only about 14 million viewers, the inflated figure lead to a flurry of investigation of the electronic church. In 1981 sociologists Jeffrey Hadden and William Martin challenged Armstrong's data and offered much smaller estimates of the sizes of the audiences of the television evangelists. Subsequent polls in the 1980s were inconclusive; particularly elusive was a method to accurately measure cable television viewing. The most sophisticated recent survey was conducted by A.C. Nielsen, Co., in 1985 for CBN. The survey reported much larger audiences for "The 700 Club" than had been previously projected, estimating an average daily audience of 4.4 million viewers. Other religious programming also fared well in the survey, although "The 700 Club" had by far the largest audience. While some viewed the survey as biased in favor of CBN, sociologist Jeffrey Hadden warned, "those who choose to focus on this as a criticism of the study will miss the enormous value it offers for clarifying a number of important issues in audience measurement."

While the general size and impact of religious television is still a matter of debate, even less can be said about the audience profiles for each ministry. Some viewers supported several ministers, but it was also clear that each of the ministries was built on the personality and style of its leader and that each appealed to distinctive audiences. Like secular television programs (perhaps even more because of the theological content of the programs), each television minister covertly or overtly pitched his or her message to a friendly audience. Critics have repeatedly argued that religious programs were supported largely by believers. "The usefulness of the broadcasts as tools of evangelism—the primary justification used to raise money," wrote William Martin, "must be seriously questioned." Early surveys indicated that religious audiences were markedly older, more Southern, more feminine, and more religious than the national average.

More than any of the other television ministries, CBN took to heart the findings of the early surveys and intentionally tried to mold "The 700 Club" to reach more diverse audiences. A 1979 CBN survey indicated that nine out of ten contributors to "The 700 Club" were "church members," and women outnumbered men two to one. The 1985 Nielsen survey indicated that the profile had changed. The audience of "The 700 Club" was decidedly younger than that of most other religious programs; 61 percent of the program's male viewers were under fifty-five years old. "The mainline audience that CBN reaches," said Tim Robertson in 1987, "is adults with families, from age 25 to 54." Because of the news content of the program as well as the suave presence of Pat Robertson, "The 700 Club" succeeded in reaching a far larger number of nonreligious people than any previous religious programming.

Robertson also reacted with some sensitivity to the other major criticisms of the electronic church. The fund-raising tactics of the evangelists were a constant source of public criticism. While little empirical research has been done to measure the "cost of membership in the electronic church," two communications scholars, Robert Abelman and Kimberly Neuendorf, concluded in a 1985 article that "explicit requests for funds are not as widespread among the televangelical population as has been previously assumed." They documented vast differences in the fund-raising tactics of the television evangelists and concluded that the most frequent appeals were made by noncharismatic ministers. Most religious programs included less time spent in fund-raising than was used by commercial television for paid advertisement. Robertson was particularly sensitive on the issue of fund-raising and CBN's annual telethons greatly reduced the need for fund-raising on "The 700 Club."

Perhaps the most persistent criticism of the electronic church is the charge that it undermines the local church and represents the final privatization of American religion. Once again, empirical information, such as it is, calls that judgment into question. Princeton sociologist Robert Wuthnow has concluded that the available data indicates a slight "positive relationship between church attendance and religious viewing." In 1980, CBN marketing specialist John Roos reported that 34 percent of the network's audience became more active in a local church after viewing "The 700 Club" and that only 2 percent became less active. In his book *Answers to 200 of Life's Most Probing Questions,* Robertson commended church membership: "You do not have to be in the church to be saved, but to continue effectively in the things of God, you must be in some type of fellowship with other Christian people, and churches meet that need." More than any other ministry, CBN established ties with thousands of local churches around the world and often cooperated with them in spiritual and humanitarian matters.

On the other hand, Robertson refused to be intimidated by pressure from institutional religion. In a 1980 confrontation with critics from the mainstream churches, Robertson observed that the electronic preachers and the churches were "serving the same Lord," but he also pointed out that a recent poll showed television personalities to be second only to the White House in "perceived power and influence," while Protestant churches rated twenty-seventh. He believed that Christians had the right to send their tithes to "any spiritual authority that is ordained of God," not just to local churches. Furthermore, all television ministers argued that their ministries were, in some ways, more personal than local churches. "Pat Robertson talks to the viewer every evening *via* television," noted communications specialist Robert V. Miller; "his telephone counselors are available twenty-four hours a day. When was the last time the local parish minister stopped for a personal visit?" In short, while television evangelists denied that they were replacing the local church, they also contended that they were meeting spiritual needs not being served by the institutional churches.

Aside from the high name recognition he gained by appearing on "The 700 Club," the political significance of Robertson's identification with religious television appeared to be of little import at the beginning of 1987. While Jerry Falwell's political forays and Robertson's own activities led many to associate the television evangelists with political activism, most religious television was remarkably apolitical. Nowhere was the privatizing effect of electronic religion more obvious, according to Robert Wuthnow, than in its "withdrawal from active participation in political life." Most of the successful evangelists rigorously kept to their messages of health, prosperity, and otherworldly hope. It was a remarkable achievement when Robertson received the support of Oral Roberts, who had long refused any association with political causes, and an endorsement from Jimmy Swaggart.

The potential impact of the electronic church on Robertson's political hopes was increased by the PTL "Pearlygate" scandal, which exploded into the news in the spring of 1987. The specter of a major ministry being destroyed by accusations of adultery, homosexuality, extortion, and financial fraud wounded the entire electronic church. It soon became clear that, next to Jim and Tammy Bakker and Jerry Falwell, Pat Robertson had the most to lose. A *USA Today* survey published on April 1, 1987, showed that over half of those polled felt that the scandal had damaged the "presidential aspirations" of Robertson. In the summer of 1987 the electronic church turned from a dubious asset into a very large potential liability for Pat Robertson.

As the PTL scandal sucked one evangelist after another into its vortex in 1987, Robertson tried desperately to stay clear of the mess. His initial terse assessment, "God is cleaning house," expressed his obvious shock and disgust, but for the most part he remained discreetly quiet. In an appearance on the Larry King Show, Robertson distanced himself from the Bakkers, pointing out that their association with CBN had been terminated for well over a decade and that his contacts with them since that time had been few and casual. On "The 700 Club" most of the editorializing about the PTL scandal was done by Tim Robertson and Ben Kinchlow; in general, the controversy was handled with balance and objectivity.

Some of the negative fallout from the PTL scandal was probably short range. Nonetheless, most of the ministries reported an immediate drop in financial support in the wake of the affair, and as the summer drug on, the crises deepened. By June CBN was faced with its "worst financial crisis" in the history of the ministry. The CBN budget was trimmed by $25 million and nearly five hundred employees were laid off. While most of the television ministries lost some loyal supporters, it was those who already distrusted the electronic church who reacted most negatively to the PTL scandal. And it was precisely those people whom Pat Robertson was attempting to influence, both as an evangelist and as a politician. Those who were inclined to stereotype television evangelists as charlatans found ample confirmation in the PTL fiasco. If Robertson was not Elmer Gantry, he at least was consorting with him. It was ironic that the PTL scandal seemed likely to injure most of those evangelists farthest removed from it. The most faithful supporters of the electronic church had a seemingly infinite capacity to excuse the misdeeds and extravagances of their charismatic leaders. On the other hand, those evangelists with more discriminating supporters bore the full brunt of the bad publicity.

While theological differences had long separated the television evangelists into fundamentalist and charismatic camps, the Bakker scandal became the basis for another, more significant division. In the heat of the conflict, the Bakkers' religious critics were mostly those ministers with substantial ties to organized religion, with more orthodox theological beliefs, and with more responsible ministry life-styles—Falwell, Swaggart, and Robertson. On the other side were ministers with much more tenuous relations with organized religion, people who operated in a freewheeling theological environment and with little financial supervision, including many of the faith teachers. That division, always present in the electronic church, was obscured in the 1970s and 1980s by the evangelists' camaraderie and mutual respect as well as their growing political consensus. The unity of the television ministers had few organizational expressions other than the Association of National Religious Broadcasters, but there was an unwritten law that forbade criticism of one's fellow evangelist. The more radical evangelists sometimes behaved erratically, but they were rarely called to account by their peers.

The PTL scandal ripped open this breech in the electronic church. Jimmy Swaggart began the attack, lashing out at the "false brethren" who were "specializing in 'get rich quick schemes,' the 'prosperity Gospel,' 'Dominion teaching,' plus outright crooked dealings." And Jerry Falwell's exposé of Jim Bakker soon broadened into wide-ranging attacks on unscrupulous television evangelism. From Robertson's point of view, the collapse of unity in the electronic church pitted his potential supporters against one another. How could one retain the support of both Oral Roberts and Jimmy Swaggart? Not only had those two evangelists exchanged verbal blows in the midst of the national clamor, it had also become increasingly clear that they represented different approaches to Christian ministry.

On the other hand, the PTL scandal had at least one positive effect on Robertson's political aspirations. For the first time, the television ministries were raised to a level of visibility that made their differences apparent. Newspeople and the intelligent public were given crash courses on the beliefs of evangelicals, fundamentalists, pentecostals, and charismatics. Newspapers and magazines were flooded with graphs and diagrams defining each television minister's style and theology. If millions of Americans were inundated with the bad news about Jim and Tammy Bakker, they were also introduced to the more ethical religious world of Pat Robertson. Politically, Pat Robertson's best hope was that Jim and Tammy Bakker would disappear from the national news before the spring of 1988. His second hope was that a discriminating public would not hold him accountable for the sins of others.

PART THREE

A Political Portrait

16.

Political Inklings

P AT ROBERTSON is a presidential aspirant who has never run for public office. While the successes of Jimmy Carter and Ronald Reagan served notice that political outsiders could win presidential elections, both Carter and Reagan had been governors before running for president. Robertson's supporters point to Dwight Eisenhower as a successful president who had not previously held a public office. Barring military heroes, however, few candidates without political experience have gained major party nominations; Republican Wendell Willkie in 1940 was the most recent. Robertson has argued that his experience as a businessman, lawyer, and economist would serve him as well in the White House as a political background. His "enormous business decisions" and the humanitarian and educational programs he had created and supervised at CBN would, he believed, prepare him to solve the problems of government. "In terms of foreign affairs," he told a reporter in 1986, "I have talked with the heads of state of many nations, and I have done business in many countries. My father went to Congress when I was 2 years old and I've been brought up in politics all my life."

As his political ambitions have become more and more focused, Robertson has rummaged in his past, particularly his memories of A. Willis Robertson, to discover the moorings of his political beliefs. In a 1986 article in the *Washington Post*, writer Garrett Epps concluded: "Pat Robertson is very much his father's son. This simple fact is often overlooked by political analysts, and it may be why they so often underestimate him." Epps noted, as others have in recent years, the startling similarities between many of the public statements of Willis Robertson and those of Pat Robertson thirty years later, particularly in their allusions to the Constitution and the Supreme Court. Robertson readily acknowledged an indebtedness to his father; particularly he has studied his father's conservative economic views.

But, in fact, Pat Robertson was not a political clone of Senator A. Willis Robertson. Their relationship was much too distant and the younger Robertson's habits much too frivolous for much direct transfer of political knowledge to have taken place, but he was broadly exposed to the American political system. Robertson went with his father to the Democratic National Convention in 1952, and he worked for Adlai Stevenson in 1956. In his book *America's Dates with Destiny*, Robertson remembered wandering "beneath the ornate rotunda of the United States Capitol building fascinated by the statues honoring heroes of the then forty-eight states," visiting the White House with his father, and watching the proceedings on the Senate floor. But it was these general memories, rather than specific lessons, that were Pat Robertson's legacy from his father. "I don't recall us discussing the Supreme Court and the Constitution and these various rather precise issues," Robertson said in 1987. He and his father talked about history and about Virginia politics, but otherwise the similarity in their mature views, observed Robertson, was "almost like it's something innate."

The similarities, of course, were not genetic; they were cultural. Both A. Willis Robertson and Pat Robertson were products of their past—of Celtic pioneers and entrepreneurs, of the South and Virginia and Lexington, of independent and pious kinsmen. In the Introduction to *America's Dates with Destiny*, Pat Robertson took a short but telling tour through his upbringing, mulling over those names from the distant past that remained buried deep in his subconscious—the Shenandoah Valley, "Stonewall" Jackson and Robert E. Lee, Lexington, and Washington and Lee. Much happened to Robertson in the years between leaving Lexington for a tour in the Marine Corps and his running for the presidency. During those years he reformed his life and revitalized his religious convictions, became a business success and a world-class Christian spokesman; but he did not change the character or the patriotism that were his legitimate bequests from Senator A. Willis Robertson of Lexington, Virginia.

There was an interval in Pat Robertson's life when he did ignore his political heritage. Partly, he simply became engrossed with his growing and successful business. But partly, the urgent need to proclaim the gospel rearranged his priorities, making all earthly pursuits seem trivial. Robertson never changed his political views; he simply sublimated them. But that sharp separation of the spiritual and the secular slowly eroded in Robertson's mind in the 1970s, as it did in the minds of many evangelical Christians.

There was a surety about Robertson's early disdain for politics, however, even a degree of righteous pride that he had elevated himself above such mundane matters. It was a common feeling among the more zealous followers of Jesus. Symbolically, his rejection of politics was expressed in his aloofness during his father's unsuccessful 1966 campaign for renomination to the Senate. He later recalled that "the Lord refused to give me the liberty" to enter the campaign because "I have called you to my ministry." Robertson subsequently became convinced that his father's defeat was for the best, because it removed him from Washington during Lyndon Johnson's Great Society, a period when the Democratic party gave "itself over to pressure groups which advocate causes and initiatives which are contrary to the Bible and contrary to the Christian faith." During those years, wrote Garrett Epps, "Pat Robertson renounced the secular political world his father lived in, turning to the religious devotion his mother taught him."

Most lives are not quite so neat, however, and Pat Robertson's quietus from politics in the late 1960s and 1970s was never so total as it seemed, not did he wear otherworldly spirituality as naturally as many of his charismatic and evangelical brethren. Tim Robertson recalled that his father had always offered television commentary on national elections, even in the 1960s, and that he was "very interested and concerned about the national consciousness." But it was in 1974 in the midst of the Watergate scandal that Robertson "broke silence" and appeared on "The 700 Club" with "fear and trembling and calling upon our President to . . . confess his sins before the Lord." Along with many conservatives, Robertson was "shocked by the profanity, and the seeming lack of regard for the common good that the Watergate tapes showed." By the end of 1974 Robertson was offering regular commentary on world affairs to his supporters and had clearly rekindled his own interest in politics.

In the mid-1970s, Robertson moved rapidly toward political activism. He commended Gerald Ford in 1975 for declaring Thanksgiving a day to give honor to God. He spent two days in Chicago in a prayer meeting with 135 evangelical and charismatic leaders, including Bill Bright, a meeting that hinted at the potential for political cooperation among diverse evangelical leaders. In the fall of 1976, he joined with the major party candidates Gerald Ford and Jimmy Carter in calling the nation to a day of prayer on September 17. He wrote to his "Faith Partners": "God wants to give good government. God wants spiritual revival in a nation. . . . And he has commanded us to pray that these things might exist in America." In 1976 in what Robertson believed at the time was the "most significant single ministry CBN has ever undertaken," the network aired the special "It's Time to Pray, America," featuring such evangelical and charismatic personalities as Billy Graham, Charles Colson, Pat Boone, Bill Bright, Demos Shakarian, and Rex Humbard.

But for Pat Robertson as well as for most American evangelicals it was the nomination of Jimmy Carter that fired the political imagination. "I thought it would be wonderful to have a man who was a born-again Christian as president," Robertson recalled in 1987. For the first time in years, he wholeheartedly plunged into the fray, giving Carter "some quiet help behind the scenes in the Democratic primary that may have been responsible for winning Pennsylvania for him." Carter's election was exhilarating to Robertson, and in 1977, just a month before Carter's inauguration, Robertson began writing his "geopolitical newsletter," *Pat Robertson's Perspective*. The initial intent of the newsletter was to track the progress of world events under the presidency of a Christian.

For five years Robertson wrote *Perspective,* spending "countless hours reading, analyzing and praying about world events in the light of the Bible." CBN supporters were told: "Through his many contacts in Washington and around the world, Dr. Robertson has become one of the most informed watchers of the current scene. As a frequent participant at seminars on economics and global politics, Dr. Robertson is made privy to the thinking of leading experts in those areas. And, through his thorough knowledge of the Bible and his total reliance on God's Word, Dr. Robertson is able to provide spiritual insights for a much needed perspective overlooked by many." By 1978 Robertson was ready to return to campaigning; in that year he backed an old friend, G. Conoly Phillips, in an unsuccessful race for a Senate seat in Virginia, briefing him on national and international issues. By 1979, like most evangelicals, Robertson had concluded that the "country was in desperate condition," betrayed by the evangelical president who had inspired and given hope to conservative Christians.

More than any other single event, the Washington for Jesus rally on April 29, 1980, crystallized Pat Robertson's political conscience. The march was the brainchild of John Gimenez, the minister of Rock Church, an independent charismatic congregation in Virginia Beach, and a long-time friend of Pat Robertson. Gimenez hoped to bring a million Christians to Washington "to dramatize to the nation and the world that the church of Jesus Christ means business with God." Most of the early planners of the campaign were charismatics, but they soon attracted as "national sponsors" such leading evangelical figures as James Kennedy, Ben Haden, Robert Schuller, and Charles Stanley. The success of Washington for Jesus was assured when Bill Bright agreed to join Robertson as cochairman. "It is hard for the evangelical, and even worse for the fundamentalist, who has damned me and everybody like me to hell," recalled Gimenez, "to say, this is my brother. That's why I honor and respect Bill. . . . He joined us." Significantly, Jerry Falwell and other fundamentalists were not among the supporters of the rally.

The Washington for Jesus demonstration was deemed a success by its architects. The leaders of the movement estimated that 500,000 people participated, although the secular press reckoned the number as low as 200,000. The speaker list at the rally read like an evangelical celebrity roster, missing only Billy Graham and the absent fundamentalists. The day's activities were aired on all of the major religious television networks. Among the political dignitaries who welcomed the marchers were Senator Orrin Hatch and Congressman Jack Kemp.

In the long run, no one was influenced by Washington for Jesus more than Pat Robertson. In 1987 he recalled: "It was a very moving thing. . . . It was a drawing together of the evangelicals, pentecostals, the blacks, the Hispanics, the Roman Catholics, the Episcopalians, Lutherans, . . . the Southern Baptists, we were all there together. Which I think was the symbol of what was to come. The unity that we now experience in the Christian body is more profound that I can ever remember. Bill Bright is convinced, and I am convinced, that the prayers offered that day had a profound impact . . . on the whole thrust of America." For months afterward, Robertson heralded the spiritual results of the national confession of Christ. In 1981 he wrote: "The events of 1981 can be considered a clear answer to the prayers of 500,000 earnest Christians who assembled in Washington. . . . In answer, God has given our nation wise leaders, confusion to our enemies, and a year of peace and prosperity." The quickening of the nation's spiritual life in the 1980s, symbolized by the rise of the huge charismatic megachurches, seemed to Robertson to be directly linked to the national demonstration of faith and repentance.

Most important, however, Pat Robertson saw in Washington for Jesus the potential of a unified evangelical response to the nation's political problems. Surely, as the thousands of faithful mingled before the podium, there was a spark of curiosity about where he fit into God's plan. Robertson later recalled that during the Washington for Jesus rally several people suggested to him that he ought to run for president—chance remarks, no doubt, not to be taken seriously, but made in the midst of a euphoric environment of faith that was hardly bounded by reason.

It is difficult to say when the idea of running for the presidency began to seep to the surface of Pat Robertson's consciousness. Some of his public statements in the 1960s showed that he had not completely forgotten politics, although he never hinted at any specific personal ambitions. Conoly Phillips believed that God was using his senatorial campaign "to get Robertson more involved in the political arena." While Phillips did not believe that Robertson had any political ambitions in 1979, he was sure that if God ever did show him that he should run, "he'd do it at 90 miles an hour. Who knows the mind of the Lord?"

In spite of these ruminations, in the early 1980s Robertson seemed to draw back a bit from politics. When he stopped publishing *Perspective* in 1982, he wrote to his supporters: "Last spring the Lord made it clear to me that my job with the *Perspective* was coming to an end. . . . He clearly spoke to me, 'You take care of My work, and I will take care of the world's crises.' His clear direction to me and to CBN is to give all of our efforts to our primary mission of bringing the knowledge of the kingdom of God and of His salvation in Christ to entire nations around the world. And as this has happened His anointing upon me to write the *Perspective* has lifted." He was "very pleased" with the administration of Ronald Reagan, and in the early 1980s he had other challenges that demanded his attention.

After 1984, however, the presidential idea resurfaced. "Suddenly things just came together," he recalled. "From various sides, people who were significant were saying you should do this." Robertson listed among those who urged him to run an unnamed former president and three senators. He apparently was encouraged by several members of the staff of Senator Jesse Helms as well as an array of conservative lobbyists in Washington, including Paul Weyrich and Howard Phillips. In March 1985 the *Saturday Evening Post* publicly launched the idea with a highly supportive article. After having checked "out rustlings in the grass roots," the magazine reported "wide interest in the possible candidacy of this multitalented broadcaster." By the end of 1985 Robertson's response to media inquiries was that he was "prayerfully considering" a run for the Republican nomination.

In early 1986 Robertson outlined for *Charisma* magazine how he would "crystallize a decision": "The first step was intense prayer, and the second was consulting a number of Christian leaders. The third part is assessing the reaction of Christian people. The fourth will be to observe some of the political races in 1986 where Christians are running for governor, congressman and so on. By the end of 1986 we'll all have a much clearer picture. But I feel that God is doing something very extraordinary among His people in this country and possibly I'm a part of it." On September 16, 1986, the 199th anniversary of the signing of the Constitution, Robertson rented Constitution Hall in Philadelphia to announce his decision.

Robertson's decision, made before a live audience and shown by satellite in scores of cities around the nation, was that he would run for the presidency "when at least 3 million registered voters sign petitions committing to pray, to work, and to give toward a campaign effort." Robertson insisted that his presidential ambitions were not personal, since he was "comfortable with my ministry, my career, my home." His candidacy was a response to the urging of tens of thousands of Americans who had "stood to their feet in city after city, clapping and shouting, urging me—'GO FOR IT, Pat!'" But most of all, his explorations were "in response to the clear and distinct prompting of the Lord's Spirit." He wrote to his supporters: "I have walked with the Lord for more than 25 years. I know His voice. I know this is His direction. *I know this is His will for my life.*" Robertson gave his campaign organization, Americans for Robertson, until September 17, 1987, to secure the 3 million signatures and the necessary financial support. By March, the organization had secured 600,000 signatures and by July the figure had reached around a million. During the summer there were rumors that the petition signings were lagging and that the campaign was not operating efficiently, but frantic last minute efforts pushed the list to well over 3 million by mid-September.

17.

The Religious Right

THE RISE of Pat Robertson as a national political figure was related to the emergence of the new religious Right at the end of the 1970s, though it was by no means an identical story. The religious Right movement, led by Jerry Falwell and the Moral Majority, bore the brand of American fundamentalism. The rise of the Moral Majority has been well charted. *Christian Century* labeled the success of the religious Right the most important religious news story of 1980, and though the movement's breast-beating after the elections of 1980 and 1984 was overdone, few people doubted that the wedding of fundamentalist religion and conservative politics at the end of the 1970s had been influential. In the election of 1980 Jerry Falwell claimed to have registered four million new voters and the Moral Majority played a visible role in several crucial state elections. Jimmy Carter agreed that the religious Right had a "very profound effect" on his defeat.

The rise of the new religious Right was the result of an alliance of several major American evangelists with a group of lobbyists who had arrived in Washington in the early 1970s and welded an alliance that came to be known as the New Right. These young political conservatives viewed the older conservative leadership in Washington as sluggish and complacent, an elitist clique of East Coast snobs. In the late 1970s the New Right established a coterie of political organizations in Washington, including the Committee for the Survival of a Free Congress, the Conservative Caucus, and the Heritage Foundation. Direct-mail expert Richard Viguerie was the early financial wizard behind the new organizations and he also began publishing *Conservative Digest* to chronicle the progress of the new conservatism.

In the long run, the most important of the New Right leaders was Paul Weyrich, who formed the Committee for the Survival of a Free Congress in 1974. Weyrich also coordinated a series of coalitions in the 1970s to develop strategy "for the implementation of conservative ideas." The Kingston Group discussed economic problems; Library Court sought to coordinate the work of lobbyists concerned about education and social issues; the Stanton Group, presided over by Weyrich himself, held briefings on foreign policy. The son of working-class German immigrants and a devout Eastern Rite Catholic, Weyrich came to Washington without a college education but with a razor sharp mind that earned him a reputation as the "New Right's leading strategist" in the 1980s. Among his other contributions, Weyrich focused on the political importance of "issues," a strategy that proved to be the key to arousing conservative religion. Serious, almost austere, Weyrich nonetheless proved both flexible enough and innovative enough to encourage the New Right coalition with conservative evangelicals that bloomed into the religious Right in 1978 and 1979. While the influence of Richard Viguerie declined in the 1980s and Conservative Caucus leader Howard Phillips remained a decided outsider in Washington, Weyrich, according to conservative William Marshner, became a "more and more crucial, important and inside player in Washington."

The emergence of the religious Right, then, resulted from the fortuitous convergence of the New Right political experts with conservative evangelicals who, by historical circumstance, were prepared to claim their rightful role in the American political process. While the political arousal of American evangelicals is partly explained by the unique religious history of each subgroup of religious conservatives, the immediate sparks that set off the new religious Right explosion came from the dramatic social changes of the 1960s and 1970s. Beginning with the Supreme Court decisions banning prayer in the public schools in 1962 and the legalization of abortion in 1973, evangelical Christians agonized through twenty years of incredible social change—the drug revolution, the specter of long-haired hippies and antiwar demonstrations, the apparent collapse of patriotism, the spread of pornography, gay rights, the ERA campaign, radical feminism, and other assaults on traditional family values.

The outrage of American religious conservatives was exacerbated by the complicity of the traditional Protestant churches in the social revolution. As mainstream religious leaders struggled with liberal consciences at the outbreak of each new protest, millions of parishioners left their churches to join with conservative evangelicals in decrying the collapse of traditional values. Many religious Americans became convinced that the mainstream churches were controlled by arrogant elites who had lost their faith. While mainstream churches shrank, evangelicals grew, and with that shift came the growing evangelical conviction that they, not the National Council of Churches of Christ, represented the religious conscience of the American people.

In some ways, the trauma of the "sinful sixties" reenforced the feelings of isolation among evangelical Christians. More than ever, they retreated to their churches and to their preoccupation with spiritual matters. They began building an alternative school system to protect their children from the ravages of secularism. They voted for Richard Nixon, but they had little real sense of political power. There were stirrings in 1974, when a group of parents in Kanawha County, West Virginia, challenged the choice of textbooks in the local schools and a few months later when Anita Bryant challenged the gay rights movement. By far the most important of the early efforts to organize conservative religious discontent, however, was Phyllis Schlafly's Stop ERA campaign in the mid-1970s. Schlafly's organizing skills brought a variety of religious conservatives together in a dynamic mix, as did the White House Conference on Families in 1978. Slowly, evangelicals, fundamentalists, Mormons, Catholics, and Jews found themselves joined in common cause against the social revolution.

Jimmy Carter's election in 1976 greatly heightened evangelical expectations. Carter's presidency, typified by his support for ERA and gay rights, infuriated them. In 1981 fundamentalist Tim LaHaye wrote: "Between 1976 and 1980 I watched a professing

Christian become president of the United States and then surround himself with a host of humanistic cabinet ministers. . . . These people nearly destroyed our nation." By the end of the 1970s the evangelical community was angry and confused, ready to be organized for a fight.

While this general scenario explains much about the emergence of the religious Right, at the local level there were countless encounters between conservative Christians and the government that convinced them that their insulated religious enclaves no longer provided them with safety. Tim LaHaye's political awakening began with a zoning fight in 1975; James Robinson jumped into politics when a Dallas television station canceled his program after he attacked homosexuality. But the goad that spurred most fundamentalists to political concern was a series of government actions against Christian schools. The schools were the epitome of conservative Christian isolation, particularly for the fundamentalists. They were the citadels to which the conservatives had retired to train the next generation. The evangelical resurgence began not as an offensive manuever to seize control of American society; it began as a defensive tactic to protect themselves from the encroachments of federal regulation.

Most conservative Christians considered their schools a part of their churches. In 1978 the Internal Revenue Service, arguing that tax-exempt status constituted Federal assistance and suspecting that the schools were residual havens for segregation, began an investigative campaign that threatened the life of many of the schools. It was the last straw. "Step by step," wrote Jerry Falwell, "we became convinced we must get involved if we're going to continue what we're doing inside the church building." In the mid-1970s a few untrained lobbyists for the Christian schools began to appear in Washington. They, in turn, became educated on the other issues on the emerging conservative social agenda such as abortion. Slowly, in the last half of the 1970s, thousands of conservative American ministers underwent political conversion experiences, dismayed by the decay of American society and angered by what they considered calculated attacks on their religious freedom and their own detached kingdoms of God. What they lacked was political know-how.

The cast of characters who facilitated the union of the New Right conservatives in Washington with the powerful evangelical religious leaders included Christian school lobbyist and fundamentalist William Billings and an ebullient former advertising man and Southern Baptist layman, Ed McAteer. Their historic role was to bring together Jerry Falwell and Paul Weyrich and the other New Right conservatives. John Buchanan was convinced that the New Right created the religious Right, that the evangelists became the "creatures . . . of the secular New Right forces in Washington, D. C." While the relationship was not so tidy, it was certainly the political experts who facilitated the union and who saw the political potential of evangelical discontent. The single most portentous moment in the jelling of the movement came in the Dallas National Affairs briefing sponsored by McAteer's Religious Roundtable in August 1980. The meeting featured speeches by preachers like Falwell and James Robinson and the New Right political experts, as well as an address by presidential candidate Ronald Reagan. More impressive, 18,000 evangelical Christians attended the briefing, including around 5,000 preachers. While these early political meetings were attended by a variety of evangelical leaders, including many Southern Baptists, it was the fundamentalist Independent Baptists who, in the words of Ed McAteer, "quickly got the microphone in their hand."

In the late 1970s the Moral Majority became the most visible symbol of the new religious Right. While the base support for the Moral Majority came from Baptist fundamentalists, Jerry Falwell drew considerable backing from Roman Catholics and conservative Jews as well as from other segments of the conservative evangelical community. While the Moral Majority was probably never so influential as either its supporters or critics imagined and its prominence clouded the breadth and diversity of the religious Right, the organization vaulted Jerry Falwell to national visibility; he seemed to aspire to the kind of influence that Billy Graham had on earlier occupants of the White House. Falwell's growing influence also made him a target for criticism. When the press revealed that Falwell had talked extensively with President Reagan during the debate over the confirmation of Supreme Court justice Sandra Day O'Connor, James M. Dunn, executive director of the Baptists Joint Committee on Public Affairs, charged that the president was "misreading political realities if he believes that Jerry Falwell has to be consulted or pacified."

The influence of the Moral Majority declined steadily in the 1980s; many conservatives spurned the support of the organization in the elections of 1984 and 1986; Falwell's support for South Africa was unpopular and Moral Majority's negative rating in public opinion polls was quite high. Jerry Falwell's announcement in January 1986 that the Moral Majority was expanding and changing its name to Liberty Federation and that he intended to take a lower political profile had many nuances and constituted only a "strategic withdrawal" in the minds of political experts, but to some degree it reflected the declining vitality of the organization. The demise of Moral Majority and the strategic withdrawal of Falwell may be seen as the close of the fundamentalist stage of the evangelical political resurgence. Falwell's political foray had stretched fundamentalist theology to a breaking point, and the Moral Majority had never reached large numbers of nonfundamentalists. Falwell remained an important religious-political figure and his role as a pioneer assured him a place in history, but by the mid-1980s his political influence appeared to be declining.

The demise of the Moral Majority did not signal the end of the religious Right. That movement, in the mind of critic John Buchanan, remained a "potent" and "virulent force" in American politics. Falwell's declining influence was at least in part a result of the political metamorphosis of Pat Robertson. "I think the Robertson thing isolated him from his own constituency," observed Buchanan. Robertson was more than a new personality emerging from the shadows, he was a representative of the huge numbers of charismatic Christians who had been quasi-supporters of the religious Right. He also brought to his political activism a broad political agenda that promised to join religious conservatism and the New Right in unprecedented ways.

Pat Robertson was a fellow traveler in the early religious Right movement; he was indebted to it and identified with its aims, but he was never perfectly at ease with its leaders. Robertson's vision of a unified evangelical and charismatic political uprising was grander and less sectarian than the Moral Majority movement. His sense of independence and probably his latent personal political ambitions kept him from wholehearted participation in the first stage of the conservative religious revolution.

Actually, the political emergence of Pat Robertson paralleled almost exactly that of other conservative evangelicals in America. Step by step his political and religious sensibilities responded to the same affronts that offended other evangelicals. In its earliest stages, he supported the New Right–religious Right coalition. In 1979 Ed McAteer signed Robertson along with Falwell, James Robinson, James Kennedy, and Charles Stanley as his "big five" directors for the Religious Roundtable.

Then in 1980, at the peak of the efforts to get the religious Right launched, Robertson backed off, severing all formal connections with the new organizations. In the early 1980s observers of the religious Right tended to ignore Robertson. Robertson's retreat surprised many of his peers and his supporters. He explained to his partners that he felt called back to the original spiritual work of CBN. He wrote in 1980: "Obviously, individual Christians will enter politics; all of us owe Caesar informed and active citizenship. But, at least for the next couple of years, the church of Jesus Christ should concentrate on the salvation of the lost, rather than taking over temporal political power." Writing in *Perspective* in September 1980 he appeared discouraged: "Christians should be wary of placing their hopes in non-Christian men and in programs of secular political parties. Even the best men fail and find themselves rendered ineffective by today's systems. . . . Right now, our only hope is God's intervention as thousands join in fasting, confession, and prayer."

Although he never criticized, Robertson almost surely was disenchanted by the hurly-burly, sometimes slapstick campaign led by the fundamentalists in 1980. He clearly was unwilling to hitch his own political future to such a narrow-gauged theological and political movement. In the fall of 1980 he wrote with candor in *Perspective:* "The attackers [of the religious Right] have found an easy target in 1980 because the conservative Evangelicals involved in politics—Christian Voice, Moral Majority, and Religious Roundtable—have been, at times, unsophisticated, simplistic and inept. But, for that matter, Harry Truman and Abraham Lincoln were unsophisticated and, at times, inept. The question is the constitutional right of Evangelicals to express their concern about what they perceive as dangerous trends in our nation."

Actually, Robertson never backed away from the objectives of the religious Right, only the untidy and hastily built organizations that flowered before the election of 1980. In a 1986 article in the charismatic magazine *New Wine,* he identified himself as a part of the evangelical political crusade that began around 1978. His personal links with the New Right political analysts never diminished; they appeared frequently on "The 700 Club." Almost immediately after his withdrawal from the Religious Roundtable, Robertson began building a parallel political system. The founding of CBN's Christian Legal Foundation and the Freedom Council were welcomed by Moral Majority director Ron Godwin as new allies in the cause of the religious Right.

In short, in the 1980s Robertson's political connections were not so much with the religious Right as with the New Right. In 1985 and 1986 he served as president of the Council on National Policy, a select group of important conservatives who received periodic briefings from leaders ranging from Jesse Helms and Secretary of Education William Bennett to Oliver North. Robertson remained particularly close to Paul Weyrich, who briefed him at regular intervals.

At the same time, Robertson maintained a discreet distance from the New Right lobbyists, as he did from the Christian Right. "I think most of the [New Right experts] like him," said CBN President Bob Slosser, but "there is no real relationship. . . . There's no counsel going on." Pat Robertson shared the faith and convictions of the New Right and the religious Right, but he would do it his way. While his political views were almost totally acceptable to most conservatives, Robertson's ideas and his campaign methods were expressions of his own personal and religious backgrounds.

18.

Foreign Policy

P AT ROBERTSON has always been interested in international affairs; for the past ten years he has carefully studied world politics and American foreign policy. Until his presidential ambitions surfaced, his insights were likely to be framed in the language of dispensational premillennialism. But by the mid-1980s his prophetic dogmatism had waned. "As a close friend," said Bob Slosser, "I'd be hard pressed to say exactly what he believes regarding premillennial philosophy. . . . I am sure of one thing. . . . He firmly believes that none of those [views] can effect foreign policy and it must not be allowed to. . . . He wrote some brilliant things and he wrote some things that I wish he hadn't written." As early as 1979 Robertson confessed that he had probably been "a little overzealous" when he predicted that there "had to be a nuclear war" in the Middle East; by the 1980s radical eschatology had disappeared from his rhetoric, if not from his religious faith.

Robertson flirted with other deterministic schemes in addition to dispensational premillennialism. He exposed the readers of *Perspective* to radical Right conspiracy theories about the "one-world" ambitions of David Rockefeller and his influential allies drawn from "the elite world of international banking, major corporations, New York law firms, major broadcasting and publishing firms, ivy-type universities and major foundations," though he never endorsed those ideas. Some saw the collusion of these people as a "sinister plot," Robertson reported, while others believed that they were sincerely trying to build a "rational world order." But, whatever their motives, Robertson believed that institutions like the Council on Foreign Relations and the Trilateral Commission had worked for an "interdependent one world government" and that their influence over the United States government had created "a conflict of interest of massive proportions." In 1980 Robertson asked: "Why should a great nation have to place the control of its national destiny in the hands of a small clique dominated by one rich family?"

By 1987 such schemes rarely surfaced in Pat Robertson's discussions of foreign policy. His statements were pragmatic, rational, and informed, and they were largely in agreement with the foreign policy agenda of the New Right conservatives. In a 1987 article in *Policy Review,* a conservative journal published by the Heritage Foundation, Robertson outlined the foreign policy positions that would undergird his bid for the presidency. He postulated "two main principles" upon which to build American foreign policy. First, foreign policy must be viewed as an instrument to defend the national interest, a means of protecting "the life, liberty, and pursuit of happiness of American citizens." While reality demanded such self-interest, Robertson believed that self-defense was also a "moral responsibility, because America is one of the few truly free countries in the world, and the only free country which can raise the flag of freedom which can 'make the world safe for democracy.'" The second principle was "America's commitment to freedom beyond its immediate borders, for its allies and indeed for all people who long for freedom and are willing to struggle for it and pay the price for it." Robertson recognized that these two principles were sometimes difficult to apply in combination, that we had tolerated repressive dictators for the sake of national security and that we had sometimes failed to support those who wanted freedom, but we nonetheless had no alternative but to try to balance the two: "In general, the United States should attempt to put its two principles of foreign policy into effect with a realistic view toward what is possible, what will help more than hurt, and what is desirable, not just in the short term, but in the long term as well."

Within that framework, Robertson saw the world as an ongoing East-West confrontation, the clash of freedom with the repressive power of the Soviet Union. All other foreign policy questions were related in one way or another to the Western struggle with world socialism. The Soviet Union was a "new kind of totalitarian state" with an "all-encompassing utopian ideology" that guided it unwaveringly toward world domination: "Its theory and practice, guided by Marxism-Leninism, aims at reordering the international system by turning every encounter into a gain for world socialism."

At times in the past, Robertson believed, there had been chances for change in the Soviet Union, but those opportunities had been ignored by Russian leaders. On the other hand, the United States had been irresolute in standing against Soviet ambitions, often ashamed of our "strongest weapon—confidence in the truth of our founding principles." Robertson ticked off a series of humiliating American defeats since World War II—failure to support the Hungarian uprising, our "cowardice" during the building of the Berlin Wall, our abandonment of Vietnam, the fact that we "took five years" to retaliate against Qaddafi for his "monstrous behavior." The United States had tried to "negotiate" with the Soviet Union and Soviet leaders had consistently taken it as a sign of weakness. "Without a comprehensive and cohesive strategy," warned Robertson, "without self-confidence in our values, we will allow the Soviets to overwhelm us."

In the Middle East, Robertson believed that the Soviet Union was poised to dominate Iran after the death of Khomeini. In the meantime, "Islamic terrorism," masterminded by Muammar Qaddafi, held the United States hostage in the region. Harking back to Franklin D. Roosevelt's plea to "quarantine the aggressors" before World War II, Robertson called for the economic isolation of Libya, including the mining of harbors so that oil exports would be cut off.

Robertson was also deeply concerned by the Sandinista takeover in Nicaragua in 1979, a revolution that he believed was the handiwork of the Soviet Union, establishing a Marxist foothold in Central America. Robertson saw Nicaragua as a second Cuba and warned: "Nicaragua is well on its way to forward basing status for the U.S.S.R. on the North American mainland." The government of Daniel Ortega, he charged, had become a supporter of worldwide terrorism. Robertson threw his full support behind the United Nicaraguan Opposition (Contras), arguing that this policy rested on the same high "moral ground" that supported the Truman Doctrine's resistance of armed Communist takeovers after World War II. The problem with the United States policy in Nicaragua, Robertson believed, was that it had been shrouded in secrecy, conducted surreptitiously by the C.I.A. and nongovernment agencies. The nation needed to make a commitment to openly recognize and aid the freedom fighters, taking the war out of the shadow of "uncertainty and illegitimacy." Robertson's outspoken support for the Contras stirred public protest on a number of occasions. He emphatically denied the charge of a Catholic bishop that he had called the Contras "the army of God" and just as vehemently denied a charge published by *Sojourners* magazine that CBN had supplied funds for the Contras. A magazine spokesman subsequently agreed that CBN had only given "food, medicine, clothing and shelter to people in the border regions."

In other areas of foreign policy, Robertson's stance was consistent with his general opposition to Soviet expansion. Early in his political thinking he opposed recognition of the People's Republic of China, but by 1987 he had come to view American-Chinese relations more pragmatically. Since the establishment of relations had been beneficial to both nations, the United States should continue the relationship so long as we kept up pressure on the Chinese to abandon their "centralized totalitarian command system" that denied human rights to their citizens. As with other nations where human rights had been linked to continued relations with the United States, such as South Africa, El Salvador, and Chile, the People's Republic of China should be forced to make concessions in return for the economic benefits it reaped from reopened relations with the United States.

There were few chinks in Robertson's conservative foreign policy. He consistently supported a strong defense, including the Strategic Defense Initiative. And yet, there were a few nuances that separated him a bit from some of his right-wing allies. In a 1981 issue of *Perspective* Robertson brooded over the fact that the "monied barons in the Western industrial society realized that wars insured full employment" and that they profited from the perpetuation of the Cold War. He longed for the day when saner policies would "end this selfish madness" and allow nations to spend their resources to aid "the hungry, the illiterate, the diseased, and the miserable." He decried the "madness" of the nuclear arms race, a protest that more liberal evangelicals noted and applauded. And while Robertson never underestimated the Soviet threat, he strongly denied the charge of Democratic Chairman Paul Kirk that he favored "a massive military buildup." In fact, in 1987 he proposed massive cuts in defense spending based on more efficient procurement procedures, though he assured that this could be accomplished without weakening the nation's military strength. Robertson's harsh assessment of the defense industry provided a link between his hawkish foreign policy and his somewhat populist economic views.

19.

Economics

PAT ROBERTSON is a self-taught economist. As early as the mid-1970s he showed a keen interest in economic issues and began informing his supporters about the precarious condition of world finance. When he began writing *Perspective,* he became engrossed with the subject. "Back in those days he saw that the future was going to be governed by economics," recalled Bob Slosser. "He got off on some tangents. He basically learned. . . . Pat would every night immerse himself in this." For a decade, Robertson's economic predictions were ominous. Over and over he predicted "depression or hyperinflation," warning in 1982: "The deluge will come between 1980 and 1984." Robertson read and sometimes passed along some highly speculative economic theories, but basically, he learned.

Before 1985 most of Robertson's economic advice was directed to individuals. He instructed his supporters on how to protect themselves from the impending economic disaster. Frequently his directions were quite specific, including instructions about investing in commodities, stocks, and Treasury bonds; always they included the warning to "get out of debt." Hanging over all his economic advice was the "specter of debt collapse." In his most pessimistic period, Robertson's thinking took a survivalist turn: "Stored grain and well-watered agricultural land will probably rank as the best tangible investments for these days," he wrote in 1980. The next year he added: "Churches should begin cooperative buying and storage programs. They should establish skill banks to assist one another."

Robertson's economic conservatism was hardly unpredictable. It was a natural outgrowth of his evangelical theology. Not only did he believe that the Bible taught Christians to stay out of debt, he also cautioned against the "blandishments of easy living funded by easy borrowing." Robertson never embraced the runaway prosperity message that increasingly captured many of his charismatic friends. He was, in fact, offended by it. The prosperity message, a theological justification for the joyous embracing of the world by a generation of poor pentecostal ministers who achieved unimagined wealth, never rang true to the values that Robertson had learned in the evangelical circles where his faith was grounded.

Of course, Robertson's economic conservatism was also a response to those truths that had become so embedded in his boyhood character that they stood like eternal verities—that people should live by the sweat of their brows, that debt was unwise, but that debts honestly incurred must be honestly paid. In short, Pat Robertson's economic conservatism was a studied response to who he was. Once he began studying economics seriously in the 1970s, he reviewed the philosophy of his senator father and he was ready to learn. "I think that Pat has seen that a lot of things his dad stood for were right," said Bob Slosser.

While Robertson was supportive of the economic policies of Ronald Reagan, like other New Right conservatives, he was alarmed by the large budget deficits of the Reagan administration. Robertson promised to "take a meat ax to the federal budget." He insisted that the budget was crammed with waste, citing a report by his old employer, Peter Grace, that asserted that government spending could be reduced by $430 billion immediately and by $2 trillion within the next decade. While other conservatives talked about trimming the federal budget, there was a "ferociousness" about Robertson's rhetoric, noted The Economist, that made his economic proposals more notable. In Robertson's mind the deficit was a moral issue: "We are stealing the patrimony from our future generations. This becomes immoral because this is theft." But more than that, argued Robertson, the deficit was "just stupid." A balanced budget reached beyond left-wing and right-wing politics, he believed; it was a matter of national survival.

Robertson's commitment to a balanced budget demanded a reduction in federally funded social programs. In his book *America's Dates with Destiny*, Robertson traced the runaway growth of the federal bureaucracy from the Depression presidency of Franklin D. Roosevelt through the massive spending of Lyndon Johnson's Great Society. Robertson conceded that Johnson "loved the nation and desperately wanted to create the Great Society for all its people and the people of the world," but the idea was "doomed from its inception." No amount of government spending could solve the problems of poverty, inequality, and injustice. These were sicknesses of the "human spirit" and they could be cured only by revitalizing the spirit of the people. The legacy of the Great Society was an immense national debt and an inefficient bureaucracy that by 1985 "absorbed 90 percent of the money appropriated for the relief of poverty."

In general, Robertson advocated a return to the principle of helping those who helped themselves. He said in his September 1986 Independence Hall speech: "Our government should guarantee every citizen the right to pursue happiness; but no longer will it try to guarantee every citizen happiness." "America is a great and a compassionate society," he told the *Saturday Evening Post* in 1985; "we obviously must look after the poor, the needy, the truly destitute, those who are suffering and hurting. But it has to be an intelligent use of funds guided by the maxim of the apostle Paul: 'If any man will not work, let him not eat.' That's what the Bible says. And that's the way it ought to be." Specifically, Robertson believed that CBN's Operation Blessing relief work and Operation Heads Up literacy program provided models for helping the poor to help themselves without government funding and without the creation of an unwieldy bureaucracy.

Over and over, Robertson insisted that his economic conservatism did not translate into a blatant disregard for the poor and the needy. He was no social Darwinist; he understood the predicament of the unfortunate, that many were trapped in the ghetto through no fault of their own. CBN was in the business of dealing with human tragedy; Robertson knew that there were suffering people in the nation. He repeatedly appealed for charitable giving on "The 700 Club" and CBN distributed millions of dollars to relieve the needy and educate the underprivileged, supporting, Robertson believed, a "Holy Spirit–inspired social gospel." Often in his public speeches, Robertson harked back to his days in Bedford-Stuyvesant, to the times when he contemplated spending his life in slum mission work. In a 1986 interview with *Conservative Digest*, he said: "I gained a tremendous compassion for, and understanding of, the poor. . . . I am sincere when I say that I am no dilettante when it comes to the problems of the inner city, the difficulties of the life those people live, the many burdens and the unfairness they suffer. When I talk about those things, I am not talking about what some liberal saw from the window of a limousine. I lived in the inner city with my family, helping my neighbors with their spiritual problems." The question was not whether the poor should be aided, Robertson insisted, but how it should be done.

In some ways, Robertson's most innovative economic suggestion was his call for a thorough revision of the Social Security system. Noting the lack of any real trust fund to support the current system and the decreasing number of workers who would be forced to support growing demands, Robertson argued that the liabilities of the Social Security system represented the "greatest hidden debt in America." In the early 1980s Robertson began thinking of ways to make the system solvent. In 1981 he suggested that worker investments in "private pension plans" would be both beneficial to the nation's economy and more rewarding for workers. More recently, Robertson advised making the "hard decision" to pay the price of making the Social Security system "actuarially sound." Such a step might require funding Social Security out of general tax funds for a decade, while contributions to the system were invested to provide a trust fund to support future benefits. But the positive result would be the accumulation of a huge trust fund that could be invested in the private sector, thus encouraging economic growth, and in the end it would provide a sound retirement system that would protect the workers who purchased the insurance.

Finally, Robertson's economic platform called for a "fair tax structure." First, he demanded a renunciation of the use of taxation as a means of redistributing wealth, a concept first introduced into the American tax system by the Wealth Tax Act during Roosevelt's New Deal. "Taxes should be used to raise revenue—end of story," said Robertson curtly. Second, he supported a 20 percent flat income tax as a means of removing the "loopholes and gimmicks" that protected the rich and rewarded borrowing.

While Robertson's economic beliefs were in most ways conventional conservatism, there were nuances that were unique to him. In the first place, his ideas were distinctly New Right conservative as opposed to traditional Republican conservative. New Right conservatism spoke more clearly to the needs of the middle class and the working classes than to the interests of entrenched wealth. Robertson's disdain for powerful elites, his innate populism, led him to entertain not only ideas of "one-world" conspiracies led by the Trilateral Commission, but also made him lash out at the greed of the business establishment, which "loves the Cold War" because of government contracts and loans. During the oil crisis of the late 1970s, Robertson charged that "our society is a hostage" to the unscrupulous scions of wealth who were amassing "fortunes beyond the wildest dreams." Lurking behind much of this economic wrongdoing was David Rockefeller and the Chase Manhattan Bank.

Finally, Robertson's nonpolitical background made him willing to speak with unusual candor and, on occasion, to innovate and take risks. He was not inextricably tied to any theory or clique. He explored the idea of a biblical Jubilee Year in which all debts would be canceled to stop the inflationary spiral and a depression. In capitalistic societies the "redistribution mechanism" after the accumulation of burdensome debts was a depression. But such economic dislocations were dangerous and painful; perhaps they could be avoided if society learned the lesson of redistribution of wealth taught in the biblical Jubilee. In a more practical vein, Robertson toyed with the idea of canceling the debt of overburdened Third World nations, forestalling the ill will and world economic dislocation that would follow their inevitable repudiation of the loans. By declaring the debts foreign aid and by protecting the American institutions that had made the loans, the government could leave behind a legacy of good will and perhaps avert an international depression. In short, while Robertson and his advisors agreed that some of his ideas in the past were hastily drawn and indiscreetly stated, his thought betrayed an innovative and searching mind, a mind willing to explore options that most politicians would consider too risky to give serious thought.

20.

The Social Issues

IN THE ESTIMATION of many observers of American politics the Democratic and Republican parties have reached a "new era of consensus." To a large degree the leaders of the two parties have accepted the key programs of the welfare state and agree on the need for an expanding economy. And, for the most part, both parties support the concept of a strong military to deal with threats of Soviet aggression. On the other hand, the social issues, or the "cultural agenda," hold the potential to become the center of American political debate for the next generation and to leave distinguishing marks on the two major political parties.

For better or worse, many New Right Republicans linked their electoral hopes to the social agenda. It was those issues that made possible the marriage of the New Right with evangelical conservatives in the late 1970s. Robertson wrote in 1979: "Leaders of the so-called New Right have realized that issues such as abortion will bring evangelicals and urban Catholics together at the polls. In the 1978 elections, 26 senators and representatives espousing abortion, ERA, and antifamily legislation were defeated by carefully planned precinct-by-precinct organization." It was from both the evangelical and the New Right point of view a marriage made in heaven. The social issues were, in the words of conservative Southern Baptist Paige Patterson, "inextricably comingled" with evangelical theology. On the other hand, the churches provided the grass-roots organization to "reach people with the issues" that was needed by the New Right political lobbyists. Paul Weyrich said in 1982: "The churches gave us access to the social precincts because there are only a few places where you can reach people—their home, their work, and the place they go to church. . . . We . . . have begun to reach people in their church, or, if not in their church, in their home by means of their religious value structure." The social issues opened up the possibility of startling new political alliances, Weyrich believed: "Today values determine more where [people] end up politically, so the poor guy who goes to a Baptist church and hears the gospel preached in the worst part of town has more in common with the rich guy who may go to a conservative Episcopal church to hear the same gospel preached . . . and end up in the same place politically."

Pat Robertson stands as squarely in the center of the values-oriented political revolution as anyone in America. In his letter appealing for 3 million petitioners for his presidential nomination, he wrote: "You can successfully launch this campaign—not just a campaign for Pat Robertson—but a campaign to restore America to the traditional values upon which it was founded more than 200 years ago." There was more to Robertson's bid for political office than the social agenda and he had a much broader understanding of world politics and of economics than most leaders of the Christian Right, but it was the social issues that awakened him and his fellow evangelicals, and it was those questions that were anchored squarely in the center of his political psyche. Robertson's belief in a conservative social agenda was profound and religiously grounded. His views had nothing to do with political expediency, though he was prepared to use the social issues as a political asset.

The "social issues" embraced three related but distinct areas of concern that brought disparate pressure groups into the conservative alliance in the 1970s. The "family issues" ranged from opposition to the Equal Rights Amendment to the prolife crusade against unregulated abortion. The "moral issues" included such questions as drug abuse, pornography, and the regulation of television and motion pictures. Finally, the "education issues" included prayer in the public schools and demands for tuition tax credits for private schools.

No issue was more responsible for the broad coalition that formed the religious Right at the end of the 1970s than the prolife crusade. One of the nation's tragic "dates with destiny," according to Pat Robertson, was January 22, 1973, when the Supreme Court announced the decision of *Roe v. Wade*, abolishing virtually every anti-abortion law in the nation. The issue of abortion was loaded with moral and emotional meaning, and by 1975 Robertson along with thousands of other evangelical ministers had taken up the crusade against the decision. He began discussing the question on "The 700 Club" because he viewed it as a religious issue, not a political one: "Abortion is not a legal matter. It is strictly a theological matter not subject to judicial interpretation." Robertson was outraged by the moral implications of the decision. He warned viewers over sixty-five that the logic behind the abortion ruling "will be used in the future to destroy the elderly." Like all prolife activists, Robertson considered unregulated abortion no more than "legal murder" and kept his supporters informed as the count of abortions climbed into the millions.

By 1987 Robertson's position on abortion was clear and reasoned—he believed that an unborn child had rights that could not be subsumed to the choice of its mother. He also believed that a vast majority of Americans did not approve of the abortion ruling and that it had been foisted on the public by the shrill agitation of the "radical feminists" aligned with the National Organization of Women. But the real culprit was the United States Supreme Court. Its decision infringed "upon the rights of the people in each state to decide that complex social issue for themselves." In effect, the Supreme Court had passed its own legislation, a law "regarding the definition and value of human life that disregards the universal laws revealed in nature and in the Judeo-Christian Scriptures."

While the prolife movement has been the most visible of the family issues, particularly because of the Roman Catholic support for the cause, *Roe v. Wade* was only a part of what conservatives considered a general attack on the family. Robertson believed that the feminist movement in general was devoid of a "spiritual heritage" and that feminist demands were "tearing apart . . . the family." Robertson supported, quite simply, the traditional family based on the biblical model: "The first head of the family is Jesus Christ. . . . We believe in headship. Now, under Jesus is the hus-

band, and the husband is to be the high priest of the family. . . .
Now, the concept of headship . . . is repugnant to many in our
age, especially those who want to create a unisex society. They say
male equals female, female equals male, therefore they are equal
and there is no difference. . . . Well, that's not what the Bible says.
It doesn't say that necessarily a female is any less good . . . than a
male. But it does say that when two people gather together in
marriage they have established a type of entity which must have a
head. I don't have two heads, I have one." Robertson repeatedly
insisted that he believed in equal rights for women, and that he
believed that women had made many important contributions to
religious and political reform in America. He agreed that "women
needed help in securing equal job opportunities and civil privi-
leges." But those were not the "rights" that radical feminists wanted to protect, he contended; they rather were interested in
"restructuring the Judeo–Christian concept of the male–female
roles."

Nothing more flagrantly flaunted the threat to the family in
modern American society than the gay rights movement. "We have
people with changing sex identities," said Robertson in 1983,
"women who want to be men, and so they form lesbian relationships, and men who want to be women, so they form homosexual
relationships. And there is this tearing apart of the family and it's
not going to end until people are saying: I will give myself to God."
In Robertson's mind, as in the minds of other evangelical
Christians, homosexuality was a clear and simple matter: it was an
"abomination," and "from the biblical standpoint, the rise of homosexuality is a sign that a society is in the last stages of decay."
Under questioning from the secular press, Robertson affirmed that
he believed that homosexuals had the same constitutional rights as
other citizens, but he also observed that many states had sodomy
laws that he believed should be enforced.

If conservative Christians felt that the family had been under
attack since the 1960s, that feeling was only a part of a general
dismay over the changing moral standards of the society. The as-
sassination of John F. Kennedy in 1963, Robertson contended,

marked the beginning of the "loss of personal rights and safety" in the United States. What followed was a moral spiral downward, marked by crime, drug and alcohol abuse, and a decline in the national will to resist moral decay. Robertson saw a relentless "trend toward anarchy in the nation."

The conservative litany of moral collapse in American society was familiar by the 1980s—the abuse of alcohol and drugs, the spread of sexual promiscuity, the blight of pornography, the irresponsibility of public television. The picture that Robertson painted of modern society was enough to shock the nonreligious: "Consider the sexual revolution. Public standards regarding nudity, fornication, adultery, homosexuality, incest, child molestation, and sadomasochism have either crumbled or arc under fierce attack." Individual freedom had given way to unrestrained license. Robertson particularly feared that ratification of the Equal Rights Amendment would provide constitutional protection to "homosexuals, lesbians, sadomasochists, and to anyone else who engaged in any other sexual practice whether or not that practice was prohibited by the Bible, religious dogma, existing federal or state law."

CBN was constantly in touch with the personal misery that resulted from such license, counseling thousands of individuals whose lives had been scarred by lawless and undisciplined conduct, but Robertson felt a particular burden to address the evil influence of television. CBN was conceived as an alternative to the moral collapse of network television. In a fund-raising letter to his supporters, Robertson described his anger when he and his fifteen-year-old daughter tuned in to network TV one evening to find "scenes of a young man romping in bed with two scantily clad girls." "I was infuriated by having this sick behavior invading our home," he wrote. "Surely you feel as I do that this sort of thing is *wrong!!*"

If the Supreme Court was the major culprit in breaking down the American family, the media was the foremost contributor to the collapse of personal morality. "It breaks my heart to think of the families that are being subjected to a frightening barrage of nudity, profanity, violence, and immorality—simply because that's all the Network heads in New York have chosen to offer this season," Robertson wrote. The only motive of the "godless media giants" was "money," "pure profit"; greed was behind the "steady diet of raw sex, bloody murders, and boy-dates-boy shows" offered to the "Godless mass." Network television's arrogant disregard for traditional morality made the mission of CBN consummately important.

Finally, Robertson and other conservative evangelicals were shocked and angered by the secularization of American public education. That ominous change, noted Robertson, began in 1962 when the Supreme Court, in a session that opened with a prayer, ruled that prayer in the public schools was unconstitutional, a decision that was vigorously protested in the Senate by A. Willis Robertson. While most conservatives recognized that the school prayer decision was largely symbolic, the support of voluntary school prayer became a principal concern in the conservative social agenda. One 1984 survey indicated that 92 percent of evangelicals strongly supported the return of prayer to the schools.

The 1962 school prayer decision was symbolic of a profound transformation in American public education; the changes were subtle but nonetheless clear, especially to religious parents. Prior to the 1960s, the public school systems in most communities in the United States remained profoundly, if informally, Christian. Clergymen were frequent guests in public schools and not infrequently were instructors. Traditional moral values were both revered and taught. Although the anti-evolution struggle of the 1920s foreshadowed the intrusion of secular thought into the public schools, in most American communities, particularly outside the major cities, education remained firmly in the hands of the believers.

The first reaction of many conservative evangelicals to the secularization of the public school system after World War II was withdrawal. Nineteenth-century Roman Catholics built an extensive parochial school system to protect their children from the dominant evangelical public schools. In the 1960s and 1970s, millions of evangelical Christians built private schools systems to protect their children from the secularized public schools. Pat Robertson's establishment of CBN University was a response to these pressures. He wrote in 1980: "Christians must educate their youth in new schools which teach biblical principles and a biblical life-style in which the Lordship of Jesus Christ is acknowledged in every facet of their lives."

The growing Protestant educational system provided the spark for the politicizing of evangelicals in the 1970s. The school system, more than any other institution in modern American society, brings millions of parents into direct confrontation with government regulation. Beginning in the late 1970s, the Christian school movement fought and by and large won a series of battles against government regulation. Increasingly, conservative support for its parochial school system took the form of urging tuition tax credits for those whose children attended private schools. Like the prolife movement, the support of tuition tax credits showed considerable potential to coordinate the religious and political interests of conservative Catholics and Protestants.

By the 1980s, however, it was clear that the overwhelming majority of evangelicals in the country still used the public school system, including most Southern Baptists. Politically aroused and better trained in the methods of legal confrontation, in the 1980s evangelicals launched a campaign aimed at recapturing the public school system, or at least influencing it. It was in this context of confrontation that Pat Robertson could emphatically deny that he intended to destroy the American system of public education; on the contrary, he intended to save the system. By the mid-1980s the most sophisticated pressure on secularized public education was being applied by the CBN-sponsored National Legal Foundation, established in 1982 to protect traditional religious values. In 1987 Robertson's legal foundation was prosecuting several "landmark cases" designed to place religion on an equal footing in public education with its secular competitors for the minds of American youth.

The most visible litigation in 1987 was a case in Mobile, Alabama, designed to force public schools to present Judeo-Christian views. Robertson agreed that the anti-evolution laws of the 1920s had been misguided in attempting to bar Darwin's theory from public education. However, Robertson personally rejected the "theory of scientific evolution," and he supported a series of "creationist" laws passed in the early 1980s that demanded that the biblical account of creation be taught as an equally valid explanation. When those laws were struck down by the courts as efforts to teach religion in the public schools, conservative evangelicals developed a new, more promising tack. In a March 4, 1987, decision, Alabama Judge W. Brevard Hand agreed with the attorneys of the National Legal Foundation that forty-four textbooks used in his state either taught religion in the form of "secular humanism" or presented inadequate or distorted views of the role of Christianity in the development of the United States. When the decision was reversed by the Circuit Court of Appeals in August, Robertson announced to the press that he would back an appeal to the Supreme Court.

Of all of the elements in the New Right political platform, the social agenda has the clearest religious base. And yet, the recent Republican support for traditional values and the corresponding identification of the Democratic party with nontraditional interest groups have clearly caught the attention of other Americans as well as evangelical Christians. Evangelical Christians were not the only Americans to decry the influence of television on American society. As early as the 1960s, organizations such as Action for Children's Television deplored the impact of television and challenged the autocratic control of the networks. Nor were evangelical Christians the only Americans to complain of the unresponsiveness of television executives. One reporter commented in 1981: "The most offensive characteristic of TV networks is their arrogance. They carefully foster images of omnipotence and infallibility, and like governments, they abhor the thought of publicly admitting errors."

Nor were evangelical Christians alone in their concern over the public school system. Many Americans agreed that textbooks had become unbalanced in the historical treatment of religion in the United States; Roman Catholic professor of psychology Paul C. Vitz charged "the publishing industry of systematically deleting

religious references from elementary and high-school textbooks."
People for the American Way and Americans United for Separation
of Church and State, two organizations committed to religious pluralism, reached startlingly similar conclusions about American
textbooks. Even more important was a growing American concern
about the quality of education offered in the public schools. It was
the deterioration of public education that perpetuated the Catholic
parochial school system, argued Catholic scholar William Marshner, and many Catholics in the nation sympathized with Robertson's protests against the "fraudulent education" being foisted on
the American public. The movement in the nation toward teacher
testing signaled a pervasive discontent with the quality of public
education.

In short, the social issues aroused the moral conscience of a wide
variety of Americans. After a Robertson speech in Nashville that
featured family issues and attacks on the secularized public school
system, a Dallas journalist wrote: "Quirky, pre-modern concerns,
these? Not to all modern voters, it would seem. When Brother Pat
recently addressed a gathering of Southern Republicans, he was
roundly cheered and atta-boyed."

Writing in *Harper's Magazine* in 1980, *Washington Post* columnist
Dick Dabney described his reaction as he listened to Robertson
condemn the sordid "homosexual prostitution" that thrived in
every major American city: "This, Robertson said, in a common-
sense voice, was *wrong*. And that was one of the damnedest things
I'd ever heard on TV. For in spite of the fact that I, too, suspected
it was wrong, I had never heard such a view publicly expressed.
Of course, the main-line clergymen, who conducted the sleep-in-
ducing discussion groups on Sunday morning television, had addressed that topic. And, as with most other things they discussed,
they had admitted that it surely was a 'problem'—their favorite
word. After that, predictably, they had turned the matter over to
a psychiatrist to get some 'insight.' But here was Robertson saying
it was *wrong*." Indeed, such clear moral pronouncements expressed
the gut feelings of millions of Americans—religious and nonreligious. Some things were wrong, and they needed to be put right.

21.

Religion and American Politics

Pᴀᴛ Rᴏʙᴇʀᴛsᴏɴ's political agenda presupposes a battle between secular humanism and the Judeo-Christian tradition. Whether such an overt conflict is actually under way, whether or not the public believes that politics is the proper arena for the struggle, and whether a majority of the American people agree with Robertson's values are all questions that lie near the heart of his 1988 presidential campaign. This much was certain: Pat Robertson raised such questions more intensely than any recent candidate, even though others, including Ronald Reagan, probably agreed with his answers. One charismatic journalist wrote in 1986: "With a firm political viewpoint and a strong grasp of biblical truth, Robertson can drive home a message that other candidates might accept but would not articulate."

Robertson's broad political expertise contradicted the assumption that Christian political conservatism was single-issue and simplistic. On the contrary, theologian Richard John Neuhaus suggested, religious conservatives were "maddeningly multifaceted" in their concerns. But all of the issues, Robertson told an audience in 1982, were "the myriad expressions of two conflicting philosophies— secular humanism and evangelical Christianity." Those who supported Christian values were under a grave and organized attack: "A firm, clear voice for moderation will no longer be tolerated. The abortionists, the drug addicts, the homosexuals, the promiscuous, the financial spoilers, the Marxists, the humanists will make an all out assault on God's people." Secular humanism carried with it the "unmistakable scent of the Antichrist spirit," Robertson warned, and it would destroy any society that did not resist it.

Robertson's fear of secular humanism was neither ahistorical obfuscation nor sheer hysteria. He fully comprehended the profound intellectual changes that had shaped the West in the nineteenth and twentieth centuries, changes that placed humans at the center of the universe and did much to undermine the supernaturalism that had made Christianity the intellectual base of Western society. Robertson believed that the steady march of modern thought from Darwin to Marx to Freud to John Dewey was away from God toward a totally secular society. Like most other evangelical conservatives, Robertson viewed the *Humanist Manifesto*, a document signed by thirty-four American humanists in 1933, including John Dewey, as a declaration of war on traditional Christianity. Humanism was a calculated plot to replace the Judeo-Christian value system with a new humanistic one. While not all Christian intellectuals saw humanism as such a clear-cut and orchestrated movement, many agreed with Robertson that modern humanistic thought had first neutralized religion and then had attacked it as a nuisance that should be eliminated.

While conservative evangelicals have had little success in legally defining secular humanism as a religion, few historians would contest their descriptions of the transformation of modern thought. Evangelicals borrowed the term "secular humanist" from conservative Roman Catholics who for well over a century waged war against secular thought on the Continent. "Secular humanism is real," acknowledged John Buchanan of People for the American Way. Although neither "secular" nor "humanist" were "bad words," Buchanan argued, if there were a genuine plot by humanists to destroy religion in America, "I'd be as concerned as they [evangelicals] are about them." But, argued Buchanan, religion was hale and hearty in America, as opposed to its decadent condition in Europe where government had sheltered it. In short, one might argue about who was winning the secular-religious battle or what legal rights each group had, but few people were prepared to argue that there was no war.

No one would convince evangelical Christians that there was not a "militant secular influence out there." "Movements don't spring up in a vacuum," wrote Southern Baptist conservative Russell

Kaemmerling. "They rather are in response to perceived griev-
ances." The crumbling of the Christian foundations of the nation
might simply be a natural evolution to modernity, but evangelicals
thought they could spot specific enemies. And so, in part, the evangelical political revolution was a populist protest against the intellectual elites who presumed to speak for the people. "Conservative
Christians, long ridiculed or ignored, are a force to reckon with in
public life," wrote Nashville religion reporter Ray Waddle in *USA
Today*. "Many feel their world of values has been ignored by politicians, institutions, reporters." More than ever, in modern society
the lives of common people were controlled by mediating elites
who often did not share their values.

Pat Robertson repeatedly listed the coterie of institutions that had
collaborated to undermine the nation's values. It was, he believed,
an odd and contradictory confederation: "I perceive . . . a group
that would be called secular humanists who have made a concerted
effort to subvert the traditional Christian values in our country.
Now interestingly enough this isn't a rightist/leftist, conservative/
liberal kind of thing. These people are well-entrenched in such
things as the Chase Manhattan Bank, the Trilateral Commission,
some of the big investment banking companies, the think tanks,
and some of the major universities and major foundations." In his
1986 speech seeking support for his candidacy, Robertson denounced the "small elite of lawyers, judges, and educators" who
had "taken the Holy Bible from our young and replaced it with the
thoughts of Charles Darwin, Karl Marx, Sigmund Freud, and John
Dewey."

The most sinister institutional manifestation of secular humanism was the American Civil Liberties Union; in his book *America's
Dates with Destiny*, Robertson marked January 20, 1920, the birth
date of the ACLU, as the beginning of the "loss of the rights of
the majority." It was the "incessant hammering" of the ACLU, "a
group formed . . . to defend Bolsheviks," Robertson warned, that
led to increased restrictions on religious freedom. The ACLU's
crusade to protect the individual rights of the minority had resulted
in the oppression of the majority. The fight to preserve spiritual

values in America, Robertson believed, was a battle between the ACLU and "the rest of us."

In recent years, the more direct institutional enemy of the Christian Right in general and of Pat Robertson in particular has been People for the American Way, founded in 1980 under the leadership of television producer Norman Lear for the specific purpose of protecting "pluralism, individuality, freedom of thought, expression and religion, a sense of community, and tolerance and compassion for others." The founders of People for the American Way maintained that the 1980s and 1990s would be "troubled times," and that the television ministers were poised to take advantage of social discontent. The strategy of People for the American Way against Robertson was to publicize the evangelist's most extreme religious and political statements; the organization promised to track him to the end of his political journey, making certain that the public knew the complete content of his beliefs. Robertson was infuriated by the tactics of People for the American Way; in 1986 he labeled the group "anti-Christian atheists," although John Buchanan, its director, was an ordained Southern Baptist minister. Of course, other conservatives agreed with Robertson. Paul Weyrich believed that People for the American Way was composed of "people who mask themselves as believers who are really unbelievers and who are approaching this thing in a way that all religion offends them."

In Pat Robertson's mind, the chief federal instrument in undermining traditional values was the Supreme Court. Few historians would question the immense significance of the judicial activism that began with the Warren Court as a means of achieving progress in civil rights and continued in a long series of decisions in the 1960s and 1970s that pushed American society in a more liberal direction. Of course, throughout American history the Supreme Court has piqued the resentment and criticism of the public and of elected officials by issuing decisions that were at odds with the popular will. Robertson's criticisms of the Supreme Court echoed the "court packing" fight waged by Franklin D. Roosevelt in 1936 and 1937 when conservative justices imperiled the New Deal. In fact, Robertson's proposals were remarkably similar to those of Roosevelt—suggesting the addition of justices to the Supreme Court to bring its decisions into conformity with the popular will.

Robertson's criticisms of the Supreme Court have sometimes been stormy and intemperate. In 1986 he warned: "The Christian people who are coming along will no longer allow the Supreme Court to be a runaway maverick organization without any dealing whatsoever with the wishes of the general public." But in a more serious vein Robertson explored two long-debated issues in his criticisms of the Court. First, he attacked the concept of legal realism that developed in the early twentieth century. Progressive jurists argued that the Constitution was not a static document, that it could not be interpreted in the light of the unknowable intents of its framers, and that it should be construed in the light of the needs of contemporary society. Robertson sharply disagreed. "Without believing in the Constitution as our ultimate authority," Robertson wrote, "we have no trustworthy standard by which a law can be judged. Without believing that we can understand the original intent of our forefathers, modern jurists give up the attempt to understand it altogether."

In a more quixotic protest Robertson questioned the concept of judicial review, the tradition established in the case of *Marbury v. Madison* in 1803 that vested in the Supreme Court the power to rule legislation unconstitutional. While judicial review is not likely to be reversed, Robertson argued that it was not intended by those who framed the Constitution, and he concluded that it had been a vehicle throughout American history for frustrating the desires of the American people as expressed through their elected officials. In short, like both liberal and conservative critics of the Supreme Court in the past, Robertson believed that the Court had arrogantly distorted the democratic will. He judged that Congress and the president could, if they so willed, disregard a Supreme Court ruling, arguing that President Lincoln had done precisely that in ignoring the Dred Scott decision that upheld slavery in 1857. Of course, in the end Robertson knew that his quarrel was with the decisions of the Court, and in the 1980s he and his National Legal

Foundation took their case to the courts. But Robertson and his fellow conservatives also thought that the most serious imperative in the election of a conservative president in 1988 was continuing the Reagan administration's change in the composition of the Supreme Court.

At the most general level, conservatives saw secular humanists as an intellectual elite who controlled the nation's educational system and the media. The courts had operated in concert with "the leftist-oriented American Civil Liberties Union, a handful of atheists, unitarians, and liberal Protestant and Jewish groups," Robertson argued, adding to his list the major foundations, the nation's elite universities, and the media, particularly television. In short, the battle against secular humanism was an assault on those elites that presumed to speak for society. It was a people's revolt against the new "third class" in American society, an intelligentsia that perceived itself as enlightened and socially compassionate, but was, in turn, perceived as arrogant and condescending. This elitist minority had captured the schools, the universities, the television networks, and ultimately the government. It was that powerful minority that Robertson and other conservatives sought to unmask and to unseat through the injection of evangelical values into the American political debate.

Secular humanism aside, the rise of the religious Right set off another debate about the relationship of religion to politics in America that will be expanded further by the candidacy of Pat Robertson. At the most obvious level, Robertson's political ambitions raised questions about the peculiar American experiment in separation of church and state. Throughout most of American history, church and state managed to coexist in relative harmony, allowing for the general acceptance of Christianity as the national religion but guarding against government favoritism for any particular sect. Such, in general, was the consensus understanding of the constitutional prohibition against the establishment of religion. Since the early 1960s, however, the courts have systematically challenged the practices of the past and have attempted to secularize American public life. While early American concerns had been to separate church and state, more recent debate has focused on the separation of religion and state. Ironically, that shift may be related to the diminution of sectarian conflict in the nation; increasingly, generic Christianity became one of the religious competitors in a religiously pluralistic society. Whatever the causes of the shift, Robertson believed that recent interpretations of the "establishment-of-religion clause in our Constitution" were greatly at variance with the intent of the founding fathers.

At the heart of the separation of religion and state debate was the question of the place of religious ideas in the public sector. In fact, though it was not often perceived so by the religious Right, this was also the point of their confrontation with public education. Many Americans have come to view religion as a totally private matter, unacceptable in public discourse, indeed, unconstitutional. That opinion often presumed the existence of a value-free, scientific body of knowledge that had replaced religious superstition in the public forum. Of course, few modern social scientists imagined that modern learning was value-free; indeed, few pure scientists contended that their research was value-free.

The evangelical battle in the public schools and in politics, rightly framed, was a struggle between conflicting value systems that carried with them great social import. Evangelical Christians perceived that their value system, which they believed was shared by a majority of Americans, was in effect boycotted by an intellectual elite on the grounds that the Constitution prohibited teaching religious values. On the other hand, a competing value system, just as laden with subjective assumptions but disguised as objective truth, was given free reign. "Book burning," conservatives believed, was a term better reserved for those who on constitutional grounds banished from public debate the traditional values of the nation. Such reasoning, according to religious conservative Richard John Neuhaus, was "a profound distortion of how separation of church and state in fact has been understood and practiced throughout most of American history."

Most American religious leaders believed that the combination of religious values and public policy decisions was both natural and essential for the nation's health. Harvard theologian Harvey Cox wrote: "The two most prominent religious traditions in the U.S., the Jewish and the Christian, are not accidentally or peripherally concerned about politics. They are essentially and intentionally concerned. They are religious worldviews in which the political arena is enormously important because they are religions of justice." All systems of law and public policy have a moral base; evangelicals insisted that the United States had been well served by its Judeo-Christian foundations. "Politics is an inescapably moral enterprise, in the sense that it is asking moral questions about how we ought to live together," wrote Richard John Neuhaus. "In a democracy, the way we answer those questions should be shaped by the moral beliefs of the people, who are increasingly convinced that their moral vision is derived from the biblical tradition." In short, while some Americans rejected any insertion of religious rhetoric into politics, both liberal and conservative religious leaders agreed with John Buchanan that "religious concepts belong in the political sector."

The point, of course, was that politics cannot be value-free. Politicians, like all human beings, confront questions that have no clear and simple answer. When in doubt, all resort to the first principles of their value systems. Combining those values with elements of reason and a worldview based on faith, they make decisions. What was more basic in evaluating a political candidate than his or her ultimate moral convictions?

Of course, American religious leaders on both the Left and Right have long been active in espousing political causes and the Christian Right's activities differed little from moral crusades in the past. However, there was little precedent in American history for the presidential candidacy of a person perceived as a religious leader. In some ways, Jesse Jackson was a welcome foil for Robertson. But Robertson did not embrace the comparison because he considered himself a more serious candidate, one with a broader political constituency and a more balanced political platform. On the other hand, most Americans were more open to a black minister in the role of political activist. The black church in America had never been so concerned about the niceties of separation of church and state as its white counterpart. While no one challenged a minister's right to be president (James A. Garfield had been a Disciples of Christ minister), everyone agreed that Robertson's most pressing need was to establish his credentials as a politician. "He has to show his ability to function as a political figure to his own base," commented conservative William Marshner. "Because neither his base nor anybody else in America believes in electing a preacher. You elect a statesman or somebody you think could be a statesman."

In reality, distrust of the religious Right and of Pat Robertson was based not on their religion or their injection of moral principles into political debate, but on the political ideas that God was being called upon to support. "The argument about church and state," wrote columnist Jeff Greenfield, "has nothing to do with theology or pluralism, and everything to do with whose political ox is being gored." "The fatal flaw of the religious Right," argued John Buchanan, "is to baptize the mentality of the John Birch Society." For better or worse, more than any other person, Pat Robertson hoped that the American people would judge him on his political views rather than on his religious reputation.

Robertson's political opponents raised one other serious issue about his injection of religion into the presidential campaign. It had to do with rhetoric. Richard John Neuhaus acknowledged that American democracy was a "raucous enterprise," and all candidates resorted to conscious oversimplification and passionate rhetoric to rally the troops. But Robertson's rivals charged that his "harsh condemnations" of those who opposed him "poisoned the atmosphere of politics" and that his intemperate language was "especially inappropriate" for an American presidential candidate. In its founding Statement of Purpose, People for the American Way proclaimed: "What is at issue, then, is not the political activism of the new evangelical right wing. That is not in itself inconsistent with the American Way. What is at issue is the form of their political action. When the main-line religious groups issue 'policy statements' on political subjects, it is with the explicit recognition that on complex questions there will be inevitable differences of judgment. . . . This new evangelical right wing, however, claims that America's purity and strength can be restored only if the nation submits to answers which they see as Biblically self-evident." "The problem," concluded People for the American Way, "lies in their refusal to respect those who differ." All of American politics, argued John Buchanan, was based on "consensus" and "compromise"; the rigidity of Robertson was wrong "in the context of Christianity itself," and it destroyed the "kind of civility that has marked our pluralistic society."

Many evangelicals and political conservatives agreed that extremist rhetoric injured their cause. A 1980 Harris poll showed that Americans overwhelmingly disapproved of the notion that one could not be both a Christian and a political liberal. Conservative political analysts acknowledged that some religious Right activists had "crossed the line" by implying that God was on their side or that the devil was sponsoring their opponent. It was one thing to call on moral principles in support of one's beliefs, but quite another to charge that an opponent's platform was immoral. And it was foolish to claim God's personal endorsement. Of course, Pat Robertson understood these nuances well. He repeatedly declared that "no one should say, 'I am God's candidate.'" But his supporters were not always so circumspect; conservative Paul Weyrich noted: "If I were the opposition, I would try to make Robertson pay for the sins of his most extreme supporters."

The demand for civility, countered conservatives, could be used to curb public debate. Evangelicals insisted it was their right to proclaim their religious values with certainty. The clash between liberal and conservative religious models was the issue—the one tolerant, genteel, and uncertain and the other narrow, abrupt, and confident. However one felt about those two religious models, argued William Marshner, one could hardly accuse Robertson of injecting "sectarianism and bigotry into the American political debate" because he spoke his views frankly. "I reject that as an absolute insult to every religious person in America," protested Marshner. It was precisely this commitment to doctrinal truth that had drawn together conservative Catholics, evangelicals, and other religious Americans.

Is there a place for such bimodal thinking, this "Manichean style of thought" in the words of its critics, in the American political system of compromise and consensus? Does not such divine certainty inevitably end in intolerance and oppression? Precisely the opposite, argued William Marshner. The religious Right was built on religious diversity: "We tend to think that each other are going to hell." "What we insist on," said Marshner, "is that if the American proposition proves anything at all, it proves that people can be good neighbors . . . and can cooperate civilly without attaching salvational value to each other's religion." The danger was liberal intolerance. Liberals believed that "heresy consists in calling another person heretic." The genuine threat to religious liberty in America and to political freedom came not from those who pursued the heated and fervent defense of their religious convictions while at the same time respecting the right of majority rule, but from those who flinched at the sound of arduous debate in the public square.

22.

Christian Populism

"THE ONLY chance that Pat Robertson has is not as a Washington insider," commented political expert Paul Weyrich, "but as an outsider much in the mold of Ronald Reagan." In Washington, Weyrich continued, Reagan's candidacy in 1980 was a "joke," and in 1988 Robertson would have difficulty finding "fifty people in this entire metropolitan area that would openly commit to his candidacy." Robertson savored the Reagan comparison; he often asserted "there isn't a dime's worth of difference between me and Ronald Reagan." And he, like Reagan, set out to run on the assumption that the "inside-the-Beltway" mentality in Washington was a political "counterculture" that was out of touch with the people. The media controlled the news, but since 1976 the people had elected the presidents.

In 1987, Pat Robertson embarked on a calculated populist campaign. While he sought advice and received counsel from New Right conservatives, particularly Paul Weyrich, his campaign organization was virtually devoid of political professionals. A March 1987 letter circulated by the Robertson for President Support Committee noted: "We do not intend having a large Washington, D.C., based staff. Instead, our efforts are concentrated in the states, identifying support for Pat Robertson in communities across the nation by getting thousands of petitions signed." "They have gone very much their own way," remarked William Marshner in 1987. Pat Robertson's campaign was reminiscent of the forays of A. Willis Robertson through the Virginia countryside, doing it himself, with neither help nor obligation to the party organization. "Politics is a matter of simple organization, a lot of hard work," Robertson confided to Michael Barone of the *Washington Post*.

By 1987 the grass-roots organizing for Robertson had been going on for several years. Since 1981 Robertson's Freedom Council had been educating charismatics in conservative political tactics. By 1986 the Freedom Council had nearly 50,000 members, most of them committed to influencing politics at the local level. In 1986 *USA Today* reported: "He and his council hierarchy have built a sophisticated political machine with paid organizers in 11 states. . . . In each state, supporters at church, precinct, county, and congressional district levels are educated and then urged to run for office." In meeting after meeting the faithful were told that "working for God is getting involved." "The results of this massive education effort," Tim LaHaye confidently asserted, "will show themselves in '88 and on into the 21st century." Pat Robertson entered the campaign of 1988 with the most formidable trained cadre of workers in modern electoral history.

It was the grass-roots organization of the Robertson campaign that most clearly distinguished the charismatic phase of the Christian Right from the Moral Majority movement lead by Jerry Falwell. In 1986 a *Washington Times* story noted that "after several years of cozying up to Washington power brokers and going along, the Falwell groups are refocusing their efforts 'outside the Beltway,' and they believe other conservatives will follow suit." Actually, the charismatics had always taken a grass-roots approach to political organization. While the Independent Baptist–led Moral Majority had been strongly managed from the top, noted Maryland conservative activist James Wright, the "charismatic movement is not a top-oriented movement." Because of their religious history, charismatics were well acquainted with cell-type arrangements and were grass-roots oriented. While the Moral Majority in Maryland courted publicity and staged rallies, Wright's charismatic lobbying group mobilized cell groups all over the state: "We deal with the small unit instead of the big unit. And because we deal with the small unit, we can beat them every time." In short, charismatic polity lent itself to the politics of a devout and organized minority. Pat Robertson was the first candidate to test the strength of that minority in national politics.

If Pat Robertson's organizational strategy was aimed at the grass roots, his campaign message also had a populist ring. Like the agrarian populists of the nineteenth century and like George Wallace in the 1970s, Robertson believed his was the voice of the people speaking against the elites who ruled and oppressed them. He spoke the fears, the prejudices, the hopes, and the aspirations of the common people. Like populists before him, Robertson seemed a demagogue and fascist to those who opposed him, but a hero and defender of the people to those who supported him.

In the absence of dominant candidates in either party, the election of 1988 holds particular promise for a populist candidate. In an intriguing article published in 1984 in the New Right journal *Election Politics,* Kevin Phillips argued that both the Democratic and Republican parties have been captured by elites that do not have broad popular support. The Democrats, while sensitive to the economic problems of the majority, were cursed by a "malingering McGovernism," a captivity to "middle-class intellectuals—teachers, do-gooders, strayed law school graduates." Democratic candidates "rarely voiced the cultural and patriotic complaints of constituencies disgusted with crime, busing, permissivism, . . . [but rather followed] the general liberal pattern of placating every minority in the Manhattan telephone directory." On the other hand, the Republican party, while embracing the "populist appeal on cultural or nationalist issues," consistently backed conservative economic policies and would do nothing "to rouse the dander of their well-heeled contributors in California, Texas, or Colorado." A real populist upheaval might be in the offing if a candidate offered a genuinely attractive economic and social platform.

Robertson pictured his candidacy in populist terms. He was out to "puncture the complacency of mainstream Republicans," Robertson told *The Economist,* warning that evangelicals would not support the party without having a voice in framing policy. Some conservatives were deeply distributed by Robertson's attacks on the Supreme Court and his strict interpretation of the Constitution. Calling Robertson a "court-stripper," Edwin M. Yoder, Jr., wrote, "Whatever else it may be, this is hardly conservatism. And it is certainly unwise." In some ways, Robertson's beliefs fit well the long list of tags hung on the religious Right by perturbed intellectuals—"neopopulism," "the anticonservative right," and "rampageous democracy." Garry Trudeau captured Robertson's populist self-image in a 1986 Doonesbury strip lampooning a fictitious Robertson press conference. Asked by reporters if he was aware of the "widespread snickering in the press" over some of his proposals, including the Jubilee Year, Robertson replies: "Well, I certainly don't blame the reporters. Most reporters are simply doing their jobs. It's their secular humanist masters, the editors, who are forces for evil, Satans in eye-shades." "No argument here," "Got that right," "This guy's okay," grinned the startled reporters in the strip.

Whether Robertson can develop a genuinely populist agenda to go with his populist rhetoric and organization remains a central question of the campaign. "I am not a traditional Republican," Robertson insisted. "I have a great heart for the poor and the needy and the downtrodden. I understand their hurts." Over and over, he emphasized his experience with poverty and his commitment to alleviating suffering in the nation. "His acquaintance with inner-city and rural poverty has stimulated him to work out schemes for educating and helping people that are certainly cheaper, and may be better, than the current one," reported The Economist. Oral Roberts's endorsement of Robertson highlighted Robertson's rapport with the poor: "Pat Robertson knows what it is to be hungry. I know you've heard about his pedigree. But I remember when he didn't have enough to eat." If Robertson can convince the poor that he has their interests at heart while convincing the middle-class that he will reduce the federal budget, and at the same time be the defender of traditional moral values, he could be a formidable populist candidate.

Whatever the outcome, Pat Robertson is a classic outsider candidate. He comes from a privileged background, but not a wealthy one. His roots are in the middle-class society of the Valley of Virginia. He is literate and informed, but he is not wedded to any political ideology. "He reaches conclusions on his own grounds,"

observed William Marshner. "He developed his right-to-life position on his own and not in cooperation with the New Right. . . .
He developed it on his own from what I take to be very old-
fashioned Dixiecrat principles. . . . I guess you might say that he
is much more of a Harry Byrd type than any of us here." Actually,
one should probably say he is more of an A. Willis Robertson type.

23.

The Quest

TOWARD THE end of the May 1987 CBN telethon, Pat Robertson and Ben Kinchlow talked nostalgically for several minutes about the telethons of the past. Robertson recalled the hectic days when he traveled from city to city conducting one exhausting telethon after another. Then for several minutes he pondered the thought that this might be his last telethon. His years as the builder of a television empire were drawing to an end, and he was about to embark on a new quest. There was no apprehension in the conversation and little exhilaration, only a reasoned reflection on what was about to happen.

In early 1987 most political observers did not think anything striking was about to happen to Pat Robertson. Over and over, polls indicated that Robertson had very high negative ratings; large numbers of voters reported that they would never vote for an evangelical minister for president. William F. Buckley, Jr., noted that Robertson "said everything conservatives wish to hear," but he agreed that there was a pervasive "indisposition to believe that any minister is, ultimately, a serious candidate." Robertson compared such prejudices to the early religious opposition to John F. Kennedy, and he believed that he could overcome the negative ratings once the campaign was under way. But he knew that he was fighting a phantom image that would be very difficult to change in the popular mind.

Furthermore, although Robertson tried to conduct his presidential race on his political platform rather than on religion, his religious beliefs were not likely to become invisible. His Republican opponents for the nomination relished comparing his candidacy to that of Jesse Jackson. Potentially more embarrassing were caricatures of his charismatic theology and practice. Art Buchwald ridiculed Robertson for saying that he would run "in accordance with God's wishes." People for the American Way promised to "follow his candidacy with great interest," helping him to "bring his case to the American public." In addition to such responsible challenges to Robertson's candidacy, he was subjected to countless scurrilous attacks that associated him with the seamiest excesses of the faith healing subculture. A critic wrote in *Gallery* magazine in early 1987: "Seemingly fleecing the poor and the elderly and the dimwitted by perverting the teachings of Christ is bad enough, but their alliance with the New Right is nothing short of ominous. Where will it end? . . . Will we one day reach the point where religious law and secular law are one and the same?"

Less serious, but important nonetheless, were the reservations of many of his fellow evangelicals about his entry into politics. Some expressed fears that Robertson's political ambition would damage CBN, the most respectable and formidable voice of charismatic Christianity. Others feared that Robertson would be "humiliated," and that evangelicalism would be damaged. Or, some evangelicals suggested, the candidacy of Robertson would separate the evangelical voting bloc into an outsider minority, killing its potential to influence the practical politics of the nation. And some of his close friends worried about the impact of his presidential ambitions on his ego and his spirituality. At the end of 1986, Jamie Buckingham, the coauthor of Robertson's autobiography, asked a series of questions: "Will Pat the Candidate no longer be our friend, our source of inspiration and accurate information, our analyzer of world affairs, our number one ministerial statesman?"

Some political observers wondered if Robertson and his backers were tough enough to handle a presidential race, to survive the abuse and disrespect that would come his way. One reporter who covered his Independence Hall speech in September 1986 sensed that Robertson was genuinely shocked by the rough handling he received at the hands of the press, that he seemed to think that the respect he had won among evangelical Christians would carry over into the rough-and-tumble world of presidential politics. Robertson demonstrated through the years a quick temper and a tendency to shoot from the hip when under pressure. He fired back angrily when his Marine service was challenged, when People for the American Way targeted him for a press conference, and when Democratic Chairman Paul G. Kirk, Jr., circulated a scathing letter attacking Robertson's "radical political views." Kirk seemed bemused by Robertson's heated reaction and commented to the press that Robertson would have to "have a little thicker skin" if he hoped to run for the presidency. On the other hand, Robertson supporters were convinced that he was prepared for what lay ahead. "Robertson is very tough," observed supporter Tom Dunkerton; "he knows how to deal with tough cookies, when to speak out and when to keep quiet."

Nothing threatened Pat Robertson's candidacy more seriously than the belief that the religious Right was in decline. Many political observers believed that the movement crested in the election of 1980 and diminished in influence in each subsequent election. After the election of 1986, when many Republican candidates rejected the support of the Moral Majority and other conservatives were defeated, the *New York Times* commented, "The message is not going to be lost on Republican professionals. Ideological politics, the stranger that took their party by storm, is beginning to lose its charm." Political analyst Albert J. Menendez was more cautious, noting that the election results "by no means signal the end of the Religious Right." Still, he concluded, "Religious Right activists . . . seem to have failed to convince Americans that the nation would be better off under their rule."

Those assessments did not go unchallenged. Immediately after the 1986 elections, Paul Weyrich wrote an open letter to Republican leaders arguing that "those who identified with our issues and welcomed people into the campaign won, but those who went out of their way to keep our people from being involved did not." From Robertson's point of view, the question was whether the backlash against Jerry Falwell and the Moral Majority would carry over into his campaign, or whether his new charismatic-based evangelical coalition could pump new vitality into the sagging religious Right.

On the positive side, Robertson believed that he had the ability to address a broad range of political issues that would ultimately make him an attractive candidate far beyond his evangelical base. Some Republicans agreed that Robertson was the best candidate to "continue those principles of Ronald Reagan of less government, states' rights, and more individual integrity." And Robertson candidly explained to his religious supporters that in politics there were few "absolutes," that his campaign would be guided by "pragmatic decisions that should be made through compromise." As a minister, he preached absolutes and demanded conformity, but as president he would never use coercive powers to impose his beliefs on people. Rather, he would try to improve society through "coalitions and some degree of compromise."

Most political analysts believed that this flexibility, this willingness to build a broad political coalition, must be the leading edge in Robertson's campaign. As long as he was perceived as a religious figure, he could only be a "spoiler." But if he could present his broader views to the public, he might attract additional support. "I am the kind of person who can swallow all that religion when I see his understanding of economics," observed John Exter, professor of economics at Harvard. He suffers from a "high name ID," commented Paul Weyrich; most people think they know him, but very few understand his political platform. To develop a secular image, he needed exposure outside his religious constituency, and early indications were that the Robertson campaign would rely heavily on television appearances calculated to showcase his political sophistication.

While Robertson supporters talk excitedly of his intellectual prowess, his skills as a communicator, his good looks and presence, they consider his chief asset his aura of integrity. He "projects integrity," observed Tim LaHaye; indeed, one of the founding principles of CBN was "we will demonstrate integrity." Personal integrity could, indeed, be a major issue in the campaign of 1988 in the aftermath of the Iran-Contra affair and the collapse of Gary Hart's campaign. Robertson's image of integrity would be fair game once his candidacy was declared. His vehement reaction to the charge that his father kept him out of combat in Korea reflected the crucial importance of image in his campaign. When the *New York Times* reported in December 1986 that CBN was under investigation by the Internal Revenue Service regarding issues that did not involve flagrant misconduct, the importance of image was again highlighted. And, as the PTL scandal lingered into the summer of 1987, Robertson squirmed under the inevitable guilt by association. If integrity was important to all presidential candidates, it was critical to Pat Robertson.

The first test of strength for the Republican candidates came in the complicated election in 1986 of 9,000 delegates who will choose the Michigan contingent to the Republican convention. Robertson campaigned vigorously in Michigan, as did George Bush and Jack Kemp. Early assessments of the results announced that Robertson had suffered a major setback and had "demonstrated little appeal beyond his own hard-core, fundamentalist flock." Robertson protested that such reports were biased readings and claimed that he had won a majority of the delegates. Later assessments indicated that Robertson was close to the truth. Barring a successful challenge by Bush supporters in the courts, Robertson is likely to leave Michigan in January 1988 with a majority of the state's delegates, with the vice-president running a poor third to Jack Kemp.

Pat Robertson clearly caught the other Republican candidates off guard in Michigan with a well-organized and well-financed campaign. Most Republicans did not believe that he would be able to mount similar campaigns in other states. On the other hand, many political observers were convinced that Robertson would be a force at the Republican convention. "He has enough strength that he can win delegates at the convention," warned John Buchanan, pointing out that in New Hampshire the Republican party had 8,000 names on its contributor list while Robertson had 20,000 on his. Religious Right forces had virtually seized control of the Republican party in several states, Buchanan believed, including Washington, Minnesota, and Iowa. Democratic Chairman Paul G. Kirk, Jr., warned that Robertson had become "one of the most powerful public figures in America today" and that he was in control of "the most powerful political organization in America."

As the primaries drew near, Robertson's strengths and weaknesses became clearer. His ratings in public opinion polls remained low, but his dedicated workers were forging ahead in the crucial early primary states. In July 1986 *USA Today* reported that evangelicals had elected 60 percent of the delegates to attend the Iowa Republican convention that summer; in Nebraska evangelicals controlled party conventions in Omaha and Lincoln; in the summer of 1986 Robertson's Freedom Council in New Hampshire had 48 members running for the state legislature and around 200 running as precinct delegates. In September 1987 Robertson stunned his opponents and won media attention by winning a party straw poll in Iowa. Everywhere in the South Robertson workers had the Republican party in some stage of seige. Visiting Birmingham, Alabama in September, Robertson announced that his workers had collected 58,000 signatures supporting his candidacy—perhaps enough to secure a majority of the state's Republican delegation. The primary sequence in 1988 seemed to favor Robertson's chances. If he emerged from Michigan with a sizable delegate count and if he secured any support in New Hampshire and Iowa, in March he would find himself in the Southern primaries, in the heart of the Bible Belt, in states where candidates can win by getting the votes of Southern Baptists.

Still, for all of that, few analysts were willing to concede that Pat Robertson was a serious contender for the Republican presidential nomination, though John Buchanan confided that he had heard rumblings of a Robertson vice-presidential nomination. While Robertson insisted that he was not running as a "spoiler" and his staff believed that "it is do-able," even his friend Paul Weyrich acknowledged that it would require an "extraordinary situation" to get Robertson nominated. But each Robertson victory in the early going makes him a more serious contender. If he could persuade the public that he was "electable," his talent would make him a formidable challenger for the nomination.

But Robertson's emergence as a politician had ramifications beyond the election of 1988. When Robertson first told Weyrich that he thought the Lord wanted him to run for the presidency, Weyrich's response was to ask if God had given him a "timetable." Whatever the short-range political potential of Pat Robertson, Weyrich believed that he was a "viable candidate in the long run." However the 1988 presidential contest ends, Robertson looms as a political name to be reckoned with. If he is not a factor in 1988, then perhaps 1992, or 1996, or the year 2000, when Pat Robertson would be turning seventy.

Everyone agrees that Pat Robertson's candidacy is a no-lose situation for him and for his political views. "Even if Robertson runs and loses," wrote the editor of the student newspaper at Oral Roberts University, "he will have given Christians plenty of visibility. . . . The establishment of a Christian voting bloc with special interests and concerns is a much needed tool for Christians to exert influence and express their needs." Whatever the outcome, Robertson will have established himself as the leader of a conservative coalition that dwarfs the Jesse Jackson constituency in the Democratic party. Barring an unforeseen catastrophe, Robertson will arrive at the Republican convention with delegate support, he will speak to the assembled delegates and the American nation, he will have the bulliest pulpit that any Christian minister has ever mounted. "All of that," observed his friend Tucker Yates, "is good."

Everyone does not agree, however, that Robertson's candidacy will be good for the Republican party. Robertson's strong early showing sent the other candidates scurrying after the support of the religious Right. Robertson's candidacy forced the other Republican candidates to "pay attention to his base," observed William Marshner; his presence in the campaign prevented "the Republican party establishment from trying to write off the religious Right aspect of its 1980 coalition." Particularly, Robertson wrung from the other Republican contenders resounding support for the social agenda of religious conservatives. His candidacy will surely have an impact on the Republican platform. New Right Republicans were delighted by all of that, regardless of who emerged as the candidate. Moderate Republicans and Democrats, however, warned that Robertson's influence would push the Republican party farther and farther from the political mainstream in America and would ultimately weaken its popularity. All of that remained to be seen, but, even though the temptation lingered to ridicule Robertson's candidacy, there was no doubt that he would be, in Washington parlance, a "major player" in the election of 1988—and beyond.

24.

For a More Holy Future

PAT ROBERTSON's political organization buzzes with all the same frenetic energy and practicality that characterizes all such organizations. Robertson and his advisors live in the real world, but like all candidates they also live in the midst of the adoration of the crowds that press upon them. Running for president is a heady and euphoric business, but Robertson believed that he had reason to be optimistic: "Our people tell me that we are much better organized than Reagan was in '76, or even in 1980."

And yet, beneath the organization and the campaigning, beneath the frenzy and the public appearances, there was a calm sense of spiritual mission that made.Pat Robertson a genuinely Christian candidate. Robertson insisted that he was not the first candidate to place his fate in the hands of God, that others had undertaken the arduous campaign only because they sensed that it was a divine calling. Probably so. But dependence on God had likely never been so central.

Robertson's core constituency, his charismatic friends, easily entrusted the whole affair into the hands of God. "If he does make a run for the presidency, it's going to be because he heard from the Lord," said Bob Slosser. "Therefore it will be all right and CBN will be all right." Sure, it seemed far-fetched. Charismatics read the newspapers. "But when I put on my spiritual hat," said Tucker Yates, "I can see God doing it." No one was willing to predict that Robertson would end up being president, but those close to him had tucked in their memory one of Harald Bredesen's visions. Harald, Robertson's celebrity-conscious friend and confidant, had a vision of himself in the White House at a "very critical time," joining with the president in "beseeching God." There was no date on the vision, but . . .

In a 1987 interview Pat Robertson insisted that the presidency "isn't something that I particularly desire." It was a "matter of service": "I serve the Lord. I serve the people. If this is the area of service God wants me in, I'll do it." But how could he be elected? How could a Christian, a minister, a charismatic be elected president of the United States? "If He wants me," Robertson answered, "He wants me like I am and not somebody different. And so He will have to make the people want somebody like me." That was the fact. If it happened, it would be not only Pat Robertson who had received a message, but also the American electorate.

Bibliographic Essay

Much has been written on Pat Robertson in the past decade, but there has been no serious book about his life and thought by an outsider. The most important authorized books about Robertson and his family are: Pat Robertson and Jamie Buckingham, *Shout It from the Housetops* (Plainfield, NJ: Logos International, 1972) and Dede Robertson with John Sherrill, *My God Will Supply* (Lincoln, VA: Chosen Books, 1979). Robertson's autobiography is sketchy about his early life and ends in 1971, just as the Christian Broadcasting Network was beginning to expand. Dede Robertson's book is filled with interesting family detail. Another book that gives insight into Robertson's early years is Harald Bredesen with Pat King, *Yes, Lord* (Plainfield, NJ: Logos International, 1972).

Several books have been written by Pat Robertson. Taken together, they contain his basic beliefs. Two works explore Robertson's charismatic religious beliefs: Pat Robertson and Bob Slosser, *The Secret Kingdom* (New York: Nelson, 1982) and Pat Robertson with William Procter, *Beyond Reason* (New York: Bantam, 1984) outline Robertson's personal faith in God's miraculous intervention in human affairs. More wide-ranging and practical is Pat Robertson, *Answers to 200 of Life's Most Probing Questions* (Nashville, TN: Nelson, 1984). For the first time in book form, Robertson outlined his political beliefs in a survey of American history, *America's Dates with Destiny* (Nashville, TN: Nelson, 1986).

Since the founding of the Christian Broadcasting Network, floods of promotional and instructional literature have been published by the organization. And, of course, thousands of hours of television programming have been taped and preserved. In my study, I found the ministry's regular publications to be most useful. *The Flame, TouchPoint,* and *Focus* are newsletters and magazines published by various wings of CBN. Through the years they have included hundreds of articles by Robertson and about him and CBN. *Pat Robertson's Perspective*, published for about five years beginning in 1977, represents Robertson's thinking at that stage of his career. In addition to these sources, the ministry's partner letters and promotional brochures are valuable measures of Robertson's thinking through the years. They also chronicle the major achievements of the ministry.

While Robertson's beliefs have been repeated over and over in a variety of places, I found it more difficult to collect reliable biographical information. Unlike many public figures, Robertson is not given to copious reflection on his past. I gained some insight into Robertson's roots in a visit to Lexington, Virginia, browsing through the files of the *Lexington News-Gazette* and other local publications. Even more enlightening was a visit to the A. Willis Robertson Papers at the College of William and Mary. The large collection of Senator Robertson's papers includes much family correspondence, including scores of letters written to his son Pat. Restrictions placed on the collection forbid quotations that relate in any way to a living person. While I do not quote from the correspondence, I feel that I gained considerable insight into the family relationships by reading the senator's letters.

Much of this book has been built on a series of personal interviews I taped in late 1986 and early 1987. In Norfolk, I interviewed Pat Robertson, Timothy Robertson, and Ben Kinchlow. I also interviewed most of the other members of the governing board of the Christian Broadcasting Network past and present, including Bob Slosser, Harald Bredesen, Tucker Yates, Robert Walker, and George Lauderdale. At Robertson's political headquarters, I interviewed David West. In the past, I have interviewed other former leaders at CBN, including W. LeRoy Harrelson and Richard H. Gottier. Of course, I had countless unrecorded conversations with other individuals in the Robertson organization.

I found particularly helpful an interview with Matthew W. Paxton, Jr., editor of the newspaper in Lexington, Virginia, and a college friend of Pat Robertson. I also taped interviews with Dr. William Lumpkin and Elmer Hamilton, both of whom knew the Robertson family when Pat was a youngster. I had informal telephone conversations with a variety of other former friends in Lexington. William A. Weisenbach was helpful in explaining the history of New York Theological Seminary.

I conducted a number of interviews in Washington, D.C., to measure the feelings about Robertson's political ambitions. William Marshner and Paul Weyrich gave me informed conservative perspectives. John Buchanan of People for the American Way talked with me extensively about his objections to Robertson's politics and gave me access to materials developed by his organization. Kathy Palen voiced reservations about Robertson from the vantage of the Baptist Joint Commission in Washington, D.C. While one is hardly dependent on interviews to learn the pros and cons of Pat Robertson as a political candidate, it was useful to talk personally with his supporters and his foes.

Over the past two decades, I have conducted scores of interviews with people who know Pat Robertson and understand the workings of the religious Right in American politics. I have drawn on those interviews in this book. Most useful have been discussions with John Gimenez, Ron Godwin, Ed McAteer, James Wright, Paige Patterson, Bill Billings, Paul Weyrich, William Marshner, and Connaught Marshner.

There is an assortment of religious periodicals that cater to charismatics, evangelicals, fundamentalists, and other Christian subcultures. I have used many of them, but two journals are particularly important in researching Robertson's charismatic background. *Logos Journal* was published from 1970 to 1981 and in the early 1970s it was the most important voice of the charismatic movement. Since the late 1970s the most successful charismatic magazine has been *Charisma* (1975–). In August 1985 that magazine published a particularly interesting issue outlining the "decatrends" within the charismatic movement.

Hundreds of articles about Pat Robertson have been written by journalists. I have referred to many of them in my text. The best remains Dick Dabney's article in *Harper's Magazine*, "God's Own Network," August, 1980, pp. 33–40, 45–52. Others that I found to be particularly useful were: Garrett Epps, "Pat Robertson's a Pastor, but His Father Was a Politician," *Washington Post*, October 19, 1986, p. H3; Michael Barone, "Pat Robertson's 'Noble Cause,'" *Washington Post*, June 3, 1986, p. A19; Daniel J. Nicholas, "Pat Robertson: A Profile," *Religious Broadcasting*, February, 1986, p. 66; James Wooten, "Who, Exactly, *Is* Pat Robertson?" *Southern Magazine*, November, 1986, pp. 46–53, 66; Jamie Buckingham, "Still Shouting from the Housetops," *Charisma*, April, 1983, pp. 19–22, 24–25; "Standing Tall for Moral Principles," *Time*, February 17, 1986, p. 66; David H. Van Biema, "Heaven Only Knows," *People*, August 11, 1986, pp. 27–31; Russ Williams, "Heavenly Message, Earthly Designs," *Sojourners*, September, 1979, p. 17–20; "Politics, Power, and the Christian Citizen," *Sojourners*, September, 1979, pp. 20–22; C. Ser Vass and M. G. Stoddard, "CBN's Pat Robertson: White House Next?" *Saturday Evening Post*, March, 1985, pp. 50–57; Diana Scimone, "Pat Robertson," *New Wine*, February, 1986, pp. 25–27; "Pat Robertson," *Charisma*, May, 1986, pp. 31–35; "Buckingham Report," *Ministries Today*, September/October, 1986, pp. 19–22.

There is a large body of secondary literature on conservative religion and politics. Two books that raise particularly suggestive questions in my mind are Richard John Neuhaus, *The Naked Public Square* (Grand Rapids, MI,: Eerdmans, 1984) and Jeremy Rifkin with Ted Howard, *The Emerging Order* (New York: Putnam, 1986). I found the writing of Albert J. Menendez to be a good introduction to the influence of religion on politics, beginning with his book *Religion at the Polls* (Philadelphia: Westminster, 1977). The most informed observer of the electronic church is sociologist Jeffrey K. Hadden. For a brief summary of his latest views, see "The Great Audience Size Debate," *Religious Broadcasting*, January, 1986, pp. 20–22.

INDEX